STAY

in the

RIVER

Celeste C. Delaney

Acknowledgments

First and foremost, let me say thank you to the only wise God who makes all our stories possible and allows us to be part of HIS story. I am so grateful, Lord.

Thank you to **Donna Chisholm,** my best friend from high school, who taught me to love reading and writing and set such a high standard with her award-winning journalism.

Thank you to those who have helped with the early read-throughs—**Vicky Bartlett, Carol Clark, Sandy Snavely, Jennifer Jones, Joseph Delaney, and Mikeah Sleigh**. Your insights and encouragement have been invaluable.

Thank you to **Gerry and Janel Smith,** who have loved and encouraged me with unlimited hospitality throughout this long journey of writing.

Thank you to **Lynne Worcester,** who created the "stay in the river" analogy and let me use it here to encourage others to trust God in all circumstances.

Thank you to my siblings, **Teesha, Jim (Jamie), and Trudy,** who allowed me to share our often-painful and difficult stories.

A *huge* thank you to **Erin Jennings** for taking *so* much time to read through and edit this long manuscript multiple times, adding your humorous comments and much-needed edits. You have made this book so much better than it would have been without your loving support.

And a special thank you to Rachel Bradley, Bethany Clark, and Shannon Herring at Christian Editing and Design for your patient work to turn a manuscript into an amazing book.

Contents

PART TWO
Celeste's Story: You and Me, Lord

Welcome

I know that no one likes to read the introduction, no matter how helpful the information is, so I'll keep this brief. I have taken the time to record my story because I want future generations of my family to know who God is and what it means to be part of His story. I've added in some of the lessons I have learned along the way, hoping others will not make the same mistakes I have made, but if they do, that they will also find that God is always ready to forgive and show us a better way.

My mother Eunice's story is included in part one, as her words help to explain my early years and the struggles I inherited. Although our personalities are alike and we had similar childhood experiences, we took different paths in later years. Hers was not a journey of faith in God but rather one of looking for truth. God used her search in my own life, and I am grateful for all I learned through her. Of course, my husband's story was added in as well because thirty-six years of marriage has a way of changing you. Our journey together was not easy, but we learned to trust God, and He used us to lead many others into His kingdom.

So here we are. This is not a "how to live your life" lecture. This is my story of finding my place in God's story. This is trusting Him when I don't want to keep going. This is learning to feel His love and then learning how to extend that love to others. This is watching Him work through me despite my failures and, sometimes, because of them. This is constantly praying with my husband for our children in hopes they will do better than we did. This is learning to abide with God because without Him, I can do nothing.

Our wonderful heavenly Father delights in those He calls His children. He takes us through times of abundance and times of suffering to teach us that we can trust Him in *all* circumstances. It is such an incredible journey of perseverance and hope, and it is so worth the living. My prayer is that you will find the same to be true in your life. He waits to make it so.

Celeste

Let this be recorded for a generation to come, so that a people yet unborn may praise the Lord.

Psalm 102:18

PART ONE

Eunice's Story: Where There's a Will, There's a Way

Eunice F. B. Scott
Edited by Celeste C. Delaney

Dedication

*For all my children, grandchildren, and great-grandchildren.
May you learn from my mistakes and do better than I
did. May you have the tenacity to hang in there when
it's tough, try new things, and never stop learning.*

Standing on a lower deck of a Pacific-bound ocean liner, I search the waving crowd on the pier below for a glimpse of my husband. Our seven-month-old daughter is in my arms, and I wonder briefly if this child will ever see her father again. It seems our fifth wedding anniversary will slip by with us separated by this great ocean, he in New Zealand and me in America. How has it come to this?

Hundreds of long, colorful paper streamers flutter in the harbor breeze, stretched between excited passengers and their loved ones below, a final link, a final affirmation of love before the moving ship drags them apart. There is no such connection to my family, but finally I see them, my mother and my husband with two family friends. Nick is laughing hysterically. What could possibly be so entertaining at a time like this? His pregnant wife and child are sailing away into an uncertain future, and he is amused by something a stranger said?

His laughter ignites a deep sadness in me—I cannot stand here any longer. Pushing my way through the waving crowd at the railing, I climb the steel ladder that leads to the lifeboat deck above. I stand alone with my babies, looking over the railing into the murky water far below. And it occurs to me—I could jump.

chapter one

Beginnings—Three Years Old

I sit in a white iron crib, my legs held straight by plaster casts from thighs to ankles. Unable to stand or even move much, I lean back against the cold bars and watch the nurses through the spaces in my cage. Other white cribs line the ward, and there's a desk near the door where a nurse sits most of the day, keeping an eye on us. The walls are pale green, but everything else is white: the cribs, the sheets, the floor, the nurse's uniforms—all white. On narrow tables in the center of the room, vases of all shapes and sizes hold brightly colored flowers that bring some cheer to the space. These are removed every night; when I see the flowers being taken away, I know that the lights will soon be dimmed, the curtains drawn, and another long night will follow. I hug my small, tattered rag doll and try to move into a comfortable enough position to sleep.

The only relief during the routine of these lonely days is when "Carry Nurse" comes in, scoops me up out of my crib, and carries me around on her hip while she does her chores. She's my favorite person here. There are, of course, other children in this place, but they are sick, and I don't get to play with them. The door beside the nurse's desk has a small rectangular window at eye level, which people glance through as they come in. I often look there out of habit rather than expectation. I saw my mother look in at me there once, but she never came in. I waited and waited, hoping she had come to take me home.

I wanted so desperately to stand up, but I couldn't. I wanted to cry out to her, but I was far too shy. She was talking to a man in a white coat. She never came in. It has been such a long, long time since she left me here. *Why didn't she come in? Maybe she doesn't want me anymore. Maybe I'll live in this horrible place forever.*

I wake up groggily, briefly aware of the pain in my legs. I find it hard to shift these bulky casts. It's still early; the morning routine is beginning, and it will be time for breakfast soon. I hear a commotion at the far end of the ward. Carry Nurse is holding a baby as she hurries toward me. She sits the squirming bundle on my ankles and hands me a full milk bottle.

"Can you feed her for me, Eunice?" she asks as she turns toward the group of nurses gathering around a distant crib. I obediently take hold of the bottle and look down at the tiny face looking back at me. The baby is a lot smaller than I am, too small to sit up alone, so I use my feet to support her. I lean toward her to put the bottle in her mouth and feel pain shoot through my legs. I lean back, but as soon as I do, the bottle pops out of the baby's mouth and she begins to wail loudly. *Carry Nurse chose me to feed her. Of all the children, she chose me.* It's this thought and the fear that I will anger my friend that keeps me pushing forward, feeding the hungry baby. I hold the bottle as long as I can before I have to lean back for just a little relief. Again, the baby cries angrily, and I push forward. Back and forth, over and over I struggle against the pain. *Please come back. Please take this baby.* It's not that I don't like her. I very much enjoy feeding her. I like watching her. I like the company. But I don't know how much longer I can handle the pain. Finally, Carry Nurse returns.

"Thank you so much for helping me," she says as she carries the baby away. I lie down, relief flooding over me along with a newfound sense of importance.

When the day finally arrives, the nurses argue about who is going to get me into my beautifully embroidered dress. I don't care who does it, because I'm going home! Mother soon arrives and talks to the nurses for a moment. At last, she picks me up with my heavy casts still on my legs, and we head out the door. I chance one final look back. *Goodbye, Carry Nurse. Goodbye, baby. I'm going home.*

———————

Home for us is a small, square stucco house with a corrugated-iron roof near the end of Waiatarua Road in Remuera. It has three small bedrooms, a narrow kitchen, and a large sitting room with windows at one end that open out onto a large wooden porch. Flowers of every kind surround the building, and a long dirt path leads away from the house to the orchard. Apples, oranges, limes, lemons, pears, plums, grapes, peaches, and nectarines grow side by side in the subtropical climate of northern New Zealand. Chickens and ducks wander the orchard during the day and are called into their pens at night. The property ends at the banks of the gently flowing Orakei Creek, where the ducks swim and the children play until dark most days.

Near the back of the house, the path separates two halves of a well-tended vegetable garden. Along each side of the path are the clotheslines, which are really just long wires held up by tall, forked tree branches. Throughout the year, my mother makes sauces and chutneys, jars and jars of bottled fruit, and delicious jams and jellies. She strings onions up under the house, places pumpkins on boards to keep them out of the soil, and preserves eggs in a slimy solution in large metal cans. Our family practically lives off the land. Even the soap she uses for washing clothes and dishes is made from the Sunday roast's meat fat that has been rendered down, mixed with lye, allowed to set, and cut into bars.

Annie Ethel Frances Johnston is my mother. She is a well-built woman with a matronly figure, dark hair streaked with gray, and hazel eyes. She prefers to be called "Ethel" and, if asked, insists she is from England, which is partly true. She was actually born in New Plymouth, New Zealand, but spent time in England and Scotland while she was growing up. Her family farmed in Hawera on New

Zealand's North Island, and a statue of her maternal grandfather, Arthur Albert Fantham, still stands in King Edward Park there.

We're finally home, and I'm hungry.

"Mother, I want something to eat," I announce.

"You'll have to wait until dinner. It will be ready soon," Mother assures me. But a tired, hungry three-year-old can't wait, so I go looking for Pop. I find him in his workshop, where he is always busy making something.

"Pop, I'm hungry, and Mother says I have to wait for dinner."

He smiles and takes me by the hand. Walking in these casts isn't easy. We slowly make our way down to the orchard, and I scarf down three warm, juicy nectarines. I'm still hungry, but he refuses to get me another one from the tree. I angrily bite his hand. Quickly realizing my mistake, I cower and wait to be hit, but instead, he takes me by the hand again.

"Come on, Old Thing," he mumbles as we head back to the house. I sit on the porch, listening to the sounds of the garden, relishing the smells of home, so happy to be out of that iron crib and that cold white room. The ducks and chickens are still looking for grubs in the orchard like they were before I left, but the plants in the garden seem bigger now. The flowers and trees smell so deliciously familiar. It feels like forever since that day when our family doctor was visiting us because my sister, Gena, had the measles.

He had noticed me walking by and asked my mother what was being done for this child who walked on her ankles.

"Nothing," she had replied. "She'll grow out of it."

Upset, the doctor had insisted that I be taken to the hospital for an examination. The next day, that's where I went, and I haven't been home until today. I have rickets, which is weakness in my bones caused by a lack of vitamin D. It is not common in a sunny climate like ours, and the doctors are glad they caught it before it caused permanent problems. The long leg casts are straightening each leg, and daily exposure to sunlight along with a diet of healthy vegetables is highly recommended. Mother is making sure that happens, but some neighbors are questioning why this happened to me in the first place and why she didn't seek help earlier.

Mother grew up with a strict governess and was groomed to belong to the gentry. Her maiden name was Macrae, and, as members of that clan, she and her sisters enjoyed visiting the "family castle" in Scotland when they lived there. Eilean Donan Castle is just off the coast of Dornie, not far from the Isle of Skye. Our family line can be traced back to the 1600s, and it's clear Mother believes this makes her a cut above other people. Circumstances and some poor life decisions have brought her to this situation during the great depression, but she has adapted and works hard to make sure her family is well-fed. Even though we live in the poorest house on the street, we have a refrigerator and a car, luxuries not everyone in our community has yet. Her garden is full of spectacular Iceland poppies, which she sells to a local store. Our neighbors buy eggs and asparagus from her, so she can buy meat and butter even during the lean years. The dinner table is always laid with a starched damask cloth and fine English bone china. However, though she works hard to provide for us, I never feel loved by her. Her care seems like it comes from a sense of duty rather than any true affection.

Walking in these awful casts is painful and slow. I often fall, so I have a permanent scab on my forehead. Sometimes Mother puts me in a big old pram and takes me for walks around the neighborhood and up the road to the store. I love to be outside in the sunshine, and I enjoy looking at all the flowers and beautiful gardens as we go along. After a few months, I am back at the hospital because they have discovered that my skin is adhering to the plaster casts and has become infected. My father suggests that some kind of splints would be better than the casts, but there aren't any available in my tiny size. It would take months to get them sent all the way from England.

"Order those splints, and in the meantime, tell me what you need. I can make them," Pop confidently tells the doctor. He goes home and constructs a pair of metal splints that clamp into the heels of my shoes. They have bars on either side of my legs that go all the way to the top of my thighs. Straps at the knees and around the thighs keep them in place. They don't bend, but they are a lot cooler to wear and hold my legs in the correct position. Walking is still very difficult, and the splints are horribly heavy, so I spend a lot of time sitting. Eventually, the St. Thomas splints arrive from England, and Pop's splints are hung from the rafter in his workshop underneath the house. The new splints are lighter, and I can take them on and off by myself. Now I can get to almost everywhere I want to go around the house without help.

George Forbes Johnston, or "Pop" as everyone calls him, is short and heavyset, with blue eyes and a balding head. His teeth on either side of his mouth are worn down almost to the gums where his pipe hangs, not always lit but always in his mouth. He rarely speaks, but when he does, he has a Scottish accent. He arrived in New Zealand as a young man and served in the armed forces. As a result of the injuries he got during WWI, he receives a pension and spends his days reading and fixing things for his family and neighbors. He is very good at whatever he does, though his wife doesn't think so and regularly makes sure he knows her opinion.

Mother and Pop used to share the gardening, but they argued over every detail—what kind of tomatoes to buy and how many, where to plant them and when. In the end, he gave up arguing with her and now stays in his own room. Porridge and tea are taken to him there every morning along with *The New Zealand Herald*, which he reads from front to back. I sometimes take his tray to him and get to see the big shortwave radio that he uses to listen to the BBC news every day. It is one of two such radios Pop made. They stand about four feet tall and have fancy dials and strong wooden cabinets. I'm not allowed to touch them, but I love to sit with him and listen to the news.

I desperately want to know Pop, but I am so scared of him. Yes, he can be kind and loves to help people, but he is also very quick-tempered, and I have felt his strap many times. Besides, it is hard to know someone who rarely talks. He joins us for dinner each night but usually doesn't look up from his meal. If a visiting guest directly asks him a question, he looks at them and answers briefly before falling silent again. Many have stopped coming. We children sometimes try to talk to him, but he doesn't usually answer us. His thrashings are so violent that Mother forbids him to touch us, so he withdraws from the job of parenting as well.

Now that I have splints that I can remove easily, Mother takes me to the Tepid Baths for swimming practice to strengthen my legs as the doctor recommended. I wear a blue woolen bathing suit with a wide maroon stripe around the waist. I hate it because I think it makes me look like a bumblebee, but I love the water and take to it easily. This downtown pool complex has two saltwater pools: a smaller one for women and children and a larger, deeper one that anyone can use. The swimming instructor is reluctant to include me in his group lessons because, at three years old, I am "too young to understand." So my older sister Gena gets to take lessons, and I watch from the side of the pool.

I listen carefully and do everything he says from the other end of the pool. A few weeks later, when I am the first in the group to swim the width of the women's pool, he is very pleased with himself. A newspaper reporter and photographer arrive to write a story about "the youngest child to ever swim across this pool," and they take my picture. The article appears in *The New Zealand Herald* the next day.[1] I continue to go swimming regularly to strengthen my legs. I love the freedom the water gives me to move, and I *feel* strong. I also like

---

1   "Remarkable Swimmer," *The New Zealand Herald*, June 2, 1938.

that I'm better at it than most of the other children, especially my sister Gena.

Georgena Frances Johnston is my big sister. Two years older than me, she is everything I am not—loud, sassy, and always in trouble. Every morning, our mother stands brushing her hair into shoulder-length ringlets that bounce around prettily as she skips along—not like my dead-straight blonde hair that is always cut really short. She has hazel eyes and lots of freckles. When the milkman arrives with his horse and cart early each day, she sits on the curb, talking to him nonstop. As she prattles on, he ladles the milk from a large metal can into our billycan. Once it's full, he hands it to her to carefully carry inside. She loves reading and always gets books for birthday and Christmas presents. She also loves to pinch or hit me and then get me in trouble when I retaliate. Mother always takes her side, and I get spanked more times than I can count for things I didn't do. I don't like Gena, and I don't trust her.

On Sunday mornings, we have a ritual of climbing into Mother's narrow twin bed with her so she can tell us stories. Gena always gets to pick which one we hear, but I'm just happy to be included. Mother never goes to church. She says she always had to go when she was a child, and she hated it. Some neighbors take me to Sunday school most weeks, and I love it, even though Gena teases me and calls me "Goody Two-shoes" all the time.

Gena shares a bedroom with Mother. They have the one off the sitting room that has a large picture window facing the river, while I share the small room near the back door with our sister, Daphne. Fifteen years older than me, Daphne Maud Macrae Morrison is technically my half-sister. She never knew her father, as he drowned in a tidal wave while visiting Japan when she was very young. Mother and Daphne were still living in England when they received a photo of his grave near Yokohama and a letter explaining what had happened. When they got back to New Zealand, Mother borrowed money and opened a boardinghouse in an old Victorian home in Mt. Eden to provide for herself and her child. That was how she met and married Pop, who had been one of her boarders. Daphne works as a salesgirl for Woolworth's department store in Newmarket. She is painfully quiet and very dependent on Mother. We have little in common, never talk, and rarely do anything together. I don't feel like I know her nor do I really want to.

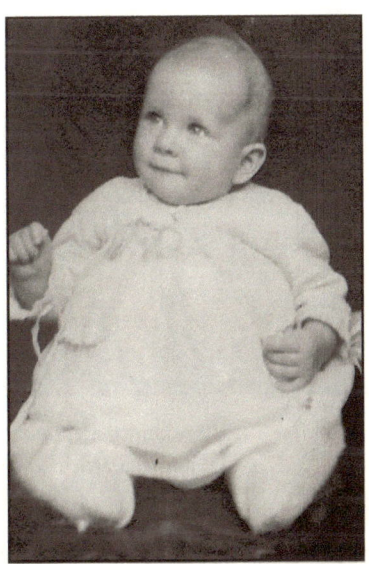

Eunice Fantham Bruce Johnston.
5 months old.
Born September 14, 1934.

Eunice's Waiatarua Road home. Photo taken in 2019.

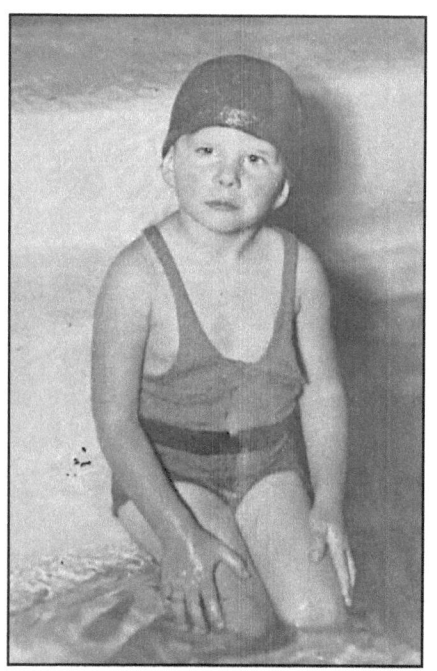

REMARKABLE SWIMMER

GIRL THREE YEARS OLD

Remarkable ability as a swimmer is posessed by Eunice Johnston, of Auckland, whose age is 3½ years. Learning only recently, she can already swim about 20 yards.

The child's instructor was Mr. D. B. Anderson, who said yesterday that she took enthusiastically to the water and quickly learned to swim in the Tepid Baths. She shows no fear, and delights in diving from the springboard in the ladies' pool at the baths. It is very uncommon for New Zealand children to become swimmers so young as this small girl.

Eunice—a proud swimmer at 3½ years old.
Photo and article in *The New Zealand Herald*, 1938.

Gena (five) and Eunice (three), 1937.
Their mother made the dresses from crepe paper.
Eunice still has casts on her legs.

Gena (ten) and Eunice (eight),
1942.

chapter two

Trust Lost

It's early August of 1939, and there's talk that war is about to start in Europe. I'm almost five years old, and I am back at the Auckland hospital for my final checkup. I watch as those horrible braces are handed over the counter to the attendant—I'm free! Noticing all the crutches along the wall, I'm so glad I don't have to use any of them, and I can't wait to get home and try out these knees that bend. As soon as the car stops in the driveway of our house, I eagerly jump out and ask if I can walk up the road.

"Be home in time for dinner!" Mother yells to me as I head back up the long driveway to the street.

I turn left and walk past the lush green paddocks dotted with grazing cows and horses, past the tall hedge around the neighbor's fancy house, and on toward the little school. My knees are working fine. I look into well-kept gardens, peer through manicured hedges, and stand on my tiptoes to see over wrought iron gates. All the swimming I've done has kept my leg muscles strong and my joints mobile. There is no sign of the deformity from nearly three years ago, and I'm relieved I will begin school on time later this month with no braces for others to tease me about. I'm standing in front of the school contemplating this when I suddenly feel sad and tired. I turn and walk slowly back to the house. I'm not looking forward to this new adventure called "school." I'd rather stay home.

As always happens, the dreaded day arrives all too soon. Early this inescapable morning in late September, Mother takes me by the hand, and we trudge up the road to Meadowbank Primary School. Both my sisters attended here, but that is no consolation for a painfully shy, awkward child. We stop at the first classroom door, and I take cover behind Mother, hoping to be invisible.

"Sit over here," the teacher says, pointing to a desk near her. I reluctantly sit down as Mother leaves, and class begins. I get through the day without saying anything or getting into any kind of trouble. By the time I return to school after the Christmas break, I have been moved up to primer two. When the teacher realizes I can already read, they quickly move me to a new classroom and primer three.

I like reading, but every day, after the morning roll call, we each have to stand at our desk and read aloud from the daily reader. Somehow, I have picked up my father's Scottish accent, rolling my *r*'s every time they appear in a word. My new teacher is not at all happy about this and constantly corrects me. One day, after trying to make me change and having no success, she takes me to the front of the classroom and makes me face my classmates. After giving me another chance to say the word "correctly" and listening to my failing again, she makes me put out my hands and hits them with a ruler. Over and over she demands the correction, and over and over I try, only to fail and be hit. I refuse to cry, but I can hear stifled sobs from the children watching. My hands are numb when the recess bell finally rings and the word comes out of my mouth without an accent. On the playground, some of the children gather around me to ask if I'm all right and want to play. Broken and embarrassed, I just want to go home. I never want to come back here again, but there's no choice. Despite all this, I do well in school, although I never really like it, and I certainly never trust a teacher again.

The war in Europe is heating up as the new school year starts. With all the young men off fighting, Pop and a few other men volunteer to build underground air-raid shelters at our school and the orphanage across the river from our house. He starts getting up earlier, now that he has something useful to do. His mood improves as he helps with the initial digging and makes plans for the steps leading down into the reinforced structure, the seating for the children, and an air vent at the top. As a former engineer, he is in his element and enjoys the company of other men who have made themselves available to help the community. It takes several months to complete the arduous work, and there is a well-attended ceremony to thank the volunteers. During the building of the shelter at the orphanage, the children there have gotten to know Pop. They call out to him and walk down the road holding his hand whenever they can. I am so jealous of this because I would like to hold his hand too, but I am too frightened of him. I cross the road rather than pass him on the sidewalk. I wonder if things would be different if I lived at the orphanage too.

Gena and I do occasionally play together, like the day we decide to include the new girl, Lee, who has moved in across the street. After going to her house to ask her mother if she can play, the three of us head down the path that leads to the creek and across the bridge, talking about what to do next.

"Let's make a hut in the bracken ferns down by the water," Gena suggests.

"I want to go up the hill and see the cows," I reply.

"Why can't we play in the trees and make a hut?" Lee asks.

As we cross the bridge, we see two rough-looking workmen repairing a fence. One is fat and unshaven; the other is thin and has a cigarette hanging out of his mouth. They look up at us, and, of course, Gena immediately starts talking to them.

"It's time for a break anyway," the skinny one says to his friend with an irritated look.

Gena chatters on and on while Lee and I wait, hoping we will soon be able to go on our way and play. The men soon tire of it and send us to look for some wire they "need" to fix the fence. I think there might be some near the barbed wire fence around the cows and go to look. As I walk into the trees, the fat man follows me, catches up to me, and roughly throws me onto the ground. Shocked, I don't know what to do or think. He climbs on top of me, groping, moving around, and breathing heavily. I try desperately to yell to the others, but nothing comes out of my mouth. After a terrifying eternity, he slowly gets up and lumbers off without looking back. I sit up and look around, uncertain of what to do, unsure of what just happened. *I have to tell the others.* I find them on the other side of the trees and try to explain it all. Lee is horrified and immediately makes us go to tell her mother, who is equally upset and hurriedly takes us to tell our mother. She seems surprisingly calm about it all but calls the police.

They soon arrive and catch the men as they walk up the road on their way home. The fat man is arrested, put into a police car, and driven away. I am shaking and don't understand what has just happened. No one explains anything.

"Don't worry about it," my mother says. "The police will take care of it."

But what does it mean? Did I do something wrong? What if that horrible man comes back here again?

The next day, a detective arrives to question us. He asks for the underwear I was wearing the day before. I want to give him a clean pair out of my drawer, but my mother says that won't do.

"They need the ones from yesterday," she tells me. I wonder why, but I do as she says. The unsmiling policeman talks to me alone in the sitting room, trying to coax information out of me about what happened the day before. I know you're not supposed to talk about the parts of your body he is trying to get me to name, but he won't go away. After more than thirty minutes, I finally whisper what I know, and he leaves. I run into my bedroom and cry. He comes several more times and explains that there will be a court case and we will have to answer questions in a courtroom. *I can't talk about this in front of people. I just can't go. Maybe Gena could explain it for me.*

Several months go by before our mother takes all three of us girls to the courthouse. I have been trying not to think about this, hoping it would just go away and I wouldn't have to do it. We sit in the waiting room, wondering what will happen next. Every so often, the big wooden doors open and a uniformed man comes in. He announces someone's name in a loud voice, and they follow him out. We can hear their footsteps echoing down the hallway as they disappear. I am the last one called. I am too frightened to look at the fat man as they walk me up the aisle to sit in a chair near the judge. A man in a black robe and a funny white wig comes forward and begins to ask me questions. I know to never disagree with an adult, so I just agree with whatever he says, nodding and saying "yes" very quietly. No one has explained what they will ask me or why. I just want to get it done and go home. Suddenly, it is all over. The fat man is found "not guilty," and we all get to go home at last. I don't know what he was supposed to be guilty of doing, but I instinctively know that what happened that day in the trees is nasty, and I will never forget it. Nothing else is ever said about it again in our house, like it never happened.

You can't trust adults, especially teachers and strangers. They will hurt you with no explanation when you haven't done anything wrong. They are powerful and always right. They will always win. I can't wait for the day when I am a grown-up so I will know everything, and no one will hurt me ever again.

Japanese and German submarines have been seen in New Zealand waters as early as 1940. American troops are sent to help protect New Zealand, as most of our able-bodied men are already serving in the dreadful wars in Europe and Africa. The handsome American soldiers bring chewing gum for the younger children and silk hose for the older girls. I don't know much about the war, but I notice the nightly blackouts and the rationing of some food products and petrol. My mother puts the car up on jacks to try to keep it in good condition until the war is over and she can buy petrol again. As the war drags on, she eventually sells it to a farmer, since he gets an extra petrol allowance for his farm equipment, and he can afford to run it.

Making ends meet is even harder for Mother than it was before the war. She trades eggs for sugar and flour coupons, buys butter from a local farmer, and goes without meat at some meals so that her children can have it. She always manages to feed us well, and we are all healthy. At school, the war is a daily reality, as we each wear a small cotton bag around our necks that contains a cork and some cotton balls. We often practice air-raid drills: running to the shelters, putting the cork between our teeth, and placing the cotton balls in our ears in anticipation of loud explosions from falling bombs. It's just how life is. I never worry about it, because everyone is in the same situation. What does bother me is that we are poorer than our neighbors, and I don't like that they have nicer houses and newer clothes to wear. I'm always in hand-me-downs from Gena, and I never want to invite friends over to our tiny old house.

———————

Daphne loses her department store job when she is fired for giving a customer the wrong change. Mother sets up for her to sew military uniforms at home, but she isn't a good seamstress, so that doesn't last long either. She doesn't care, though, since she's with Leo. They have fallen in love and will soon be married. Leo is a tall, thin man with dark skin and black hair. He loves children and plays tirelessly with me and Gena whenever he is at our house. We like him a lot and are ecstatic that he is going to marry our sister. He brings so much laughter and joy into our home.

The wedding is planned for a Saturday afternoon at the nearby St. Aidan's church in Remuera. Mother makes stylish dresses for the bride and her delighted bridesmaids. War brides are expected to wear a dress that's just below the knee to save fabric for the war effort, so she sews a pretty blue dress for Daphne, a green one for Gena, and an apricot one for me. On that much-anticipated day, Daphne wears a hat with a veil over her face and carries a small bouquet of flowers from the garden. Gena and I have big bows in our hair that match our dresses. We feel absolutely gorgeous as we walk slowly up the aisle behind the bride in time to the classic "Bridal Chorus" ringing out from the church organ.

Although it is obviously a solemn occasion, I have never been to a wedding before, and I am amused by the demeanor of the serious minister at the front. I have to keep from giggling all the way through the ceremony. I am delighted to find myself sitting next to this fascinating man at the reception that is held afterward in our home. Guests are seated in chairs that line the edges of the sitting room. The bridal party is seated at a table made from a long wooden plank held up by boxes and covered with a cloth. Mother has spent days preparing a delicious assortment of festive food, including her famous duck-egg sponges. Gena and I helped her go from shop to shop buying enough hard-to-find bananas for all the trifles and fruit salads she had planned. Everything looks so elegant for a wartime wedding.

As I nibble on my food, I watch the unsuspecting clergyman right next to me. When he stands to lead the last of the formal toasts to the bride and groom, I notice that he is seated in one of the dining room chairs that has a removable leather-covered seat that rests inside the oak frame. I just can't resist. While he talks on and on, I covertly remove the seat from the frame and wait expectantly. As he finishes his speech, everyone drinks a toast, and he sits down. His bottom immediately goes through the gaping hole in the chair, his legs shoot up in the air, and he is stuck! I am laughing hysterically, unlike my mother, who is mortified. She runs over to him and pulls him up and out of the chair while apologizing profusely.

"Just a childish prank," he mutters as he glares directly at me. I try to look innocent and hope I won't get spanked too hard later on.

After the guests leave and the bride and groom are happily off on their honeymoon, Gena gets in serious trouble with Mother for having pulled such a mean prank on the poor, unsuspecting minister. When she insists it wasn't her, Mother doesn't believe her.

"Don't be ridiculous. Eunice is way too shy to do anything like that," she insists. I cannot believe my good fortune. Not only was the prank successful and hilarious, but now I've gotten away with it too. The tables have turned. For once, Gena knows what it feels like to be blamed for something she didn't do. It is a small victory for me and one I will no doubt pay dearly for in the future, but for now, I savor it. I still laugh out loud when I remember how absurd that shocked man looked, stuck in our dining room chair.

chapter three

It Is Better to Have Loved

I'm an aunt! Daphne has had her first baby, and she's a beautiful little girl named Lorraine Ann Meyer. She has blonde hair and green eyes, like me. I wish they lived closer and I could see her all the time, but they live way up north from us. Mother asks if I would like to go stay with them during the school holidays. Of course I say, "Yes! Yes! Yes!"

We leave for the Newmarket train station early in the morning, and I watch for the steam engine while Mother buys my ticket. I didn't realize she meant I would be taking the train by myself, but here I am. *I'm ten now*, I reason to myself, *and I can read. I know not to talk to strangers, and when the conductor comes around, I will give him my ticket to punch.* I sit in my seat by the window, watching the scenery go rolling by, looking for the sign that says W-H-A-N-G-A-R-E-I at every station like Mother told me to do. I hope I don't miss it. The rhythmical clickety-clack of the train makes me so sleepy, and I'd love to just fall asleep, but I'm way too nervous about missing the stop. The little cardboard suitcase that Mother packed with some clothes for me and a letter for Daphne now sits on the luggage rack above my head. I keep reminding myself not to forget it.

It helps that there is a lot to look at as we chug along: farmhouses with big milking sheds and red barns, rolling green fields with cows and sheep grazing contentedly. At each street crossing, the train slows a little and the engineer toots the loud horn while the people waiting for the train to pass wave at us. When we stop to take on water for the steam engine, I open the window and stick my head out to watch the long, heavy hose from the tall water tank being pulled over to the waiting engine. After a few minutes, we are steadily on our way again, and when we pull into the next train station, I finally see the sign I've been looking for. I pull my suitcase down and wait for the train to come to a complete stop. Carefully, I make my way down the stairs as the guard puts some extra steps at the bottom for me to step down on. I run excitedly over to where Daphne and her precious baby are standing on the platform. Lorraine is asleep, snuggled in a pink crocheted blanket with only her darling little face showing. I can't wait another minute to hold her. I drop my suitcase and put out my arms. Daphne carries the suitcase home.

Daphne and Leo have rented a small one-bedroom flat that is part of a large old house. I am assigned the job of keeping the baby quiet between feedings so the nearby neighbors won't be disturbed by her crying. I'm looking for ways to help when I remember that I brought my favorite rag doll with me. She is my most treasured possession, but that evening, I gently tuck the tiny doll into Lorraine's blanket and bend her soft chunky arm around it.

"I want her to have it," I tell Daphne. "I love her so much."

Daphne knows how much that old doll means to me, and for a second, she looks like she might say no. Instead, she smiles and says, "Thank you, Eunice. She will love it."

I hope she will love it as much as I do and have it for always.

I love sweet Lorraine more than anyone, and I love all the attention I get from her parents. I don't feel homesick at all. Every afternoon, Daphne takes me to get ice cream at the local dairy. I *love* ice cream, and Mother hardly ever buys it. At noon each day, Leo comes home for lunch and eats a bread and cheese sandwich.

"We need to get a bigger loaf of bread while Eunice is here," he suggests one day.

"We don't have enough money for that," replies Daphne.

If she stopped buying me ice cream, she could afford the bread. I wonder why she is spoiling me so much. The time passes way too quickly, and soon I am back on the noisy train platform, waiting to head home. I kiss the baby over and over. I just don't want to leave. I wish I could live here. Daphne promises to come and visit soon, but I know it will be a long time before I see them all again.

The war in Europe is over in May of 1945, but we still have troops fighting in the Pacific. When victory is finally declared in August, there are joyous celebrations in the streets as we wait for our troops to slowly return on ships. New Zealand has lost nearly twelve thousand people, and more than fifteen thousand have been injured.[2] Many lives change, as some come home to marry their sweethearts while others file for divorce after the long separation. We are all glad when the rationing is over and more products are available in the stores. I don't have any close family members who fought in the war, but lots of our friends and neighbors do. Like Pop, many are permanently disabled and never return to work. On the other hand, many more women are now working than had been before the war. Some are happy to give up their jobs to the returning soldiers, while others are enjoying having a paycheck and the freedom that comes with it.

Robert Barry Meyer is born a year later, a little brother for Lorraine. She loves to help take care of him, and Daphne keeps busy with two little ones. Leo is delighted to have a son and is looking for extra work to help provide for his growing family. His parents have a dairy farm in Dargaville, about fifty miles west of where they live, and Leo decides to spend his vacation helping them bale hay. He isn't used to the long hours of hard work in the hot sun anymore. One afternoon, he passes out, and when he doesn't seem to be recovering

---

2   "Second World War," New Zealand History, accessed September 5, 2025, https://nzhistory.govt.nz/war/second-world-war.

quickly, his concerned family take him back to Daphne. Weeks pass, and he is getting weaker and weaker. It seems like more than just exhaustion or heatstroke. Daphne decides to move her family back to our parents' small house on Waiatarua Road so she can have help with her ailing husband and two young children.

A carpenter is hired to enclose the front porch to make a room for them. Leo continues to feel dizzy and weak and finally goes to see a doctor. The report is not good—he has Tuberculosis. Because this is a dangerous and very contagious disease, he should be immediately moved to a TB hospital, but they are all full. We must make do for now and hope no one else in the family catches it. Leo is moved into Mother's room, and she labels a set of silverware and china with his name so the rest of us won't use it. Only Daphne and Mother are allowed in his room. Lorraine and baby Robert sleep with Daphne and me. Months go by, and Leo is still in the house and still very sick. So far, all the children are well. Despite the house being really crowded, we are managing.

Mother decides to buy a bike, and Pop attaches a big wooden box to the luggage carrier so she can do her shopping with it. Sometimes Lorraine rides in the box, but on several occasions, she complains that her legs are hurting afterward. Mother rubs her tiny limbs, thinking it is just "pins and needles," but soon Lorraine is complaining that her legs are giving way on her, and she seems to fall often. The doctors at the hospital examine her but can't find anything wrong. A few days later, her temperature reaches a scary 103°F. The bed under the sitting room window becomes hers, and she lies in it all day and night, too sick and weak to move. Our family doctor is away on vacation, so his replacement comes to the house. He looks at Lorraine's throat, decides she has tonsillitis, and prescribes aspirin and rest. She lies in bed, hardly moving for several long days.

When our doctor finally gets back into town, he comes to check on Lorraine. He takes one look at her and orders she be taken to the hospital at once. She has TB meningitis, and there is no cure. She dies in the hospital three short weeks later, not long before her third birthday. Despair and disbelief blanket our household. In shocked numbness, I attend her funeral. I stand next to the graveside, looking at the tiny white casket with little silver handles. People talk, and someone sings a song; I can only think about holding her and playing with her such a short time ago. Now I will never see her again. As they lower her into the ground, a bright light goes out for me. *Goodbye, sweet Lorraine. I will always love you. I will always remember you.*

Soon after, a bed is found for Leo in the TB wards at Greenlane Hospital. He is in a long white room with large windows, and I can stand on the grass outside and wave to him. After Lorraine's death, though, Leo seems to give up trying to get well and slowly passes away after being sick for a whole year. His family comes down from Dargaville for his funeral. His sister is married to the son of an important Māori chief, a good-looking man named Johnny.[3] I love the loud fun and laughter he brings into the home, but Mother won't let him sleep in the house, because he's Māori. She makes him sleep in the car in the driveway because "there's just not enough room in the house." That makes me angry, but I don't say anything.

Gena has finished school and is working as a florist, so she makes the beautiful wreaths for the funeral. Leo is buried in the same grave as his daughter in the Waikumete Cemetery in another heart-wrenching ceremony. *Thank you, Leo, for bringing your special joy into our lives and sharing Lorraine with me. You will always be part of our family.*

---

3   "Māori are the indigenous Polynesian people of mainland New Zealand. Māori originated with settlers from East Polynesia, who arrived in New Zealand in several waves of canoe voyages between roughly 1320 and 1350." "Wikipedia: Māori People," Wikimedia Foundation, last modified September 1, 2025, https://en.wikipedia.org/wiki/Māori_people.

chapter four

Oh, Those Carefree Days!

I am so happy to graduate from primary school at the end of 1946 and begin high school at Epsom Girls Grammar School in January. At twelve and a half, I'm the second to youngest student, and I wear a uniform now. This makes me feel more equal to the other girls, as it doesn't matter if I have many clothes, because we all look the same. I had to visit the headmistress to fill out a form for financial aid to get my uniform and books. That was embarrassing, but I don't think many of the girls know about it. We have two and a half hours of homework assigned each day, but I don't usually do it. I'm passing all my classes, and my parents don't encourage me to study. As long as I'm home in time for dinner, I don't get in trouble.

As the school year comes to an end in December 1947, a polio epidemic breaks out, and the schools are closed for four months. This delays the start of the new school year and gives us the whole summer off instead of the five weeks we usually get. Polio is a serious disease that can cause paralysis or death. It is spread through contaminated food and water, so we are not allowed to swim in the Orakei Creek near us.

Wendy McGill lives across the street. We went to primary school together, but she was the class delinquent and only came when she felt like it, so we didn't know each other then. As teenagers, we have become friends and are enjoying our newfound freedom to do whatever we want for the summer. When we get bored of riding our bikes and playing tennis every day, Wendy comes up with a new plan.

"We have an old rowboat behind our house that we could fix up," she announces one morning.

"That's a great idea. Can I see it right now?" I ask.

"Sure! It's actually the lifeboat from my dad's sixty-foot ketch called the *Inyala*," Wendy informs me as we run to her house. "He anchors it off Schoolhouse Bay, where we have a beach house that he lets us stay at sometimes. It's on Kawau Island, and there are wallabies there and a big old hotel where Governor Grey lived when he was the governor of Auckland years and years ago."

The boat sounds like a great idea, but I'm not sure whether to believe Wendy's stories or not. I've seen her tell lies before. Her parents are divorced, and her father lives in a big house a few miles away. Wendy lives with her mother and sister in a dilapidated old house, struggling to make ends meet. Her mother seldom leaves the house, so most of the errands are Wendy's responsibility.

We set to work sanding, caulking, and painting our boat. We finally drag it down to the water's edge and christen it "The Wendice," a combination of both our names. It has a narrow deck about five inches wide all around it, and even if we jump and rock the boat as hard as we can, we never capsize her or get her to take on a drop of water. Even though swimming is forbidden, we are allowed to row all the way up the creek to the Orakei Basin. We get to know every bay and peninsula along the way and give them romantic names of our own.

A month later, a most wonderful gift arrives by ship for Wendy's mother, Mrs. McGill. Her brother in England has sent her a little Morris Minor car! She is too scared to learn to drive, so my mother teaches Wendy how to drive, and suddenly we are free to go anywhere we want. We go to the beach, the park, and up into the hills. Naturally, we take her mother shopping or to the movies whenever she wants to go. One day, Wendy realizes that she can go to her father's house and see if it still looks like it did when she lived there. She calls his office.

"Hello. Is Mr. McGill there, please?" she asks politely.

"No, I'm sorry. He's not in the office today," his secretary replies.

"This is his daughter, Wendy. Is he in Australia on business?"

"Yes, he is."

"When will he be back?" Wendy inquires.

"Not until Sunday."

"Thank you for your help. I'll call him next week."

As soon as she knows he's going to be gone for a while, we drive to his house to have a look around. Wendy knows where the keys are kept in the garage and is able to climb through a small window to get in. The house is spacious and modern, with opulent carpets and furnishings. There's every kind of liquor in the bar area and drawers full of neatly arranged clothes. Nothing is out of place.

In the garage, we find two shiny black luxury cars—a big American Studebaker and a French Citroën. Wendy's mind is working overtime.

"Let's borrow one of these cars," she says with a shameless grin.

"You'll get in big trouble if we do," I warn her.

"How would he know?" she reasons.

"People will see us and tell."

"Oh, come on. What if they do? I'm his daughter. What can he do to me?"

So we take the Studebaker, drive to Wendy's house, and pick up her mother. She's more than delighted to be in on the deception, and we spend the day having a lovely picnic at Piha Beach before driving home in style.

The next day, we're back at his house again. This time we take the Citroën and have a wonderful time driving around like royalty until almost dark. Back at the garage, we realize we need to make it look like the cars haven't been driven. We find some old potato sacks stored in a neat pile in a corner, and we each take one to shake up and down until a fine layer of dust covers both cars. After we return the sacks to their storage place, we squeeze through the window and head home in the Morris Minor. We're ecstatic about our bold adventure and pleased to get back at Wendy's father for leaving her mother to live in poverty with two children while he lives his lavish lifestyle.

A week or so later, Wendy is at the petrol station in her Morris when the attendant says to her, "Your father was in here the other day. He was telling me that while he was away, someone broke into his garage and siphoned the petrol out of his cars." Winking at Wendy, he continues, "No one likes your father. Your secret is safe with me."

Apparently, he knows what we have been up to, but Wendy's dad never finds out about our adventures. Now we have the perfect inside joke to retell whenever we want a laugh at his expense.

———————

By March of 1948, the polio epidemic is over, and we're back in school. Wendy goes to a private school, paid for by her father. We still hang out together after school and on weekends. We spend our time playing tennis, swimming, and diving off our boat. Saturday nights there's roller skating at the local rink. My mother won't let me go, because she's convinced the boys there are "too rough." I sneak out and go anyway.

———————

After the second polio epidemic in ten years, the government is becoming aware that they need to be more proactive about children's health in our country. Back in 1935, they started giving us a half-pint of milk to drink at school each day, and apples were added to the menu during the war. Now they are adding in free dental care for children up to age sixteen and beginning measures to test for and control tuberculosis. Free education for all children in the country is also starting. They have developed regular kindergarten and preschool programs, and the age to leave school has gone up from twelve to fifteen years old. With some mothers now working, there is concern about children not being supervised in the afternoons when school is out. Wendy and I are fortunate that both our mothers stay at home but still let us roam free most of the time. Our quiet community is an ideal place to grow up, and we make the most of it.

We have settled into a daily routine of school and fun when Mrs. McGill receives a stern letter from the headmistress at Wendy's school. The letter states that Wendy will be expelled from the school if she doesn't leave voluntarily. Apparently, she misbehaves there as much as she did in primary school. The unforgivable offense this time involved a girl who sits in front of Wendy in one of her classes. The girl had been constantly complaining about having to do her long hair every day, but her mother wouldn't let her get it cut. So Wendy helped her out by taking scissors to school and cutting off one of her braids, forcing the girl's mother to take her to the hairdresser and get the bob she said she wanted. At this point, the outraged girl decided she loved her long hair, and now Wendy is her worst enemy! Wendy gladly leaves school and goes to work for a milliner in Newmarket. She's happy to be free and making money, and we still see each other every weekend.

Music is new to me, as no one in my house sings and Mother won't allow us to listen to singing on the radio.

"Please buy me a uke," I plead with Mother day after day. "Wendy always plays her ukulele when she sings, and I want to play with her." I'm about to give up begging for one when one evening, Pop walks into the dining room with a parcel and gives it to me. It is wrapped in brown paper, and I'm sure it is my uke. I tear off the paper and stare at it in disappointment.

"What is this?" I ask a little too rudely as I open the black case. My father picks up the violin he has made and hands it to me.

"This is for you, Old Thing."

"But I'm tone-deaf. How am I supposed to learn to play this thing that has no frets?" I complain, feeling the disappointment flood over me. "I want to be able to play with Wendy when she sings. I can't use this." I cry and cry, trying to explain to my mother how all my happiness is wrapped up in having a ukulele. Mother finally relents and buys me a uke with two palm trees painted on the front. It's definitely the most beautiful one in the whole world. Now Wendy and I play together while she sings.

However, despite my protests and lack of interest, Mother insists I make use of my violin as well. Every Wednesday morning for several years, I have to lug the violin to school so I can take it to my music teacher's house in the afternoon for lessons. I will never be a great violinist, but I do play in the school orchestra and am also accepted to play second violin in Auckland's Junior Symphony Orchestra.

Boys are looking better and better to us, so Wendy and I decide we want to go to one of the dances at Johnny's, a dance studio where teenagers can learn to waltz, foxtrot, and rumba. Our mothers agree, but we have to go with Gena. That seems like a small price to pay, so we plan to go to a dance being held in two weeks. The problem is, I have absolutely nothing to wear. A neighbor gives me a blue crepe dress with pin tucks on the yoke and sweat stains under the armpits. My mother loans me a pair of stockings and brown lace-up shoes. I look hideous, but either I don't go or I go looking like a waif. I spend most of the night waiting on the sidelines and only get to dance once when the teacher instructs a boy to dance with me.

I decide I have to get a job so I can earn money for a dress before I go to another dance. By lying about my age, I find work at the local market garden, hoeing weeds around the tomatoes, picking flowers, and doing chores in the owner's house. When I finally have enough money for fabric, Wendy helps me make a simple dress, and I feel very proud that I've earned the money and made it myself.

During the next school holidays, I work at the milliner's shop, sewing flowers onto hats, serving customers, and sweeping floors. I have had my eye on a little silver pitcher in a store window I pass every day. I desperately want to buy it for my mother, so I go back frequently to make sure it hasn't sold. By the time school begins again, I have the money for three pieces of fabric and the coveted pitcher. I wrap it carefully and give it to Mother. To me, it is the most beautiful thing I've ever seen, and I'm so happy to be able to give it to her. She proudly puts it on the sideboard in the dining room and never tells me it is chrome plated and not real silver. Every weekend when I dust, I always give it an extra wipe and make sure it is positioned so everyone can see it.

During this time, I learn an important lesson. Mrs. McGill takes Wendy and me on holiday at their family beach house on Kawau Island for several weeks. It turns out, Wendy's story about the *Inyala* and the beach house was true! We have a wonderful time climbing the rigging of the boat to dive off into the clear water and sunbathing on the deck all day. We row around in the sister lifeboat to the *Wendice*, run through the pine trees on the island, and listen to the wallabies hop gracefully across the roof at night. There's only one rule—don't ever go on board one of the mullet boats anchored in the bay. Apparently, the boys who work on them party a lot, and girls who go on board get a bad reputation.

As luck would have it, several days into our time here, we are rowing around the harbor when we notice a mullet boat anchored not far from the *Inyala*. We casually row near it and get invited to go on board for lemonade. In our ignorance, we're thinking it's all innocent fun, but Mrs. McGill doesn't see it that way when she notices the rowboat tied up to the stern of their boat. She starts yelling our names across the water. We hastily return to shore to receive a good tongue-lashing and get sent to our room. I'm sure that this will be the end of our good time and we will never hear the end of this story, because that's how it would be at my house. But the next morning, to my surprise, everything is normal, and Mrs. McGill never mentions the matter again. We have a great time. I make a mental note of this lesson: In the future, if I ever have children of my own and they do something wrong, I will have my say and let it drop, just like she did.

Eunice (far left), Rae, Beverly, and Dawn on the first day of high school, 1947.

chapter five

Independence Brings Decisions

When I walk through the door with my starched white collar signed by my classmates at the end of 1949, Mother knows this is a sure sign that I have decided to leave school. I hang the ruined, old blouse in my closet, a souvenir of my high school years, never to be washed or worn again. I'm only fifteen and a half. I would like to get a job that involves using math skills, as that is my favorite subject at school, but I don't know how to and won't ask for help. Instead, I accept an apprenticeship learning to sew at the exclusive dress boutique next door to where Gena works. Mrs. Vera Jones owns the high-end shop and does all the designing and cutting out of the dresses. Only one of each style is made, and after one of the two seamstresses completes the work, it is displayed in the window and usually sells within a few days. Although this is not what I really want to do, I'm grateful that I have a way to make some money.

I have nothing suitable to wear to work, so I sell my school uniform at a used clothing store and buy a piece of brown woolen fabric to make myself a skirt. I wear that same skirt with a short-sleeved olive-green sweater and a yellow scarf every day for the next four months. Even though I'm saving everything I can and even walking the two and a half miles to work on fine days, it takes a long time to save enough money for another sweater. I'm cold at work, but I'm so happy to be working and to be able to pay my mother room and board. I'm making my own way, being responsible, acting like a grown-up.

Mrs. Jones starts me off with the simplest tasks of hand sewing hems, attaching shoulder pads, and doing the beadwork and drawn thread work on the fronts of the bodices. I also arrange a vase of flowers in the corner of the big storefront window every Monday morning. Maitland and Selene are our seamstresses. They are both well trained and very efficient at their jobs. I learn a lot just by watching them.

When Maitland leaves to get married, I get moved over to train on the big industrial Singer sewing machine and discover it's a lot faster than Mother's machine I usually use at home. Mrs. Jones is an experienced teacher, and I learn all kinds of proficient sewing tricks. As my sewing gets faster, it also gets neater. Before I know it, I am ready to make my first dress for sale. Mrs. Jones chooses a style from *Seventeen* magazine and buys a beautiful white voile fabric with multicolored dots embroidered on it. The scoop neckline is trimmed in the same satin ribbon as the sleeves, and it has a gathered skirt with a satin ribbon belt around the waist, tied in a small bow. I'm excited and nervous all at the same time.

Two days later, when it is finished and displayed in the front window, I make sure my mother goes by to see it. I'm so proud. And two days after that, someone comes into the shop and buys it. By then, I am already working on the next one, and so my sewing career begins.

Among my most rewarding accomplishments is making a regal white gown for Queen Sālote of Tonga. She went to school in New Zealand when she was younger and sometimes has us make formal gowns for her. She is six feet, three inches tall with a big build, so it's quite a task, but she looks magnificent in the gown I create and is so nice to work with. Although being a seamstress wasn't my first choice, I'm happy to be doing really well.

Selene becomes a supportive friend and mentor. She introduces me to her brother Jimmy, and we go to a few dances together. I spend some time at their home, going for walks and watching their younger brother play rugby. But it is a different young man who captures my heart. Every other Saturday night, there is a dance I love going to at the community hall for the farming township of Pakuranga. It's family oriented, so lots of teenagers and their parents bring homemade desserts and have a good time dancing and talking. Des is a tall, blond twenty-one-year-old with a polite, easygoing country manner. He is wonderful to be around and has cared for his twin brother and three younger siblings since their mother died. Their father left the family years ago, so the five of them get along as best they can. He starts picking me up for the dances and includes me in family gatherings. Our relationship is so comfortable and safe; how could I not fall in love?

Just when I'm making private plans for a long future with this wonderful man, his Australian grandmother dies, and he immediately leaves the country to help with the funeral and the settling of her estate. He writes twice before his letters stop coming. Heartbroken, I wait and wait. Months pass and still nothing. I never hear from him again, I never go to a dance at the Pakuranga hall again, and I am left to always wonder what happened.

You would think that sisters working next door to each other would travel to and from work together, but Gena and I do not. We neither know nor care about what the other one is doing. Even at home we usually keep our distance, until the day she arrives home with a rifle on her arm, excited to try her hand at marksmanship. I look around as she walks over to the open window and aims the gun out into our backyard. *Surely one of our parents will stop her.* But no one does. She takes careful aim, pulls the trigger, and shoots our cat in the head. Smokey lies dead in the garden, and Gena is jumping up and down, excitedly exclaiming what a great shot she is. "First try and I get a bullseye!"

Smokey was a small, fluffy gray kitten who looked half starved the day Gena brought her home and insisted we keep her. As cats will do, she had chosen her favorite human, and that was me. Every day when I got off the tram at the top of our street, she would be sitting there waiting and would walk home with me. Every time she had kittens, she would find me so I could gently rub her back as she gave birth.

And now she is dead.

In stunned disbelief, I pick up her limp, still-warm body and carry her down to the orchard, where we have buried several pets over the years. I cry for days; no one says anything to Gena.

"Get in the car, and we'll go for a ride," commands Gena a few months later. But I don't want to go.

"No, I don't think so," I say reluctantly.

"Go look at his car in the driveway and tell me you don't want to go," Gena challenges.

I have to at least look at the white Buick convertible with the open black top. It's striking, like nothing I've seen before, and driving around in it would be special. I still don't really want to go with Gena and her new boyfriend, Frank, even if his friend Nick does own this amazing car. It feels as if I'm being forced into a double date. Nick is much older than any man I've dated and is tall and thin with a receding hairline. I eventually agree to go, reasoning it will just be this once. But when I get home from work a few days later, there he is in our sitting room. Mother seems to enjoy inviting him over each week after that, even though I ask her not to. A month later, he asks me to go out with him on Saturday night.

"I don't think so," I say, trying to be firm but polite.

"Oh, go on," my mother insists, embarrassing me in front of Nick and making me feel obliged to go.

Privately, I explain to her that I don't like him or the way he puts his hands all over me.

She says nothing, and I end up going out with him. I do enjoy his funny English sense of humor, and we go to all kinds of fabulous places I didn't even know existed. He is sophisticated and worldly, while I know nothing. I rely on his judgement and let him make all the decisions.

We often hang out at friends' parties on weekends, drinking whiskey, rum, or beer while Frank plays the piano and everyone sings. I love being accepted as part of this popular group.

Most of the men are Englishmen who have jumped ship after the war and are hoping to not get caught. As long as they don't get in trouble with the police, they can live in New Zealand illegally without too much difficulty. Nick is one of these men, but he doesn't like worrying about being caught, so he turns himself in to the police, admits his crime, and spends two weeks in police custody as a result. I'm not sure how I feel about any of this, but I just push it aside, as I enjoy meeting new friends and getting out of the house.

Two of my new friends are John and Colleen,[4] who have been married for several years. John is a tool and die maker like Nick, so they talk shop while Colleen and I laugh our way through trying to make a sumptuous new dessert or non-lumpy gravy when we get together every Sunday. When the Gold Room nightclub opens on Queen Street, we have to go. I am completely unprepared for the wonder of this glamorous place and can't even walk through the door at first; I just stand there, spellbound, my feet glued to the spot. I never imagined that such luxury existed, let alone that I might actually be here. I'm hooked on this new life now and will go anywhere Nick wants to go. He showers me with gifts and flowers. He calls me his "Little Princess" all the time, and I really do feel like one.

---

4   Names changed.

I suppose I should have seen it coming, but I just didn't. We are snuggled together in the front seat of his car, looking out at the shimmering water of Mission Bay after an afternoon barbeque with John and Colleen. He reaches over and turns my face toward his.

"Will you marry me?" he asks gently. I sit up and look right at him.

"No." There is something about him I just don't trust. Don't get me wrong, I love going to all kinds of exciting places with him and hanging out with fun friends. I love feeling sophisticated and glamourous when I'm with them, but marry him? *No.*

"I love you, Eunice." No one has ever said that to me before, not even my parents. I treasure the sound of it and let it roll around in my mind over and over. It's wonderful to hear these words, but it's hard to accept they are true, as I'm very sure I'm unlovable. I stare out at the beach and don't know what to say next. We drive home in silence.

Nick still comes around, and we continue to go out. Then one Saturday night, he doesn't turn up, and I'm left sitting at home, alone. I don't like not knowing where he is and what he's doing. A few days later, however, he is sitting at the dining room table when I get home from work. As we take a drive that evening, I suggest he propose to me again, and, of course, this time I say yes.

He gets Frank to make me a beautiful half-carat diamond solitaire ring, and with that on my finger, it's not long before I finally give in to his pleadings to sleep with him. I'm seventeen; he's nearly twenty-seven. I'm still not sure, but the alternative seems worse, so I put my fears aside and enjoy the thought of planning a wedding and getting to move out of my parents' house one day.

"She's not entitled to it," snaps my mother.

"But you can't give to one and not the other," retorts Pop.

I'm listening in on a conversation between my parents, and I'm fascinated because they never talk to each other. I'm not sure what they are talking about, but a few days later, Pop gives Gena and me each £200. She also gets a beautiful book about floral arrangements and a handmade wooden box with florist's tools. I am given a similar box with scissors and sewing tools as well as a Singer sewing machine that Pop imported from Scotland.

He must have been saving up for a long time, because a few weeks later, we each get a set of dinner dishes and silverware as well. I go downtown to order my trousseau of sheets, blankets, and embroidered linens with the money from Pop. My fiancé is furious and insists I return it all.

"We will need that money for something important," he explains, and I go along, as I always do, cancelling the order and putting the money back into my bank account.

Gena is eager to show off the extravagant engagement ring that Frank has made for her and is anxious to get married before I do. I don't care. I'm just looking forward to her leaving the house.

Frank is Catholic, so Gena goes to special classes to be able to marry him. I get to be a bridesmaid for the second time, and the cathedral looks spectacular on the wedding day. Gena has arranged garlands of flowers down both sides of the aisle and huge urns full of cascading orchid sprays around the altar. Her dress is elegant, her bouquet is a large arrangement of flowing orchids, and her radiant face says how happy she is to be getting married.

Frank's family welcomes her with constant family gatherings, and they move into a brand-new home in a new suburb on the North Shore of Auckland. Frank takes a second job working on the docks to pay for all the new carpeting and furniture Gena insists they need, but he is happy to provide well for his new wife. I hope Gena has finally found happiness and will be nicer to him than she has been to everyone else in her life.

———

Without consulting any of us, Mother decides to sell our home and tells me we're moving across town in two weeks. I don't understand why. She finally admits to me that she's angry at Pop and is getting back at him by buying a house without a space underneath for him to have a workshop. He has been making violins and guitars for years now, ever since I asked for a ukulele and suggested he make me one. A beautiful assortment of carefully handcrafted instruments hangs from the rafters downstairs next to the tiny leg braces he made for me so long ago. He places a handwritten label in each one, and several stores downtown sell them. He also repairs instruments and is often seen carrying a cello or guitar home. When a production of *Geisha Girl* was being rehearsed, he was asked to make the Japanese instruments for the show. He studied books from the library for weeks to get them just right, and when he was given tickets for the opening night, we all got to see our first professional, live performance. Now where will he work? This is everything to him. How could she do something so mean?

After the loaded moving truck pulls out of the driveway, my two boxes of clothes and memories stuffed between the housewares in the back, I stand looking around the quiet, empty house. There have been so many days when I hated this place because it was poor compared to the others around us. I have felt sad and unloved, scared of my parents, hated by my sister, and confused by a deep sense of not belonging. But it has been my home, familiar in all its pain and sadness. I was born in that room. I sat on that porch in my casts. I ran in that orchard and swam in that creek with Wendy. Lorraine slept over there. The war, rickets, TB, and polio all touched my life here. I learned to read and write and sew within these walls. I met Nick right here, and now, after seventeen years, I'm being forced to move out. I know I'll be getting married soon and will move anyway, but I thought I could always come back here to visit. It feels so sudden, so final. *Goodbye, house. Goodbye, old life.*

The Croydon Road house is on a busier street than our old home, and the houses are much closer together. There are three bedrooms to the left off the main hallway, and I have been assigned the middle one, which suits me fine. Pop is sleeping in the musty laundry room off the back porch, surrounded by his stacked boxes of supplies and instruments. Getting to work each morning takes me twice as long, so I'm up early and out the door while it's still dark to catch two trams and a bus.

Gena and Frank have only been married for a couple of months, but she has already managed to alienate her in-laws and sue her neighbors for planting a hedge too close to her property. Things became so unpleasant they decided to sell the house and move into a friend's trailer. It didn't take long for the friend to realize that was a huge mistake, and now their plan is to move in with us. *NO!*

I don't want to be living with Gena again. She has always deliberately tormented me and was always in trouble at school, lying about children and even teachers. When we worked in town together, she stole money from the flower shop so she could ride home in taxis instead of taking the tram or walking like I did. It seems to be a game with her. She still steals money any opportunity she gets and has often been questioned by the police but never caught.

On my way to work the day after Gena and Frank move into the room next to mine, I begin looking for somewhere else to live. The first place I move into is too expensive, and the second one has a lady in charge who is unkind to me. However, on my third move within two weeks, I find Mrs. Knight, who owns a large old house on Symonds Street, near downtown Auckland. She charges ten shillings a week and provides a simple breakfast each morning out of the kindness of her heart. At seventy years old, with several boarders to care for, she washes our sheets every week for us and keeps a strict 10 p.m. curfew. I'm so happy to have found this cozy place that is closer to my job and Nick. Every evening after work, I attempt to cook dinner at Nick's, and we often entertain friends. I'm no gourmet cook, but I'm learning. Nick is good at his job but quits after an argument with his boss. He stays at home, fixing his car, and soon runs out of money to make the payments on his furniture. Before long, he asks me for the money Pop gave me so he can make the payment. Reasoning that it will soon be my furniture too, I agree and pay the bill.

Our big plan is to go to America as soon as we can get visas. Each country is assigned a certain quota of visas, and the New Zealand quota is so full that there is a long waiting list. The English quota, however, is not full, and because Nick has an English passport, we can both get on that list when we're married. It's all so exciting, and I'm working all the overtime I can get as well as sewing at home for extra money.

"When do you two want to get married?" Mother asks me one evening.

I can tell she suspects what Nick and I have known for a couple of months—I'm pregnant. I know she thinks I will want to tie the knot straightaway, but I insist on waiting until the anniversary of our engagement, October 18, 1952. I guess I'm a romantic at heart. I'm only getting married once, and I want it to be on a meaningful day. She obviously doesn't think that's a very good idea, as I'll be showing by then, but she refrains from further comment and helps me begin the planning.

chapter six

Marriage Comes with Sacrifice

O n that cool mid-October day, I nervously walk through the tall
wooden doors of St. Paul's Cathedral with my hand resting on
Pop's arm. I can't help but immediately look down the long aisle and
to the right of the altar. He's here! I wasn't really sure Nick would turn
up for our wedding, but he's here, smiling broadly and standing next
to his best man, John. I exhale for what feels like the first time today.
Colleen is right behind us as the "Wedding March" begins, and we
make the slow walk up the flower-lined aisle. Weeks of planning and
preparation, and here we are, actually doing this.

With only a couple of months to prepare, so many people helped
to make this day meaningful. A friend agreed to take photos. Colleen
stepped in as matron of honor because Gena is pregnant, and Mrs.
McGill agreed to stand in for Nick's mother. I had long counted on
Mrs. Jones designing and making my dress since she's the best, but
she suddenly became very ill and couldn't help. Selene had a dress
pattern that would work, so I borrowed it from her and spent several
Friday evenings searching fabric stores for just the right material. I
was delighted to find a silver-blue brocade, embossed with sprigs of
lily of the valley. Mrs. Jones paid for it to be custom-made as her
wedding gift to me. After the dress was completed, I could no longer
fit into the twenty-three-inch waist, so I had to buy a cinch girdle
for the big day. I made dresses for Colleen and my mother. In fact, I

spent much of today completing the hem on Colleen's dress. I didn't get to eat all day, as Mother and cousin Ann were busy preparing food for the reception and closed the kitchen. When 5 p.m. rolled around, I wasn't feeling well, but I got myself ready in time for Pop to escort me to the fancy black bridal car waiting in the driveway. Nick is always late for everything, so I was planning on being late anyway.

As we reach the altar, Pop steps away, and Nick is at my side. I glance up at him before looking down at the little white prayer book in my hand, partially covered by a small bouquet of lily of the valley. I remember how silly the solemn ceremony at Daphne's wedding seemed to me as a child and realize now the importance of this commitment. It's not just about us and our future family; it's a vow before God. There's a spiritual joining of two souls into one that I take very seriously, knowing that this is forever.

Like many brides, I can't remember many details from the wedding service. It passed like a dream, but I remember repeating my vows and crying when Nick kissed my ring before placing it on my finger. As we walk arm in arm out into the evening light, several people have gathered to throw confetti on us, including my landlady, Mrs. Knight. I'm so happy to see her. While the guests drive to my parents' house for the reception, Nick and I go to see Mrs. Jones to show her the beautiful dress she paid for and thank her for her kind generosity. She is resting in bed when we get there but sits up to give me a hug and admire my dress. It means so much to me to take this time so she can see me as a bride and I can thank her in person.

The reception is underway when we arrive at the house. Frank is at the piano, as always, and a lively celebration is in full swing. When we were planning our wedding day, I asked Nick to do two things for me: kiss my ring before he placed it on my finger and sing our special song at the reception. A hush falls on the room as Nick raises his hand and asks for silence. Frank begins playing our song, and Nick leads me over to the piano. He turns toward me, gently lifts my chin, and sings, "Because God made thee mine, I'll cherish thee."[5] Then his head turns away from me. He makes eye contact with my cousin Ann, whom he is seeing for the first time. Their eyes lock, and they remain gazing at each other until he finishes the song. I wish a hole would open up and swallow me. I feel humiliated in front of all our guests and disappointed that the song means so little to him. As usual, I say nothing.

We spend our first night as a married couple at his place then drive south the next morning for our honeymoon. We see the glowworms at the Waitomo Caves and picnic by Lake Rotorua. My favorite part is visiting the Māori Pa[6] and watching the women do beautiful poi dances. We drive around Lake Taupo and past mile after mile of rolling green hills dotted with hundreds of sheep.

In the country's capital, Wellington, we do some sightseeing of the parliament buildings and museums for a couple of days before reluctantly beginning the drive home. Monday morning finds us both back at work. It's different now that we're married. I feel as if heaven has opened its arms and taken me in! I'm in an apartment filled with teasing and laughter; gone is the negative atmosphere I grew up in. I'm so excited to be making plans for our future together. After all, we'll be a family in a few months, and we need to make some plans. My joy doesn't last long. A week later, Nick looks serious as he takes my hands in his and sits me down on the sofa.

"You can't have this baby," he says calmly.

"But we . . ." I try to object.

"No. You're still a child yourself, and having a baby now would make it hard for us to get the money together we'll need for our trip

---

5   "Because"—music and French lyrics by Guy d'Hardelot and English lyrics by Edward Teschemacher, originally published in 1902. Recorded by Enrico Caruso, Perry Como, Mario Lanza, and Bing Crosby.

6   A Māori "pā . . . can refer to any Māori village or defensive settlement, but often refers to hillforts—fortified settlements with palisades and defensive terraces." "Wikipedia: Pā," Wikimedia Foundation, last modified August 28, 2025, https://en.wikipedia.org/wiki/Pā.

to America." He isn't asking me. He's adamant about it and tells me I have to go to a certain pharmacist who will give me a phone number to call so I can make an appointment to get an abortion. I'm shocked and silent. *But isn't this why we got married? We can make this work. This is wrong.* He's still talking.

"Do not discuss this with anyone. It's illegal, and you'll get into a great deal of trouble if you get caught, so be careful. You don't have a choice," he insists.

He has obviously figured out how to make this happen. It's my fault I got pregnant in the first place. I should have been more careful. I guess it's my responsibility to deal with this. *I don't want to do this, but haven't I just vowed to love, honor, and obey my husband? Will God understand?*

On the day of the abortion, Nick doesn't want to be seen near the place, so he drops me off a block away, and I walk in alone. It is such a horrible experience, sneaking around, hoping people won't see me, wondering if I'm going to be all right, hating myself for what I'm doing. A sympathetic woman greets me at the door and asks how far along I am.

"Three months," I lie. I know I'm nearer to five months, but Nick has instructed me to say three months, otherwise they won't do it. After the doctor does the procedure, he tells me to expect the baby to abort within twenty-four hours and sends me home. After two days pass and nothing happens, I call them, and they tell me to come back in.

"Are you sure you're only three months?" the nurse asks again.

"Yes," I lie. So they do the procedure again and send me home. That night, I quietly give birth to a tiny, perfect baby boy. I want to look at him, hold him, say goodbye. Seeing the intention in my eyes, Nick quickly takes the baby and places him in a bowl, which he covers with a towel. He takes him to the outside toilet and flushes him away. Confusion and grief settle over me as Nick returns and takes me in his arms.

"You can have a baby when you're twenty-one," he assures me as I sob bitterly on his shoulder. *But I want this one. What have I done? Goodbye, baby boy. I'm so sorry. I'm so sorry.*

Nick has booked our first-class passage on the S.S. *Oronsay*, a brand-new ocean liner on her maiden voyage between Australasia and the Americas. We will leave on January 4, 1954. Time is running out, and there is so much to do. We have to get $1,500 into a bank account in the U.S. before our visas can be issued. That's a whole year's wages for us. We scrimp and save, work overtime, go without luxuries, and stay home when we'd like to be out on the town. There's an endless pile of forms to fill out, chest x-rays to have ready to present when we enter the country, passports to order, visa photos to have taken, and copies of our birth certificates and marriage certificate to be ordered. It all takes time and money. I also have to get a smallpox vaccination, which turns out to be traumatic. I spend three days with a high fever and paralysis down the left side of my body before I slowly begin to feel better. We sell almost everything we own, including the car. Mother gives us an old trunk, which we fill with the dishes and linens from our wedding, and we move into her house for the last couple of weeks to save paying rent.

This plan of ours requires a lot of sacrifice and a sense of purpose to make it happen, so it makes me angry when people say, "Oh, you're so lucky to be going to America." It's not luck! This takes hard work and determination. I am proud of the way Nick and I are working together to achieve our goal. We're the ones doing this, but then, right before we're set to leave, we see the hand of providence on us too.

We are less than two weeks from sailing when a letter arrives, confirming our visas are approved. However, we must appear in person at the American Consulate in Wellington before December 29. That is five hundred miles away, and we just sold our car. We formulate a plan to take the overnight train straight there and back so we can be home in time for Christmas. At the last minute, Mother suggests we borrow her car to make it quicker and easier. All goes very smoothly at the consulate, and soon we're on our way back home with everything in order and only ten days left until we leave.

When we arrive home on Christmas morning, expecting a day of joy and celebration, we are shocked to hear the news of New Zealand's worst train disaster ever. "Yesterday, December 24, 1953, at 10:21 p.m., thousands of tons of water suddenly burst from the crater lake of Mt. Ruapehu. It washed away most of the Tangiwai railway bridge over the Whangaehu River, just as the express train from Wellington was approaching," the radio news announcer says as we listen in shock.

"The train was unable to stop, and the engine plunged into the river with six of the eight carriages. The Forest Service and soldiers from Waitouru Military Camp, along with the police, local farmers, and other volunteers, worked through the night looking for missing bodies. The death toll is at least one hundred and fifty people, and many bodies may never be found."

We were supposed to be on that exact train! As it was, we passed that way about ten minutes before the raging water hit the vehicle bridge we had just passed over, washing it into the flooded river. We had been completely unaware of the tragedy that devastated so many lives. We sit in stunned silence, looking at each other and the gathered members of our family in disbelief. That should have been us. All our careful plans could have been literally washed away just a few short hours ago. What an eerie feeling to know we came so close to death.

Flags are flown at half-mast for a week, even though Queen Elizabeth and Prince Philip are in the country for their first trip to New Zealand since she was coronated queen earlier this year. She mentions the disaster in her radio message to the commonwealth on Christmas Day, and Prince Philip attends the funeral for many of the victims seven days later. They are saying the accident will change warning systems for railroad bridges in the future, and we will certainly always remember how it impacted our lives as well.[7]

Cyril Nichols (Nick) and Eunice F. B. Johnston.
Married October 18, 1952.

7   "Tangiwai Rail Disaster," New Zealand History, last updated January 25, 2023, https://nzhistory.govt.nz/tangiwai-railway-disaster-0.

Nick and Eunice with best friends Colleen and John.

George Forbes Johnston, Nick, Eunice, and Annie Ethel Frances Johnston.

chapter seven

Now Is the Hour for Me to Say Goodbye

"She's so big!" I can't help exclaiming.

"Biggest, newest ship in the fleet," Nick tells me proudly as we stand on the crowded dock, looking up at the brand-new S.S. Oronsay,[8] our home away from home for the next eighteen days. I've been up since before dawn, too excited to sleep, ready to get on with this long-awaited adventure. I'm sad to be leaving friends and family and know I will miss them all, but I can't wait to see what's next in this marvelous new place called San Francisco.

Pop didn't come to the wharf this morning to see us off. "Goodbye, Old Thing," was all he said as I went out the door.

Everyone else is here though: Gena and Frank, John and Colleen, my mother, and several other friends. We all go aboard for a final drink in the ship's spectacular lounge. The excitement is contagious, and everyone is talking at once, jealous we get to go on this amazing ship and wondering what America will be like.

We get peppered with countless questions about what ports we will stop at, how far the trip is, whether we stop in Vancouver, Canada, and how cold it is there this time of year. We don't have a lot

---

8   Reuben Goossens, "R.M.S. Oronsay," http://ssmaritime.com/ssOronsay.htm.

of answers, but I am happy to sit amid the anticipation, happy that we're the ones going and not the ones being left behind.

"All ashore who's going ashore!" blares the final announcement, sending us into a frenzy of hugs, kisses, and "Bon Voyages" before we're left standing at the rail as our group moves down the gangplank. When they reach the pier, we throw the traditional colored paper streamers down to them in a gesture of connectedness. The crowd grows louder as people shout back and forth, and the band plays popular tunes, adding to the jubilation. Finally, as the ship's crew disconnects the mooring ropes, the departure song plays:

"Now is the hour for me to say good-bye.

Soon you'll be sailing far across the sea.

While you're away, oh please remember me.

When you return, you'll find me waiting here." [9]

Now I'm bawling. I can't even see my friends and family through my tears. As the *Oronsay* moves out into deep water, the broken streamers float down into the ocean. The sturdy tugboat leaves us, and we head out past the familiar islands of the Waitemata Harbor. Nick and I stand on the deck, watching the ship's wake, soaking in the last views of the City of Sails, unable to move away into our unknown future just yet. We have eighteen days to explore this gigantic floating city, with its lounges, shops, deck entertainment, and theatres. It's more luxurious than I had imagined. I still can't believe I'm really doing this. *We're sailing to America!*

Eventually, we move down to the grandeur of the dining room, with its starched white tablecloths, fancy folded napkins, formal waiters, and endless supply of sumptuous foods from across the globe.

---

9 "Now Is the Hour" (Māori, Po Atarau) is a popular farewell song in New Zealand. Music by Clement Scott, Māori lyrics by Maewa Kaihua, English lyrics and arrangement by Dorothy Stewart. Recorded by Ana Hate and Deane Waetini, Parlophone Records, 1927, Ohinenutu, New Zealand.

I have never seen anything like it, but I make a quick mental note to wear a cardigan next time I come in here. It's my first experience with air-conditioning, something I'm sure I will appreciate when we cross the equator next week. It's a shame not to be able to eat much, as my stomach continually reminds me we're at sea. Three days later, I have my sea legs, and I'm ready to try it all. Nick has found a chess partner for daily games. Our leisurely days are spent eating, playing hotly contested rounds of shuffleboard and badminton, wandering the decks, and scanning the water for whales or dolphins. We look for any little green island to remind us that land does exist somewhere in the extreme vastness of the Pacific Ocean.

It looks like a hundred people have gathered on the shore to welcome our ship into port as we inch our way alongside the pier in Suva, Fiji. It is hot and humid, but I'm anxious to go ashore and set foot on my first country outside of New Zealand. Nick and I find our way to the local market full of rickety stalls stacked high with exotic fruits, vegetables, sugarcane, and unidentifiable meats. I can't help but gasp loudly when I notice a preoccupied stall owner using a small stick to play with a hairy gray spider the size of my hand! My noise frightens the creature, which disappears under some boxes, and the woman gives me a disgusted look.

A few minutes later, I'm mesmerized watching an officer in a splendid uniform standing in the middle of an intersection. He's directing the flow of traffic with a choreographed "dance" that never stops. His happy smile and precise movements draw out the tourists' cameras and delight the waiting pedestrians. For me, it is the highlight of our time in Fiji. As the sun is setting into the pink evening sky, it is time to leave, and an exuberant crowd has gathered to sing, dance, and call, "Come back again." Our floating home pulls majestically away and heads into the dark blue expanse of our planet's largest ocean once again.

As we cross the international date line a day or so later, we put our clocks back almost a whole day, and the crew prepares a sumptuous party on deck. A few days later, crossing the equator provides another excuse for a celebration. "Neptune" is on deck to dunk the passengers underwater in the pool and issue a certificate as a souvenir. It's just one incredible feast after another, and I want to taste it all!

We arrive earlier than scheduled in O'ahu, Hawaii. It is dark as we drop anchor, waiting for the pilot boat to lead us to shore. As the sky lightens, early rising vendors begin to gather on the beach to watch their potential customers arrive. Three fireboats encircle the ship, with their hoses spraying dramatic fountains of water high into the warming air. The droplets catch the early-morning sunrays, forming the most spectacular rainbows I have ever seen. We are delighted by the sparkling white sands of Waikiki Beach and the splendor of the pink Royal Hawaiian Hotel nestled among the palm trees. It is the paradise I have always imagined. Just when it can't get any more surreal, we see young islanders swimming out toward us.

"Come on, you millionaires," they shout. "Throw us a coin." They dive down to retrieve anything thrown to them and hold their treasure in their teeth as they await the next offering.

The pilot boat arrives, and a tall man in a splendid red and yellow cloak is standing on the deck beside a group of hula dancers. I assume he is the king, only to find out later that the Hawaiian monarchy ended back in 1893. A pro-United States movement overthrew Queen Liliuokalani, ending the Kingdom of Hawaii.[10] It is currently a territory of the United States, although many are pushing for statehood.

In a touching welcome, each of the almost fifteen hundred passengers is ceremoniously bestowed with three orchid and ginger leis. Their perfume fills the ship, and I hang mine in our cabin before we set off to explore the island. Our plan is to see some of the residential areas and shops, so we take a bus up into the hills and wander around. We don't have money to spend, as we still have no idea how much life in the U.S. will cost. We don't have jobs lined

---

10 *Encyclopedia Britannica Online*, s.v. "Liliuokalani: queen of Hawaii," last updated August 29, 2025, https://www.britannica.com/biography/Liliuokalani.

up either, so it's "only looking" in response to the many offers to buy local goods. The rambling homes impress us with their wide lanais and spectacular views. The vegetation has some similarities to New Zealand, with its lush greens and vibrant flowers. We could happily live here.

We go back to the ship for lunch to avoid having to pay for a restaurant meal and then explore the more touristy areas. The entry to the Royal Hawaiian Hotel is decorated with a magnificent arrangement of tropical flowers and a gold-edged sign that reads, "Welcome, *Oronsay* Passengers." Everywhere we go, people are smiling as they shout their "Aloha" greetings and encourage us to buy their beautiful seashell necklaces and bracelets. They make us feel so special and welcome on their island paradise.

"I will always remember Hawaii as the most wonderful place I have ever been," I tell Nick as we fall asleep that night.

Another surprise awaits me three days later when I discover the snow-covered deck outside. I have never seen snow before, and I just have to go out in it. A few others are cautiously making their way around the slippery deck, trying to catch the falling flakes on their hands. We are nearing Vancouver, Canada, which is snowbound following the worst winter storm they have had in years. I am not prepared for such weather, but I have to see Vancouver. I pull my new wool coat on over my warmest clothes and finish the outfit with completely unsuitable high heel pumps, then we're off as soon as we dock. We slosh through the snow, trying to walk in the ruts from the cars, and find our way to the downtown area. Nothing is open, because of the storm, and looking at fur coats and snow boots in the store windows only makes us feel colder, so we carefully make our way back to the ship for lunch.

Being aboard this ship is becoming monotonous now. We're anxious to get to San Francisco and begin the next part of this adventure. When we anchor in the harbor in sight of the Golden Gate Bridge on January 21, 1954, we watch expectantly as the pilot boat arrives with the immigration officials on board. They assemble the nervous new immigrants to check our documents and open the sealed manila envelopes with our x-rays inside. We wait in the long line for our turn, watching as they hold each x-ray up to the light, inspect each person's documents, and stamp their approval with a happy, "Welcome to America!" We're almost to the front of the line. We just have to get through this, and we'll be on our way.

Finally, we're next. The doctor holding Nick's x-ray looks straight at him as he replaces it into the envelope, but no happy welcome is forthcoming.

"Go and wait in that room over there," he commands, with a quick gesture across the hall. We join a group of elderly and rather sickly-looking people, wondering what could possibly be wrong and why we are here.

Nick is looking surly.

"It must be you. There's nothing wrong with me," he says, glaring at me. "They'll send you back to New Zealand. I didn't come all this way just to be sent back." *I hope it's not me. Would he send me back alone and stay here without me?* I begin to think he would. Nick goes forward when the examining doctor calls his name.

"There is something wrong with your throat, but I don't think it is going to cause you any problems." He finally stamps the documents, and we're ready to leave. What a relief! I'm so glad it wasn't me, but what if it had been?

RMS Oronsay at Princess Wharf in Auckland,
New Zealand, 1958. Photo by Mr. Roger Eastwood. ssmaritime.com.

Waikiki Beach—The Royal Hawaiian Hotel, 1950s postcard.
https://www.hawaiimagazine.com.

chapter eight

Living the American Dream

We get our first glimpse of downtown San Francisco as we sail under the iconic Golden Gate Bridge, the world's longest suspension bridge and the entryway to our new home. We've packed our bags, and I have on my new suit and shoes so I can arrive in style. We're down the gangplank and standing on American soil at last. An enormous pile of trunks and bags on the pier dwindles as other passengers eagerly retrieve their belongings and head over to the uniformed customs officers. Our trunk can't be found. We search the ship's empty hold twice with the purser and finally accept the fact that our trunk is not here. It was apparently put off at another port along the way. All my toes are blistered, and my patience is gone as I woefully explain our situation to the last customs officer on duty. It's already after 4 p.m. when he unsympathetically ushers us through the formal exit gates and into the street of busy traffic.

"Let's get a cab," Nick suggests. "The cabbie will know where to look for an apartment."

I'm too exhausted and discouraged to have any other suggestions. As I look around the street of this anticipated promised land, all I see are the endless piles of trash blowing all around us. We flag down a yellow cab and chance to meet an angel, Bill, who becomes our first friend here.

We quickly explain our situation to him, and he knows exactly what to do. He tells us his plan as he helps us load our bags into the trunk of the cab and gets us to our first stop—a newsstand to obtain the local paper so we can look at available apartments.

"What price range are we looking for?" Bill asks.

"Something in the middle-class range," Nick replies.

"Okay. That would be the Mission District." After a quick scan of the advertisements, he looks up at us.

"There's three I think you should look at, and I'll go with you. I'll stand behind the landlord, and if I think the price is too high or you're being told something that's not true, I'll shake my head. If it's a fair deal, I'll nod. Okay?"

"Okay. Thank you," we say in unison, amazed that any cabbie would be so helpful.

An hour later, we settle for a place with tacky furniture and a bad smell, as we just want something that will work for now so we can take time to look for what we really want and can afford later. As we settle our meager belongings into our new home, Bill says he'll be back in an hour, when he's off duty, to show us the sights in his own car.

"And incidentally," he remarks as he walks out the door, "welcome to America!"

Before we know it, we're dining in an inexpensive little restaurant with him. We drive around for a while and go to a show. He explains that he and his family just sold their house and have put their belongings into storage. He takes us to the storage building, where he retrieves bacon, bread, eggs, butter, strawberry jam, milk, coffee, and sugar from a fridge, places it into a box, and hands it to us.

"So you don't have to find a market before breakfast tomorrow," he explains as he leaves us.

I'm so grateful. The day that had been so difficult and wearisome has been redeemed by the kindness of a total stranger. *I wonder if all Americans are this wonderful.*

We're up at dawn to explore our new neighborhood. We find the nearest streetcar and market, buy a paper to look for jobs, and figure out how to get a phone connected. When we get back to the apartment, a large chocolate cake with "Welcome" iced on top is waiting on the doorstep. It's a gift from Jane, Bill's wife. I start to cry. Could these people possibly be any nicer? This is above and beyond generous.

Before our first week here has passed, Nick buys a blue 1952 Buick convertible. It is definitely the nicest car he has ever owned, and it becomes his pride and joy. Being mobile helps us look for jobs and apartments too. He soon has a good job, but I'm still looking. There don't seem to be any sewing jobs, so I settle for an office position. We are soon in a routine of work, relaxation, and apartment hunting. After trudging through many disappointing places, we find ourselves following a landlord up the stairs to yet another apartment. It has two bedrooms, a sitting room with a fireplace, a nice kitchen, and a big picture window in the dining room that looks out over the boardwalk and beach. The landlords, John and Joyce Carroll, live right next door. It's *perfect*. We only have a few clothes to move in, so we borrow kitchen essentials and begin buying used furniture as it comes up for sale in the newspaper. I can't believe we already have a lovely home, jobs, and new friends. I'm in heaven.

Our lost trunk turns up about three months after our arrival, so we return all the borrowed items and replace them with our own. Life is good, but suddenly I feel a suffocating sadness, missing all that was familiar that we have left behind. Adjusting to driving on the other side of the road is taking time. Once, I waited for half an hour for a tram on the wrong side of the road because I forgot which way the traffic moved. Shopping for even the most basic groceries takes such a lot of effort, as I have to look at every package because none of them are familiar. Some people tease me about my accent, while others think I look like Grace Kelly and ask why I'm not an actress.

"Are all the girls in New Zealand as pretty as you?" one man asks me at a bar.

"No," I reply, embarrassed by the attention. He's obviously amused, but I continue in my innocent honesty. "Some are uglier and some more beautiful." I'm too shy and sensitive to handle these outgoing people. I never know what to say, and they laugh at me all the time. I don't like it.

I'm beginning to feel disillusioned by the financial arrangement Nick and I have fallen into. When we were saving to leave home, we both stowed away every penny we could, working together to make this happen. Now my paycheck pays for the rent, groceries, phone, utilities, my clothes, and postage for letters home. Nick, on the other hand, does whatever he wants with his generous check. I am often short of money at the end of the month, but I don't say anything. He gets angry if I ask for money to help with our expenses. Sometimes, though, I just don't have a choice.

Before the alarm goes off to get me up for work, I am jolted awake by nagging tooth pain. This is a first for me, and I'm not sure what to do about the throbbing that feels even worse now that I'm up. I head out the door, hoping it will just go away soon. By the afternoon, the pain is excruciating, and I can barely focus on my work as the time drags slowly on. I don't mention it to anyone and don't dare ask for help. When five o'clock finally rolls around, I head to Market Street in search of a dentist. I am so relieved when I actually find one and he says he can see me immediately. He eventually manages to pull out all the pieces of the abscessed, crumbling tooth.

"That will be twenty dollars," he says as he puts his hand out toward me. "I'll take a check." In my frazzled state, I hadn't even thought about paying for this.

"I'm sorry. I don't have a check account or the cash. I promise I'll bring it tomorrow." He really has no option, so he agrees that tomorrow will do.

I arrive home late, and Nick is very unhappy about it, angrily questioning my whereabouts. With half my face still numb, I tell the story of my terrible day-long pain, deliriously wandering around Market Street, and finally, the relief of getting the offending tooth out.

"I need twenty dollars to pay him. I have no money left this week."

"Get your own money!" he yells, without even looking at me.

"But I promised him I would take him the money tomorrow, and I need to do that. He needs to be paid."

Reluctantly, he tosses a twenty-dollar bill toward me and leaves. No words of comfort, no understanding or empathy. I go about my chores as if nothing has happened. At least I can pay the dentist tomorrow, but I wish I didn't need to ask for money.

As we zip through traffic on the way to work the next morning, Nick announces that he wants to take piano lessons and is looking for a used piano. Even before we met, he had taught himself to play a couple of popular tunes, so I think this is a good idea and love the thought of having a piano in the apartment. Finding a good deal on one is not hard, but getting it around the curve in our stairway proves impossible. Our landlord, John, suggests we have a crane hoist it up through the big picture window. Suddenly, our inexpensive used piano is becoming a major expense. Nick has a better idea. He takes the piano apart downstairs, carries the pieces up, and reassembles it in the apartment. Apparently, this is no problem when you have an engineering mind. I'm looking forward to sing-alongs around the piano like we did back home.

In the meantime, Nick begins lessons with a woman who lives a few blocks away. I listen to him try to do a scale on the piano when he gets home. I listened to many piano lessons when I was learning the violin, and what he is "learning" doesn't seem right to me. He isn't using a book, and the way he holds his hands on the keys and plays a scale isn't correct. After several weeks, I remark that I don't think his teacher is very good. He is startled by my concern and insists I go with him to his next lesson. He asks me to wait in the car. I watch him go into the dark apartment, and a moment later, the face of a young woman, half concealed by a drape, peeps out at me from the window then quickly pulls back again. Confused, I don't say anything, but a few days later, Nick decides that he's not making the progress he hoped he would with the piano lessons and quits.

————

When the New Zealand consulate sends us an invitation to attend a cocktail party in honor of New Zealand Day, I lament the fact that I have nothing appropriate to wear. I really want to go, as it's a chance to meet other "Kiwis"[11] who live here. Nick will not give me money for a new dress, so I go in the best one I have. I'm surprised to see so many others from "down under" and relish the chance to eat some familiar foods and hear the latest news from home. In the crowd, I meet Joyce Bickel, who is the secretary for Mrs. Koret of Koret of California. When she discovers that I can sew, she offers me a job in their design department.

Two weeks later, I'm the seamstress for one of the four designers, Anne Klein, and work closely with Cora, who makes the patterns and cuts out the garments for our team. Every week, Mrs. Koret chooses fabrics from all sorts of vendors and decides what she would like each one to be made into. The designers each come up with sketches for the garments, and their sewing teams make them to fit the live models. On Friday mornings, the finished designs are paraded in front of Mrs. Koret, who chooses the ones she wants manufactured and sends those samples to the factory. All the other samples are available for the staff to buy at bargain prices. At last, I have a way of affording some decent clothes.

————

11 A "Kiwi" is a bird that is native to New Zealand, but it is also the nickname for people from New Zealand.

Even though I can sew well and enjoy working with the design team, I still feel drawn to try something more math oriented. Several months later, I ask if I can be transferred to the order department in the office. They approve my request, and soon I'm in charge of changing all the orders into numbers in preparation for keypunching.[12] During my lunch hours, I teach myself how to operate the keypunch machine and eventually get to work there as well. Unfortunately, this decision means a cut in pay, which leaves me without enough money to pay the household bills. Rather than chipping in to help pay our monthly costs, Nick decides we should move to a cheaper place, so we move across town to a small studio apartment in Daly City. I'm not happy with this move, but I don't say anything.

As we don't have much money, we often spend our Friday nights wandering around stores like Sears & Roebuck, marveling at how cheap the appliances are here compared to New Zealand. It is during one of these outings that a salesman suggests we meet a neighbor of his who is also from New Zealand. The following weekend, we visit Fred and Dorothy Wilson and their five children. We immediately become fast friends. It turns out, Dorothy lived in Remuera and went to the same primary school I did, just a few years ahead of me. I knew her brother and sister. They have been living in the area for a long time, so they have lots of helpful information and connections for us. Time spent with them is so comfortable, like being back home but with all the American conveniences.

We also meet Bob through mutual friends. He's divorced, lives in Marin County, and has a landscape business. We spend many weekends together and often stay overnight at Bob's home. When Nick decides he wants to learn to fly, Bob starts taking lessons too. Every weekend, Nick and I drive over the Golden Gate Bridge to Marin County, and I wait in the car while he learns to fly a seaplane. Eventually, he passes the exam for his private pilot's license and decides

---

12 At this time, handwritten code was transferred to a numerical "keypunch code" on cards, which were then fed into a computer.

to buy a plane. The bright yellow Luscombe has a single engine and dual controls. I help clean it up by putting in new carpeting, and he rents space to store it at an old military landing strip at Half Moon Bay. He can't take passengers until he has logged more flight time, so every weekend, he is off flying and adding miles to his logbook while I stay busy at home. I'm very excited to have a husband who can fly a plane, and I can't wait to go up with him.

———————

John and Marge are also from New Zealand and live close to us. Marge is a lot older than John and has a daughter, Jean. We soon introduce Jean to Bob, and as I hoped, they begin dating. With a long weekend coming up, we plan a trip to Reno with all three couples. We take two vehicles: John and Marge travel with us, and Bob and Jean drive together in his truck. We take along a rifle and several pistols, hoping to get in some target practice while we're there. I have no money to spend at the casinos or the racetrack, but John lets me share in his bets, as Marge has disappeared into their hotel room and refuses to join the group. On our second day, Marge still won't come out of her room, so the rest of us cross the Truckee River to have a drink in a saloon in Virginia City, visit a silver mine, and take a look inside an old mansion. We're all hot and tired by the time we get back to the hotel, so we decide to take a swim in the hotel pool. A few minutes later, Marge emerges from her room, yelling at John that she is going to commit suicide if he doesn't come out of the water and give her some attention. He tells her to go ahead and get it over and done with. I'm worried and tell John so.

"Don't worry about her," he says. "She has been threatening to do that for years. I just wish she would do it and leave me in peace."

We all agree that it's time to go home as an awkward sadness falls over our group. We pack up and begin the four-hour drive west. Fresh snow has fallen, and the snow-covered mountains make a spectacular reflection in the surface of Lake Tahoe. Pine trees laden with snow glisten in the bright sunlight, stark against the blue sky. I've never seen such a beautiful sight in my whole life.

Along the way, we stop at a picturesque roadhouse for a drink. Marge stays in the car, so I stay with her. Someone starts playing an old honky-tonk piano, and I want to see if it's Nick. Marge ignores my pleading to come with me, so I go in alone. It's not Nick, but I find the others, and we sit at the bar, watching the bartender's son and daughter performing a marvelous tango for the visitors. John is sitting beside me, and Nick moves over to sit next to him.

"Choose, Eunice. Who's it going to be, him or me?" Nick asks, obviously drunk but very serious at the same time.

"Oh, don't be so stupid!" I answer and leave the bar to join Marge in the car. The sound of angry voices causes me to look back across the parking lot, where, to my horror, I see Nick holding a pistol on John and threatening to kill him. I scramble from the car, yelling at him to calm down as I run toward them. Nick swings around and turns the gun on me. I stand still, my heart in my throat. Moving closer, he puts the gun to my chest and cocks the hammer. I hear the click and know I'm close to death. I don't care about dying, but the thought of my mother hearing I died on the side of the road upsets me.

"Nick, don't do this. The world will go on just fine without me, but you're smart and gifted. It would be a loss to the world if you were locked up in a jail for the rest of your life," I say, trying to appeal to his ego. He lowers the gun.

Jean has called the police, and soon they arrive. They take away Nick's pistol and rifle and ask John and me if we want to press charges. Neither of us does.

Jean insists her mother ride home with her and Bob. "Nick is insane," she keeps saying.

In the months that follow, the police refuse to give Nick back his weapons, and Bob doesn't invite us to his home anymore.

I decide to take a typing course to expand my office skills, and my friend Rose joins me. She and her husband, Jim, are English and recently arrived from New Zealand. My mother wrote to say they were coming, and we helped them get settled by finding them an apartment before they arrived. They have two teenage daughters, Sheila and Shirley, and twin little girls. Sheila dyes her hair and dresses very provocatively. Shirley is modest and sensible. The girls quickly find jobs, but Jim has difficulty finding work and becomes very withdrawn. They live close to us, so we see them often for meals and outings to explore San Francisco together.

Our lives are busy with work, night classes, flying, and getting out on the weekends. When September 1955 rolls around, I begin to prepare for my twenty-first birthday. I buy some pretty white fabric with blue embroidery on it for a special dress and spend every night after dinner sewing. I'm going to be twenty-one at last. I've never been really big on celebrating my birthdays, but this time, I'm looking forward to doing something special. When the day finally arrives, Nick doesn't want to take me out and doesn't even have a gift for me. Instead, he goes out and leaves me at home, alone. The rain is coming down in torrents outside as I sit on my bed, crying. I'm not usually a crybaby, but I'm *so* disappointed. This is supposed to be one of the biggest celebrations of my life.

After a few days, I move on from the devastation of this neglected birthday to the real reason I've been excited to reach this milestone age.

"Now that I'm twenty-one, I want to have a baby," I tell Nick after work.

"No. Absolutely not," he says firmly.

"But you promised!" My plea falls on deaf ears as he walks out the door. I continue to ask, and he continues to ignore me.

In March, six months later, he finally relents. Almost immediately, I think I'm pregnant. I make a plan. I won't do anything to upset him. I'll keep working for as long as possible, and I'll pay for everything myself. I won't ask him for money. I'll show him that having a baby won't interfere with his life in any way. It will be perfect, and I'll have someone to love that no one can take away. I'll be a good mother, and he'll see how much fun it is to have a baby of our own. I feel nervous and happy and lost all at the same time.

chapter nine

A Dream Comes True

A few weeks later, I have an appointment with a doctor near our home, and he confirms the pregnancy. Now to tell Nick. I wait until after dinner, anxious about his response. But he doesn't react much at all. He is not happy but not angry either. Good enough. At typing class that night, I tell Rose.

"Oh no!" she exclaims.

This is not what I was expecting, but I don't question her for details. I chalk it up to a misunderstanding and move on.

When we find out a few weeks later that Rose and Jim have decided to return to England and leave their teenage daughters here, I'm really confused. It seems like a dereliction of duty to me. What parents would leave two impressionable teenagers alone in a foreign country? We will help them as much as we can, but I don't want to be responsible for these two girls, especially Sheila, who seems to be constantly in and out of questionable romantic relationships.

Apart from feeling queasy each morning, I'm doing well. I keep the pregnancy to myself and marvel when I feel the first little movement. I search the library for a book on relaxation and practice it every day to get ready for the birth.

My doctor is concerned about my teeth, so I go to the dentist and end up with twenty-three fillings and two extractions.

I wear ankle socks to cover my swollen feet, eat well, and sew myself some maternity smocks. All in all, I'm very happy and can't wait to meet this little person growing inside me. At the same time, it feels so lonely to not be able to share the joy of this miraculous event with the child's father. It's as if this is not even happening in his world.

Dorothy is, of course, so supportive and gives me lots of ideas and advice. After all, she already has five children.

People at work are noticing and asking about the due date and whether I want a boy or a girl. I say the usual, "Either is fine by me, so long as it's healthy." I deflect questions about what my husband wants the baby to be and try to keep up the appearance of a happy couple living the good life.

Nick is still going regularly to Half Moon Bay to log flying hours. After he leaves one evening, I notice he has forgotten to take his logbook. Curious to see how close he is to completing the required hours, I take a look and am surprised that, for as much time as he is gone, there are very few hours logged. When he gets in later, I ask him about it, and he makes some implausible excuse that I don't even try to figure out. Instead, I move on to the topic of my next doctor's appointment.

"The doctor wants to show us some visual aids to explain the delivery process and teach you how you can help me through it."

"I don't want to go to that appointment or the delivery" he replies and walks out of the room again. The next day, he tells me we're going back to New Zealand. He's booking passage on the *Oronsay* for January 1, 1957.

"But the baby is due December 5. What if it's late?"

"Then you'll have it on board the ship, I guess." He sells the plane for a profit and lends his extra car to a friend so he won't have to pay for storage. The Buick is going back to New Zealand with us.

December 5 is my due date and my last day at work. Instead of just a maternity leave, it has become a permanent goodbye. I have been happier working here than at any other place in my life, and I really don't want to leave. On my last day at Koret's, my colleagues surprise me with a baby shower. I carefully open each one of the exquisitely wrapped gifts that are placed in huge stacks around me. They are all so needed and appreciated. Without these thoughtful presents, I would only have a few cloth diapers, three little jackets, two pairs of knitted booties that I made during my lunch hours, and a shawl my mother knitted for me. I call Nick to come and help me get it all home. Their generosity is overwhelming. I'm so grateful and sad at the same time, wishing we could stay and these people could be part of my baby's life.

On my first day at home after leaving work, I decide to go for a walk to retrieve a gift that was sent to the wrong address. I'm enjoying my time out in the sun on this lovely, clear fall day when I feel the first twinge of pain. I walk on. More pain. I decide to visit my doctor on the way home.

"I think I'm in labor," I tell the nurse as I walk up to the counter.

"The doctor will let you know." She laughs as she leads me back to the examination room.

"Not today," he concludes, and I head home. But by that evening, the contractions are definitely stronger and more frequent. We call the doctor.

"Don't come in until the contractions are ten minutes apart," he tells us. Nick doesn't want to go to the hospital until after midnight, because you have to pay for a whole extra day if you get there before then. The contractions are very close together when we finally pull up to the emergency entrance just after midnight. Nick sees that I'm settled into a labor room and goes home.

Doctor DeMailly comes in, smiles at me, and says, "I don't think you are in labor."

"Oh yes, I am," I insist defiantly.

"But you're not screaming."

"Would it help if I was?"

"Well, most women do." He places his hand on my abdomen for a moment then gives me a surprised look. "You *are* in labor. How come you're so relaxed?"

"I read a book about relaxation. I've been preparing for this day for six months."

He examines me and declares, "It won't be long now. We better get you to a delivery room."

At 1:09 a.m. on December 7, 1956, my sweet baby girl is placed on my tummy, all 7 pounds, 9 ounces of her. I reach out to touch her, but they whisk her away to check her first. Soon she's returned to me, wrapped in a pink blanket, and placed into my waiting arms. I gaze at her tiny face and gently rub her soft round head. I breathe in her sweet newborn smell and hug her close. She's mine. I finally have a real baby to take care of. Her eyes flutter open. She has Nick's coloring, blue eyes and brown hair. *Good. He's got to love that about her.* I slowly remove the blanket to count her fingers and toes. *She's perfect. And I get to keep her.*

Three days later, Nick arrives to take me home. I'm sitting in the front seat of our car, holding on to our new baby bundle. I look at his face as he drives, trying to guess what he's thinking. He's distant but not unhappy. He hasn't asked to hold the baby or inquired about any of the delivery details. Then I realize he's pulling into the supermarket parking lot.

"You need to get us some food for dinner. There's nothing in the fridge," he orders.

I can barely believe he expects me to go shopping after giving birth three days ago. But I don't say anything. I place the baby on his lap and slowly walk into the market. *Wait! He wouldn't hurt her, would he? What was I thinking?*

I hurry as fast as I can through the aisles, and I'm trembling violently by the time I get back to the car. The baby is still right where I left her, sound asleep, unaffected by her mother's terror or her father's indifference. I sink into the seat in relief and scoop her back into my arms, eager to get her safely home.

I've been searching for months through name books and the dictionary to come up with the perfect name. Now that I've seen her, I can finally decide what to call our tiny gift from heaven: "Celeste," which means "heavenly." Nick chooses her middle name, "Pearl," because she was born on Pearl Harbor Day. I have just under three weeks to get us ready to sail away again.

As I recover, I need to make arrangements for Celeste's birth certificate, passport, and visa, as well as find a little bed for her to sleep in on the ship. We need a doctor's certificate saying she's healthy, as she will be the youngest passenger to ever sail on the *Oronsay*. There are also packing, selling items, and farewell dinners, and I'm exhausted. But there are a few bright spots. I can't help but laugh when, in order to get her passport approved, I have to raise my right hand and swear that Celeste is not a communist attempting to overthrow the American government!

While I'm in the city, I stop by Koret's to show off my sweet girl and am overwhelmed by the affection and kindness of everyone there. Even people I didn't work with come to see the new baby and coo over her. A friend from work invites us to dinner to say goodbye. They fuss over Celeste, hugging and kissing her, obviously infatuated.

"I wish she were ours. You're so lucky!"

"I'll sell her to you if you really want her," Nick says, smiling. *He would, too!* They look at me, unsure if he is joking or not. I take her back, making an excuse that we need to get her home to bed, and we leave. *What am I doing with this man? I really thought having a baby would change things.*

January 1, 1957. We are once again standing on the deck of the S.S. *Oronsay*, this time sailing under the Golden Gate Bridge into the Pacific, moving away from the life we have enjoyed here for three years. I wave goodbye to the city I have come to love, trying to keep my tears from falling onto the baby in my arms. The hills are wrapped in the persistent fog this City by the Bay often dresses in, feeling like a shroud of mourning to me. Going back to New Zealand feels like a step backward, and I really don't want to go. Dorothy and Fred came to see us off. She told me they are thinking about going back too. I wish we were staying here, but it would be nice to have them there with us. Their friendship has kept me going through all the ups and downs.

There are few clean places on a ship to make up a baby's bottle. In the early hours of one morning, I wander down to a crew kitchen. The refrigerator there isn't working, and there's a steward sweeping the counters down with a floor broom.

"That's bloody hygienic!" I scoff.

"Don't worry, lady," he replies. "I'm going to wash them off."

"What with? The floor mop?" I retort sarcastically as I get what I need and head back to our tiny cabin. By the time we reach the tropics, I've switched to canned milk, as there's still no refrigerator. Keeping up with cloth diapers isn't working either, with nowhere to wash or dry them easily, so I resort to buying the expensive disposable kind.

Nick, in the meantime, is sleeping peacefully and flirting with the young girls on board. I've been dreading the thought of asking him for money for diapers, but I finally have no choice, so I go in search of him. I find him chatting with a cute teen on deck. She looks up at me inquiringly as I approach with a baby in my arms.

"What do *you* want?" he asks, without looking at me.

"I need some money to buy diapers," I explain.

He's embarrassed but can't say anything, so he reluctantly gives me some money. I put Celeste into his arms.

"Please hold your daughter while I go and buy them," I say as I'm walking away. The girl beside him blushes and frowns. When I return, she is gone.

Seated at our table in the dining room is a group of Australian Open Air Campaigners, who are returning home after their first six-month trip to the Americas to preach on street corners. Several have a great sense of humor, especially Frankie, the one sitting next to me. In the middle of dinner, not long into the trip, the dining room steward approaches us and asks to do a roll call.

"There seems to be someone missing every meal from this table, and I need to know who it is." He starts reading off the names on his list. When he gets to Celeste Nichols, Frankie speaks up.

"Well, it's like this," he says. "Celeste is three weeks old and a very backward child. She can't sit up yet." Amidst the raucous laughter, the steward nods and walks away to check on another table.

"Has your baby been baptized yet?" one of them asks me.

"No. Not yet."

"Then we need to do that here," he replies. Touched by their concern and love for my daughter, I watch the next morning as they mark her tiny forehead with water and pray over her. She's already blessed with people who care about her. I'm so thankful that we happened to be sitting at the same table as these wonderful Christian men.

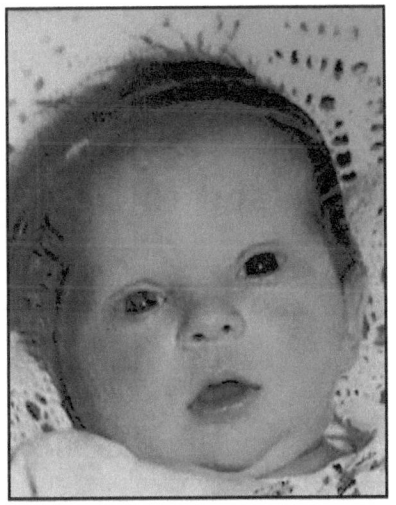

Celeste Pearl Nichols.
First passport photo, 1 week old.
Born December 7, 1956.

Eunice and Celeste ready to sail,
December 1956.

Golden Gate Bridge, San Francisco, California.
Photo credit: pexels-tae-fuller.

chapter ten

Things Aren't What They Used to Be

Much of the sadness I felt about leaving San Francisco melts away when I see the bright red Pohutukawa trees along the shore as we sail into the Waitemata Harbor. I realize that this will always be home to me, no matter where else I live. The sparkling water, the familiar skyline, and the rolling green hills draw me back in. I suddenly look forward to visiting old haunts and catching up with old friends again. Mother meets us after we get through the long customs line, admires her newest granddaughter, and drives us home. Pop is in the kitchen when we get there. He removes his pipe from his mouth and leans over the baby.

"What you got there?" he asks, grinning from ear to ear. I'm glad he's happy to see us come back.

As we're visiting our old friends over the next few weeks, I begin to see the truth of the old saying, "You can't go home again." Home has changed, and so has everyone we know. Single friends are married, and some have children. Others have moved away or have new friends and different interests. It's not the same place we left. I have new responsibilities with a baby to care for, and I'm not the same happy person who left here three years ago either.

Nick finds a job, and I take in sewing[13] to help with the bills and work from home. We're ecstatic when we hear Fred and Dorothy are finally on their way to us from San Francisco. I can't wait to have them here and raise our children together. They remember their own childhoods in New Zealand fondly and want that kind of healthy outdoor upbringing for their own five growing children.

It's so much fun to welcome them and help with their adjustment back to Kiwi life. But as the flurry of arriving settles down a few months later, they begin to realize that this is a strange new country to them and even more so for their children. Dorothy misses central heating and can't adjust to the cold and damp here. She complains that all the heat is going up the chimney, as their house is heated by one fireplace. She is used to having a washer and dryer to help her deal with the constant loads of laundry that five children produce. Hanging load after load of clean clothes outside only to have them rained on takes its toll. It's not long before they decide to return to San Francisco by the end of the year.

Oh no. I already miss them.

Meanwhile, our best man and matron of honor, John and Colleen, have just moved into a brand-new house in St. Heliers Bay. They invite us for dinner so we can catch up and see their lovely ranch home. We can't wait to visit with them again. What a night we have, laughing and talking until the early hours of the next day.

"Why don't you come and stay with us?" John asks as we hang around, obviously reluctant to say our farewells. Nick happily agrees, and by the next afternoon, we've moved into their spare bedroom. I love watching Colleen with Celeste, so tender and affectionate, a natural mother.

"Why don't you adopt?" I gently ask one evening, knowing they have been trying for years to get pregnant. "I'll go with you if you want me to."

---

13 Clothing factories deliver cutout garments to the machinist's home. She is paid for each piece that is returned sewn together to factory standards.

She smiles at me and shrugs, letting me know we'll talk about it later.

The weeks turn into a couple of months, with us women taking turns outdoing each other in the kitchen. Celeste is starting to scoot herself around on the floor, John has seeded their new lawn, and Colleen has applied to adopt a baby. All seems well in our cohabiting world, until I realize I'm pregnant again. The morning ritual beside the toilet bowl is too familiar not to recognize the symptoms straightaway. Needless to say, Nick is far from happy about it and suggests some options to induce a miscarriage. I'm in shock and not sure I'm ready to have another child to care for, but I know for sure I'm not doing anything to harm this one. I definitely want to keep it, no matter what he says.

As we are adjusting to this new reality, I walk into the kitchen one afternoon to see Colleen washing dishes at the sink, with Nick pressed against her, groping her from behind. I'm stunned that he would do that and that she is allowing it to happen. This has obviously been going on for some time, judging by the familiarity of their interaction. *My best friend and my husband? We've known each other since before we got married.* When they notice I'm standing there, no one says anything. I walk out, still in shock.

That night, Nick picks a fight with John and dramatically tells me, "Pack. We're leaving."

I know he's scared about what John will do if he finds out what I now know. I wonder what Colleen will tell John. I'm horrified by what I saw, but I'm also sad our friendship with John and Colleen is over, just like that. We can never go back.

So it's off to Mother's we go. Back to the twin beds and the candlewick bedspreads. Nick is reluctant to part with even £5 to help with expenses, so everything I earn from sewing goes toward helping Mother with the cost of our living here. Nick, meantime, spends more and more time away from home, often late into the night. It's after eleven o'clock on the night I decide to wait up for him. He sneaks into our bedroom, not expecting me to be awake and demanding to know where he has been.

"None of your business!" he snaps as he sits down on his bed.

"I want to know where you were, Nick," I reply firmly.

I have never been able to confront anyone about anything. I've always been the meek and mild little woman, walking away from arguments and letting people trample all over me. Living at home these past few weeks, I've watched my father do the same. He's a weakling who cannot stand up for himself, and I don't admire that. I don't want to be like him anymore. I don't want to be a coward. I need to find my courage. I can't go on like this. There must be something in life for me too.

Nick is livid. I have never questioned him before. Despite my determination to change, this man has been manipulating me for years, and he knows exactly what to say to get me back in my place.

"None of your business. Just leave me alone. And incidentally, get rid of that baby you're carrying, or have it adopted at birth. I'm not putting up with another kid. One is more than enough. I won't have two."

And just like that, I'm heartbroken. All resolve is gone through one quick threat to my baby. I kneel beside his bed, tears running down my cheeks as I beg him not to do this to me.

"Please forgive me for anything I've done to upset you. Please forgive me, Nick. I love you, but I love my babies too. Please, Nick," I beg.

"Shut up and go to sleep!"

But as I kneel there, it all starts to fall into place. The kitchen scene with Colleen was not the first time. There have been other women— the piano teacher who couldn't teach, the hours spent "flying" that were never logged. Then I remember Rose's strange reaction when I told her I was pregnant. I start to wonder if there was something going on with her daughter, Sheila. Maybe they were planning to have him leave me and marry her before I got pregnant. Maybe that's why he even agreed to have a baby in the first place—to avoid having to marry her. What about all those girls on the ship on the way over here? This is not a marriage. I have done everything for this man while he played around, refused to share anything with me, and demanded his conjugal rights while cheating on me with abandon. There is nothing here for me. Why am I hanging on? I make myself a promise that I will *never again*, under any circumstance, beg anyone for anything. And with all these powerful thoughts swirling in my head, I raise my hand and slap him across the face.

"Get out of my house!" he yells in shocked surprise.

"This is my mother's house, not your house," I point out, sounding calmer than I feel.

"This is where I live, and I want you to leave," he demands.

"If you give me the money in the bank account in America and pay our fares, Celeste and I will go back to San Francisco," I say. He briefly ponders this.

"First you'll have to get separation papers drawn up. Make sure you don't ask me for child support. I'll continue to give you £5 a week until you leave, and after that, you're on your own. Goodnight." He lies down, resolutely turns his back, and closes his eyes.

I climb into my own bed, weeping and shaking uncontrollably. I stood up for myself and my children. But what have I done? *What have I done?*

Everyone advises me to put the new baby up for adoption, everyone except Dorothy.

"Don't you dare give up your baby. If you do and Celeste finds out you gave away her brother or sister, she will never forgive you. We will be back in the U.S. before you give birth, and Celeste can come and stay with us while you are in the hospital. She will be okay. Everything will be fine."

I borrow her confidence and book an appointment with a lawyer whom I find in the phone book. He's very concerned that I'm not asking for child support and wonders how I'll ever manage alone with two babies. I reassure him that "where there's a will, there's a way," while inwardly hoping that is true. The separation documents are signed and sealed by the end of June. I'm glad the *Oronsay* is due to sail again in July, so I don't have to live wondering about who my husband is with and what he's doing for too much longer. Nick thinks he should be able to have one last night with me, but I emphatically decline his offer.

I've gotten used to my feelings not mattering around my childhood home, but I'm still shocked that my mother offers me no help during one of the hardest and scariest moments of my life. She isn't even angry at Nick for the callous way he is treating her daughter and granddaughter. On the contrary, she invites him to live in her house for as long as he wants. *Why doesn't she throw him out? I've been nothing but helpful, and I pay room and board. He doesn't even do that.* Like so many things in my life, it just doesn't make sense.

chapter eleven

Eagles in a Kiwi's Nest

So here I am, July 27, 1957, standing on the deck of the *Oronsay* for the third time. Now I have my seven-month-old daughter and unborn baby to care for and not much going for me. There is $1,500 in the bank in San Francisco, but I have no job, nowhere to live, and no medical insurance. I have no happy farewell over drinks in the lounge with excited family and friends this time. The ship does not look at all magnificent and glamorous anymore. Almost two weeks on board with all the celebratory parties and fascinating excursions at exotic ports of call hold no appeal. No one really seems to care that I'm leaving. I understand Nick not wanting *me,* but not caring about his own children is unfathomable to me. And as I watch him from the deck, he's laughing. He's probably feeling pretty carefree right now—no more responsibilities, no more wife to be accountable to. In my quest to be more courageous, I wish I had stood up to him and insisted he move out of my mother's home. But then, she would probably have sided with him, and I would have been looking for somewhere to live in Auckland.

I wish I'd never been born. I could jump from here and end this misery, but I'm such a good swimmer that I know I wouldn't drown. And I have no right to take the lives of my children. I'm just going to have to see where life leads next. I never knew you could feel so alone in a crowd.

The music changes to the somber strains of "Now Is the Hour" as the sturdy mooring ropes are released, and this time I cry for completely different reasons. Three-and-a-half years ago, we were leaving with hope and joy in our hearts, a bright new future ahead. Now I don't know if I'll ever be back here. I just know I have nothing and no one to hold on to right now, and I have two little people depending on me to be strong and have a plan. I hold my sleeping daughter close as I make my way to our cabin. After placing her carefully on the bunk to rest, I slump down beside her, sobbing all my fears and anguish into my hands. *I've got to hang on. Somehow this will all work out. I've got to stay strong. I'm just not sure how to do that.*

Celeste's cries wake me before dawn. A gentle rocking motion and the throbbing engine noise remind me I'm on a ship as I take a minute to get my bearings. I feel certain I'm in for a few days of seasickness as my stomach churns uneasily, but I get us cleaned up and dressed before finding my way to the now-familiar dining room. The sun is shining, and a minute sliver of hope breaks into my fog when I discover that one of the Open Air Campaigners we sailed with six months ago is sitting at my table with his lovely wife. I find out they are moving to the U.S. to begin a more permanent work there, and I share some of my story while they marvel at how much Celeste has grown. Sitting across from me is another Australian, Ron, who tells us that he is a schoolteacher, off on an adventure in Canada before settling down to become a headmaster. He explains that he wants to go out into the bush and find Sasquatch, which makes us all laugh and share stories of crazy myths we believe in. It's just what I need to help take my mind off my troubles.

As we sail north, Ron frequently finds me on deck or in the lounge, and we chat easily about our lives and hopes for the future. By Fiji, we're friends, and he wants me to go ashore with him. I explain that it's too hot for me and stay in the air conditioning I have come to appreciate so much. Even so, we go to parties together and talk for hours. He is a good-looking blond, and his attention is the diversion I need to make it through this tedious trip. I feel a renewed sense of energy building along with a tiny growing hope that everything will be all right. Ron promises that he will be there beside me when the baby is born, and although I doubt that will happen, I appreciate his sincere intentions. I'm not sure I'm ready to trust another man so soon.

Hawaii is as spectacular as ever, but today it is just a place to wait for the plane to San Francisco. I decided before the trip that I wanted to get to the U.S. as quickly as possible, so I'm not going up to Canada this time. Ron helps us through immigration and sees us safely onto the plane with a cheery, "See you in November!" before returning to the ship. The plane is packed, and Celeste cries for most of the five-hour flight. The stewardess tries to help when I ask her to warm a bottle but brings it back bouncing it from hand to hand because it's too hot to hold! After I ask for it to be cooled down, it comes back cold, and baby won't drink it. Not a great introduction to flying for my tired daughter.

I somehow manage to balance luggage and child through the customs routine and catch a bus into the city. It stops right across the street from what looks like a suitable hotel, so I leave the bags on the sidewalk, hoping no one will steal them, and dart inside to book a room. The bellhop retrieves our bags, and we settle in for the night. First stop the next morning is Koret's, where Joyce is surprised to see me back and looking for work. She quickly calls around and finds an opening in the design department until an opening in the order room becomes available.

As I walk around, people come running to see Celeste. And there I am, in the same maternity clothes I was wearing when they last saw me.

"Haven't you had that baby yet?" one of the salesmen teases. It's so good to be back here among friends. A workmate from the keypunch room suggests a good babysitter she knows, and I go to see her place. She has six children she cares for, and they all seem clean and happy. She agrees to take Celeste while I work. Now I only need to find an apartment. By the next afternoon, that is also taken care of, and I buy a used stroller, crib, and chest of drawers. I borrow a bed for myself, and we're set to begin our new life here.

———————————

Every morning, I walk eight blocks to drop Celeste off before catching a crowded bus to work. Everyone there is so kind to me. Even my boss pulls me aside one lunchtime and asks how long I plan to work.

"Until I go into labor," I reply with a smile.

"That's okay, just make sure I have the name of your doctor and the hospital you're going to, and I'll see that you get there." Looking around to make sure no one is within earshot, he quietly asks if I need money.

"No, I'm fine, thanks," I reply, blushing.

"Are you sure, Eunice? Because the company will lend you money, and you can pay it back from your wages." I fight back tears of gratitude and humiliation as I mumble my assurances. I hate that I'm in this position of needing people's help and sympathy, but it's nice that they offer.

I have no health insurance, but I'm hoping to see Dr. DeMailly again. When I contact his office, however, I am shocked to find out he was fatally shot a few weeks after Celeste was born. When they realize I have no insurance coverage, they recommend going to the Stanford University Hospital, where I had my first delivery. They are a teaching hospital, and their clinic charges only what you can afford. Of course, you must sit and wait to be seen, as there are no appointments, and most of the doctors I see are interns. Despite my gratitude for their help and kindness, this is not the happy experience of my first round of prenatal care. I decide to find out what would happen if I got sick and couldn't work. Because I'm not a U.S. citizen, the government would loan me the money I needed, but I would have to pay it back. That would be impossible. I have already spent most of the money in the bank account and have only enough left for the boat fare back to New Zealand that I'm saving in case I can't make it here. Money is so tight that I often make a can of baked beans last two meals. At one doctor's visit, the concerned physician asks if I'm afraid of gaining weight!

A note arrives to let me know Fred and Dorothy are back in San Francisco. I breathe a deep sigh of relief, knowing she will watch Celeste for free, and I finally have some friends I can count on close by. Ron writes several times, still determined to be with me when the baby is born.

I've been expecting Nick to turn up, as our visas won't allow us to stay out of the country for more than twelve months. Right on cue, here he is at my door. His seventeen-year-old fiancée wanted to come with him from New Zealand, but at the last minute, her mother put a stop to her leaving. He has exciting plans to start building their home as soon as he is back in Auckland, but he needs an immediate divorce since the separation agreement didn't legally end our marriage. He also wants me to sign over the papers for the car, which was put in my name before we left America.

"Do you still intend to keep the second child?" he asks.

"Yes, I do," I reply defiantly.

"Why are you being so stupid?" he spits back. I ignore his jab, sign the car over to him, and he leaves.

———————

Life goes on between work, home, and time with Dorothy and her children. Celeste loves it there, but I'm just managing to make ends meet. There are no fun trips or evenings with friends these days. Being a single mother is hard and lonely. Even when everything is going well, there's always a dark thought lurking in the background that things could change any day, and I'm the only one responsible for these children.

Labor begins late in the afternoon, a few days before my due date. Dorothy picks up Celeste, and I wait alone at home in the silence until I'm sure this is it. The cabbie drops me off at the main door instead of the emergency entrance, so I begin the long, painful climb up the staircase. I stop and bend over when another contraction hits.

"You okay, lady?" yells the cabbie, who's watching from the street.

"I'm fine," I yell sarcastically and continue my slow climb. Once inside, I walk unsteadily to the counter.

"Fill out these forms," the face at the window says, handing me a clipboard. I can barely stand, and I'm feeling dizzy, but I manage to get something on the admitting page and hand it back to her. A wheelchair appears, and I can finally sit down. The maternity ward is full, so they put me in a private room.

"Can I please stay here? I don't want to go to the ward," I ask the nurse who is helping me settle into the bed.

"We'll keep you here as long as we can, but if someone comes in who can pay, then we will have to move you." I pray no one does and I can stay here. I don't want to be the only one in the ward who doesn't have a happy husband doting over my baby and loving grandparents surrounding the bed with joy and cute gifts. I'm on my own with this. I did the last one alone, so I know I can get through this one too.

Before long, I'm in the delivery room, with the three large mirrors positioned behind the doctor so I can see what's happening as the baby is born.

"Are you sure you're going to keep this baby?" he asks as he prepares me for delivery. "Because if you've changed your mind, I won't let you see it."

"Oh, I'm keeping it," I reply emphatically.

"Okay then." A few hard pushes and the head crowns. "I think you have yourself a redhead!"

Baby slides out with the next big push, and it's a girl! They quickly check her and hand her to me. Through my happy tears, I see her tiny face and hold her little hand.

"I don't know how I'm going to keep you, but where there's a will, there's a way. I have the will, and I will find a way," I murmur to her. She's so beautiful and doesn't seem concerned. Her angelic face is a different shape than Celeste's, and she's a little bigger, 7 pounds, 15 ounces. She has the right number of fingers and toes—another perfect baby. I note the date, November 29, 1957, and they move me back to the private room.

He strides into the hospital room with a broad smile lighting his face and quickly hands me a fragrant bouquet of red roses.

"Thank you, Ron," I whisper as he bends to kiss me and apologizes for not getting here in time for the delivery. Seeing the hospital bassinet, he turns and peers in. His face tells a story of love and sadness—love for this sweet new baby and sadness that she's not his.

"She's so beautiful," he says, genuinely enthralled with her. "Would you have another one for me? I want to marry you." Before I can even think of an answer, he goes on. "My mother will just love you. She told me before I left that she wouldn't care if I brought home a prostitute—as long as I loved the girl I chose, it would be all right with her."

I stare at him. *I wonder what light you see me in, comparing me to a prostitute?* I don't give him an answer before he leaves.

Nick arrives later in the day, looks briefly at the baby, and asks me if I'll go to Mexico to get a quick divorce so he can return to New Zealand and marry his new love. I nod in silent disbelief.

When I get to Dorothy's the next day, Celeste is standing in her crib and staring at me with a puzzled look, as if trying to remember who I am. After a few seconds, she figures it out and smiles. I show her the new baby sister I brought with me.

"This is Diane Lynn Nichols, your sister." She reaches out and touches her. Now it's the three of us.

"Stay as long as you need," Dorothy reassures me. "I'll watch the girls while you go down to Mexico, if that's what you decide to do."

So Diane is not even a week old when I find myself sitting on a donut cushion in Nick's car, driving south of the border. I'm an emotional wreck and don't have enough clear thoughts in my head to put this all together. *How can I still feel like I love this man who is so callous, self-centered, and unfaithful? Is it him I love or the lifestyle of laughter and fun we once shared?* He's even insisting I pay half of the hotel room and half the divorce fee today. Unbelievable! Money is more important to him than his own family.

"We need to make sure that the divorce is legal in New Zealand," I tell the attorney.

"We will send it on to a New Zealand consulate in the U.S. to have it notarized," he replies. "You have nothing to worry about. We will take care of everything and mail a copy to your place of residence." He looks over the forms we have filled out. "What is the reason for this divorce?"

"Incompatibility," Nick answers.

"Incompatibility?" he asks with raised eyebrows. "She just gave birth to your second child in less than a year. That's hardly a sign of incompatibility!"

"Well, everyone has their moments," Nick replies, smiling. I sign the papers, and Nick declares himself a free man. I just want to get back to my babies.

Dorothy and I often have long talks about what I should do next.

"I just don't see how I can stay in this country, Dorothy. I don't earn enough to support my two children and myself. Someone else will always be caring for them. I won't even be a real mother if I'm missing all the new things they learn to do as they grow bigger. I can't get financial help, because I'm not a citizen. What if I get sick and can't work? They will take my kids from me."

"That's true. I wish I could do more to help you. At least back in New Zealand you would have a better welfare system to help you, and your mother is there."

"My mother wants to come over here and help me, but honestly, she gets sick so much, I'm afraid she would end up in the hospital, and I'd have to pay her bills too. I think I have no choice but to go home."

"What about Ron? He seems like a nice guy, and he's keen on you. He rented a room near here just so he could see you all the time. He's risking being here illegally just to be close to you."

"I know. But I've been thinking through so much of what he's said, trying to decide if marrying him would really be a good move. I don't like the idea of living in Australia, because it's so hot, and I don't do well in heat. He's very kind to me, but I've noticed he doesn't listen well. He'll ask where something is in the kitchen, and I'll explain it only to have him go to the completely wrong place over and over again. And he goes on and on about his mother—no one irons shirts better than she does, no one can cook steak like she can—I'm not sure I want to compete with that. And even though it's nice to hear he's close to his father, when I told him I like fishing and suggested I go with them on their weekly trips to the lake, he said, 'No, that's time for just my father and me.' I spent months sitting in a car while Nick took flying lessons. I've always allowed my needs to be put on the back burner. There's got to be more in this life for me. I'm going to wait and try to be patient. It's too soon for another commitment."

"Probably a good idea to go back home then. But I'll miss you all so much. I love having you here."

"And I love living in America. I wish there was a way to stay and take care of my children. I'd love for them to grow up here."

I book passage for my little family for just over two months from now on the S.S. *Orcades*, leaving February 12, 1958. Fred and Dorothy offer for us to stay with them until then so I can regain my strength and save a little money. Celeste and the other children enjoy celebrating her first birthday. Dorothy's youngest boy shows Celeste how to blow out the candle and gives her the biggest piece of cake, which she proceeds to smear all over her face and hair." *I'm going to miss this family so much.*

Nick has turned up again, this time to ask for my engagement ring.

"I already paid for one ring, and I want it back so I can have the diamond reset for my new fiancée," he explains matter-of-factly. I look down at the ring on my finger that once meant so much. I thought I would give it to Celeste one day, but now, with two daughters, that won't work. It means nothing now anyway. It's just another painful reminder of hopes destroyed and dreams crushed. It slides off my skinny finger easily. I place it in my palm and hold it out to him. He reaches out and takes it.

"Oh no, you don't," yells Dorothy. "How could you, Nick? That ring is not yours. You gave that to her, and you have no right to take it back. How dare you!"

Dorothy's angry reaction shames him into giving it back to me, and he quickly leaves for the airport and his flight back to New Zealand.

The new year has started, and I'm beginning to plan for yet another journey across the Pacific Ocean—my fourth time in four years. In between working and caring for my children, I'm visiting government offices to get Diane's passport and visa organized, packing what few belongings we have, and buying what I need for the days at sea. When the doorbell rings one evening, I anticipate another visit from Ron, but it is Nick who greets me with a smile, like he's an old friend coming to catch up.

"Where's the new bride?" I ask sarcastically.

Sheepishly, he averts his eyes as he mumbles, "She got together with my lawyer while I was away. She took the gifts I bought for her and then told me she didn't want to see me anymore. She dumped me!"

Good for her!

"I came to ask if we could get back together," he continues.

Are you kidding me? What nerve! After all you've done to me. Why on earth would I even consider it? The last seven years pass through my thoughts in quick succession. The confusion and excitement of our early dating days. Getting pregnant during our engagement and getting married shortly after. Watching him sing *our* song to another woman at our wedding. Letting him take my dead baby out of my arms without letting me say goodbye. Struggling month by month to pay the bills while he hoarded his own paycheck for himself. Sitting in a car for hours, waiting for him to take flying lessons, only to have him lie about his flight hours and spend them doing who knows what. Feeling the end of his gun on my chest because he thought a friend of his was flirting with me. Watching him grope my best friend. Aching for my children because of his callous attitude and neglect toward them. *There's no decision to make.*

"No, Nick. It's over," I reply.

"But I still have those house plans," he offers.

"That is not my house."

"Is it because of Ron?"

"No, it's not because of Ron. You and I are finished. That's all."

I close the door in his face before the gall of this man has totally sunk in, and I go to share this latest affront with Dorothy.

She is aghast. "I can't believe that guy. You know, when all this began, I wanted you two to get back together again for the sake of the kids, but now I think you're much better off alone," she says. After an uncertain pause, she continues, "I didn't want to tell you this, but now that he's definitely gone, I will. He used to come to see me on his way to Half Moon Bay when you thought he was flying. He would flirt with me, and I knew if I would have said, 'Let's go to the bedroom,' he would have done it. In fact, I'm positive that's why he came here. I'm sorry, Eunice."

What is wrong with this man? Is no woman off-limits for him? My best friends? Did he ever really care about me, or was I just a meal ticket while he did whatever he wanted with whomever he wanted? I have been so naïve and let myself be used. I will not do that again. I'm taking control and doing it my way from now on. Enough is enough.

February 15, 1958. I'm leaving San Francisco again, knowing this trip will seem even longer with two babies to care for. The ship's wake rushes by as we gain speed, leaving the famous skyline behind. We pass under the unforgettable Golden Gate Bridge and out into the blue ocean depths. *Why did I come back here?* I knew there was little chance I could make it on my own. I only survived for seven months. At least Diane is an American citizen; she and Celeste will have the option to return in the future. I did achieve that. I'm a Kiwi with two little American daughters. And the divorce is finalized.

Last week, Ron helped me crate up the crib, chest of drawers, highchair, and stroller. I said a gut-wrenchingly hard goodbye to Dorothy, Fred, and their children this morning at the house. They have done so much for me, and I will miss them all. Ron drove me to the pier today and promised to write to me every day. I haven't told him yet that I have no plans to marry him; he was so sad when we parted on the dock. I feel bad, but I know I can't go through with the plan he has for my life. From now on, I will do what's best for me and my kids.

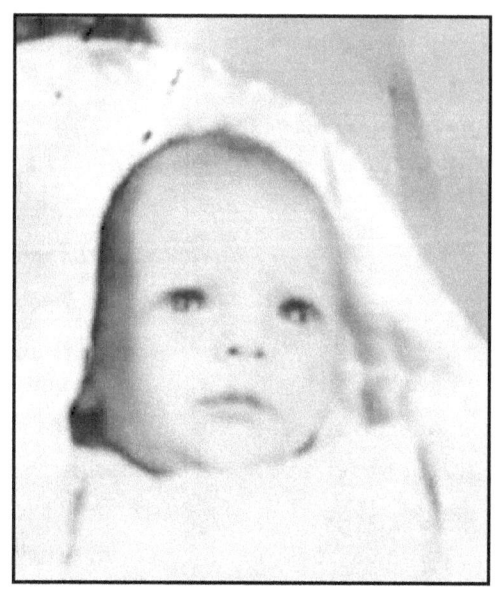

Diane Lynn Nichols, two months old.
Born November 29, 1957.

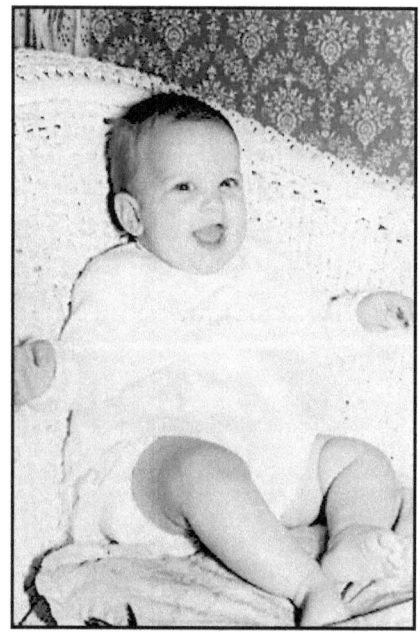

Celeste, six months old, 1957.

chapter twelve

A Marriage of Convenience

My cabin is supposed to be set up with a crib for my babies, but there is no sign of one as I try to get both children settled in. Eventually, a tall, slim man with blue eyes and a Cockney accent knocks on the door.

"I'm ya steward," he says. "Ya can call me Jimmy. I 'ear ya 'ave a problem."

"Yes, I was told they would remove the bottom bunk and replace it with some sort of a crib," I inform him.

"We could put a net up to keep 'em from rolling onto the floor," he suggests and goes off to get one. After he attaches a length of netting between the top and bottom bunks, I wonder out loud what will stop them from crawling or rolling out the ends.

"It's not going to work, Jimmy. I really need a crib." He obviously doesn't want to bother with this request, and his face shows it. He slumps off to get the necessary tools, and an hour later, I have a sturdy crib installed that will work nicely.

"Much better. Thank you. And could I have some sheets that fit it, please?" Off he goes again.

Meals on board are a problem. I can take Celeste to the dining room, but they don't allow babies. They've also let me know they won't deliver meals to our cabin, so I have no choice but to take Celeste with me and hurry through each meal, hoping Diane is okay.

After breakfast one morning, I return to the cabin to find Jimmy sitting on the floor, holding three-month-old Diane.

"She was cryin' when I came in ta get linens. I thought I'd just sit wif 'er til ya got back," he says in response to my quizzical look. From then on, he is there for each meal, and I am grateful I can eat in peace. There is no money left for disposable diapers, so I ask Jimmy to bring me a dozen crib sheets to use instead. Every day, he brings a new pile and takes away the soiled ones. There are no parties on this trip, just the cabin and the dining room.

I finally write to Ron and admit I don't want to travel to Australia or marry him. "Go look for your Sasquatch. Follow your dreams and be happy." I slip ashore in Honolulu just long enough to put it in the mail.

By the time we reach Fiji, Jimmy and I are more than friends. He asks if I will go ashore with him. "T'ere are caregivers 'oo will stay wif the children while we go," he reassures me. I could really do with a change of scenery, so I agree to go for a short trip, and we hire the help.

"Wanna get a 'otel room?" he asks as we begin walking through the crowded market.

"Of course not." Again, I'm left wondering how men must perceive me. I feel cheapened by his vulgar proposal.

We head back to the ship and spend the afternoon talking. I learn that this is his last trip at sea. He has served his five years as a steward, and that gives him the opportunity to get off the ship wherever he pleases. He has chosen Australia because he has been having an affair with a married woman there for about three years. But now that he has met me, he's having second thoughts and wants to know if I will write to him in Australia. I agree, but I'm not sure where this will lead.

The ship has barely docked when Mother comes aboard to help me get the babies and luggage ashore. She picks up Diane to have a little snuggle with her newest grandbaby.

"Gena is here with a pickup truck. She'll drive us home."

"I didn't expect to see her," I reply. "I'm glad she has a truck. I brought the baby's furniture with me." It takes a long time to clear customs and load the truck. I turn to look at the ship to see if I can find Jimmy in the crowd that's milling around, but I don't see him. I decide to come back in the evening before they sail. Back at the pier a few hours later, I see him on deck, just as the ship begins to move away from land. We wave to each other. He really does look somewhat like Nick—tall, with brown hair and blue eyes. Their personalities are complete opposites, thank goodness, but my kids could pass as his.

I'm back at the old stucco house, like nothing has changed. Mother left a pile of letters on the kitchen table for me. Ron has written every day, just as he said he would, until the day he got my Dear John letter. *I hope I've done the right thing. He really is a very sweet guy.* My huge old trunk has been sitting out on the porch for a few days by the time I finally get around to unpacking it. As I unload the things inside, I notice that the two American silver dollars I had saved for my daughters are missing. I suspect Gena took them, and I'm furious. She acts like she's helping me but then does this. I don't say anything. No one around here believes me anyway.

I call a factory that will deliver sewing to our house so I can work from home and be with my children. I rearrange the living room furniture to form a play area and set up my machine in there. Jimmy writes to say he's coming to New Zealand. He asks if he can rent a room in my mother's house, and she agrees. She has begun complaining that the children are too much for her, and she needs help to get dinner ready each night. I'm glad I didn't take her up on the offer to come to the U.S. to help me. I'd be taking care of her too. I hire a woman to pick Celeste up from the little daycare she attends and watch both girls from 4 to 6 p.m. Neither child likes her, and she soon quits.

Looking through the paper one evening, I see an advertisement for beachfront property for sale on the east coast of Auckland. I call the seller to find out more, and he comes by with subdivision plans. We drive out to see the land the next day. It seems like a great investment to me, so I buy two lots, one for each child, and slowly begin paying off the loan each month.

"At least I have a goal to work toward," I tell myself as I work late into the night.

Life with my parents is becoming unbearable. A friend suggests I get a state house and live off welfare.

"I'd rather be working," I assure her.

"But your mother is finding it hard having you here," she replies.

It's not easy for me either, I think to myself.

Pop spends months excavating beneath the house to make himself a workshop and is once again bringing musical instruments home to repair. As the evenings become noticeably colder, the fire is lit, and it becomes the focal point of the house. Mother and I often sit there, knitting and talking about the day.

"Nick never even wrote to me during all the months I was gone, even with me being pregnant and taking care of Celeste alone," I remark as we watch the logs burning in the grate.

"I used to read him the letters you sent me," she replies. "That way he kept up with what you were doing. He had a really nice girlfriend, you know."

"How do you know that?" I ask.

"Well, I met her. He brought her around here several times. She came for dinner," she says matter-of-factly.

I stare at her in disbelief. I knew he was living with my mother during that time, but I had no idea this was going on.

"You mean, you entertained his mistress while I was struggling to make ends meet in America?" I respond, stunned.

"Yes," she replies unapologetically.

I am too shocked and hurt to say anything more. I realize I have to get out of here. I can't stand to be with this woman every night, and I don't want her around my children. She seems to enjoy finding ways to hurt me.

––––––––––––

Jimmy Reason arrives with his piano accordion a few weeks later and moves in with us. I have never liked calling him Jimmy, so I ask if he would mind if I called him Jim.

"Call me whatcha like, Girl," he replies with a smile. So he becomes Jim, and I become Girl.

A short time later, Jim asks me if I will marry him and give him a son. *Why not? It will get me away from here, and that seems like a fair deal. I need financial help, and he wants a son.*

"Okay. Let's do it."

There's nothing romantic about this ceremony. We go down to City Hall, get a license, and say our vows to love, honor, and obey. Back at my mother's house, I tell her what we have done, and she is upset. She doesn't think the marriage will last, and she doesn't like him.

"Oh well, you've made your bed; now you'll have to lie in it," she says to me.

"That's why I'm telling you all this. I'm sleeping in his bed tonight."

I'm making that very bed sometime later when I find a letter under Jim's pillow. It is from his lady friend in Australia, saying she understands how women trick men into marriage, and she is sorry it has happened to him. She says the navy sweater she is knitting for him is almost finished and will be in the mail soon. A week later, the sweater arrives. It is made of a lovely navy wool, beautifully hand knitted in a cable pattern and carefully stitched together. The fire is blazing away nicely, but the sweater burns slowly and makes an awful smell in the house. No one asks me about it, and I don't mention it either.

I just can't figure out why Jim is having such a hard time getting a job. He leaves for interview after interview and always comes back with a sad tale of how they don't like Cockneys.

"I only need to open me bleedin' mouth, and that's it," he says.

When I find an advertisement for a farm job that includes a house, fresh meat, and farm produce as part of the remuneration, it seems like a wonderful place to raise our children.

"I could do that," he says when I show it to him, and he phones the farmer. I listen in.

"No, I 'aven't never worked on a farm before, but any damn fool can milk a cow."

So much for that job! Now I understand what's been happening. It's not the accent that's the problem.

Early Monday morning, I see a job offer for an untrained plasterer. I call to get the address and go to see the business owner.

"My husband is a Cockney, has absolutely no experience, and needs training. Will you hire him?"

"Yes. Send him along."

So Jim gets his first job in New Zealand and begins training as a plaster caster. He helps to pour plaster to create the tiles that become the dome for the new planetarium's sky display. His pride in this accomplishment encourages him to learn more about his new trade.

———————

Jim and my mother are having a loud argument when I walk into the kitchen. It's about him being inconsiderate and lazy and beyond help as far as she is concerned.

"You'll have to move. I can't put up with him anymore. He's just useless," she tells me.

We find an empty little house not far away and move within a week. The rent is over half what Jim earns. The backyard is mostly waist-high weeds on either side of a path that leads to the clothesline. We buy some used furniture and settle in.

"This place needs some music," Jim remarks one quiet evening a few weeks later. I take down the cardboard box I have stored in the closet and pull out a pretty necklace Ron gave me, a sapphire pendant Frank made, and the infamous engagement ring from Nick. They become the down payment on a radio/record player. It is a nice piece of furniture that takes pride of place in our compact living room and fills our silence with music. I'm happy to have something positive come from those bitter memories.

My days are long and exhausting. I reluctantly drag my tired body out of bed to face hours of sewing, washing laundry by hand, baking bread for Jim's lunches, and shopping for bargains to keep the food budget going. It won't be long before Celeste turns two and Diane turns one. And I'm pregnant again. If it's the boy that Jim wants, I hope it will reduce his obvious favoritism for Diane and fulfill my part of the marriage agreement as well. Money is very tight. We get a small children's allowance from the government, and I use it only when I must so I can save the rest for the children. We can't afford the loan payments on the two pieces of land I bought for the girls, so Jim tells me we should give it back to the owner of the subdivision. The man gladly takes them back and, of course, promptly sells them for a huge profit. It's only after I've followed Jim's advice that I realize I need to make the financial decisions in the future. I should have sold the land and gotten some money out of the deal. *I've got to think things through more and not rely on other people's judgement.*

I wake up confused, not sure what woke me in the middle of the night. It wasn't a dream—I never have dreams. And I don't hear one of the children crying. There's a warm sensation on my back, and I can hear a weird sound. I turn and see Jim convulsing, his head thrown back and his arms flailing. I get hit a couple of times before my feet get to the floor, and I realize the warm sensation on my back is urine. Standing there, I watch him writhe until the spasms stop and he starts to breathe heavily. The snoring goes on for the rest of the night. Close to dawn, he wakes slowly and looks over at me.

"I 'ad a fit, didn't I," he says groggily.

"Yes, you did. Are you okay?" I ask.

"Sure. It's been a while since I 'ad one."

"You didn't tell me, Jim. Do you think that's fair? What other secrets do you have?" I ask.

"Well, I thought I was over it. Ya mustn't say nothin' to no one. If people find out I'm epileptic, I won't be able to keep a job. Promise ya won't tell."

"I promise." *What choice do I have?*

"It started during the war. I served all over Europe. I was sittin' on an 'ill watchin' a city get bombed by the Germans when I 'ad me first one, and then it just got worse. It weren't unusual for me ta 'ave fourteen fits a day then. It's fighting that sets me off. I only need to 'ear people arguin', and that night I 'ave a seizure. It always gives me a nasty taste in me mouth, so I know when one is coming. I always 'ave 'em at night in me sleep now, so it's easy to keep 'em a secret. But it leaves me so drained I can't work the next day. Call work and tell 'em I've got the flu or something and won't be in today." He writes to his mother in England, requesting that she send his medications to help control the seizures. *What have I gotten myself into this time? What about the baby I'm carrying? Will it be epileptic too? I would never have married him if I'd known this.*

The girls are with my mother—I *so* wish I didn't have to leave them with her. I just don't trust her. Jim dropped me off at Cornwall Hospital by taxi and went home earlier today. I have been laboring all night—no medications here, just natural childbirth. It seems things are getting more complicated with each delivery I have. Finally, he arrives at noon the next day—May 9, 1959. Yes, a boy! He's 7 pounds, 9 ounces and looks perfect, but I'm still concerned he might have epilepsy. Of course, they can't tell if anything is wrong yet, so we'll just have to see as he grows. A nurse phones Jim at work to tell him the good news.

"Is he all right?" he asks.

"Yes, he's perfect."

"How's me wife?"

"She's doing well too," she reassures him. He goes back to work.

Deciding on a name is not difficult, as Jim already decided if we had a boy, he would be named after him. So James Reason it is, with no middle name, just like his dad. We start out calling him Jimmy but quickly change to Jamie, a good Scottish version of James.

He's sure a good eater but is crying so much even after nursing. They offer him a bottle, and he drinks all seven ounces straight down! At one feeding, he gets so frustrated that things aren't fast enough, he stops sucking and turns blue. I scream for the nurse, thinking he's dead. She takes him from me, and he quickly revives.

"Just frustrated and holding his breath," she reassures me. "But to be honest, when you first gave him to me, I thought he was dead too." My hospital stay is ten restful days, the usual amount here in New Zealand. I miss seeing my girls, as they won't allow children to visit the maternity ward, but I really need this recovery time too. There will be no breaks once I'm home.

Jim is working a good number of hours, and I'm at the sewing machine, churning out factory dresses whenever I can, but we're still not making ends meet. My mother arrives with a letter sent to her address. It's from Nick, and I can see it has been steamed open and resealed. I wait for an opportunity to sit outside on the step to read it alone. I'm nervous about the contents and upset that this man can still bother me. It turns out, he's applying for American citizenship and needs a letter from me stating that I didn't want child support when we divorced. That isn't true—I wanted it, but he refused to give it to me, and in the speedy Mexican divorce we got, there was no time to work it out.

"Is there anything you would like for the kids?" he asks uncharacteristically. Obviously, there's some pressure to look like he is taking care of his family in order to get the citizenship he wants.

I realize I need to be careful here and word this letter so that it serves his interests as well as my own. After some thought, I write,

"At the time of the divorce, no arrangements for child support were made. And, yes, I would like some sweaters and raincoats for the girls." A few weeks later, a check for child support arrives and a parcel containing two cheap navy sweaters and two blue raincoats.

"Another gift is on the way," his letter says, "but it is big and will take at least six weeks to get there."

At last! A little more money for the children. But we're still struggling and need to find some place cheaper to rent. A few days later, Jim comes hurrying in through the door after a long day at work, announcing that he thinks he has the answer. A friend of his at work just bought a little place in Te Atatu, and he wants to rent it.

"Can we go look at it this Saturday?" he asks me excitedly.

"It's such a long way for you to get to work," I remind him.

"But it's 'alf the rent we pay 'ere. Come on, let's at least go look at it. There's gotta be some sort of transportation from there."

On Saturday morning, the proud new owner drives us out to look at it. The tiny house turns out to be a shed attached to a garage. It sits on a half acre of weeds, with a tiny patch mowed at the front. Inside the front door, a small kitchen leads into a main room. There's a little bedroom with a sleeping porch and a bathroom. The roof is flat but doesn't leak. It will do.

"Can we dig up these weeds and plant a vegetable garden?" I ask Jim's friend.

"Sure, you can. This would make a great garden. It used to be a chicken run, so you won't have to fertilize for some time."

I look around the neighborhood. There's a grocery store, a hardware store, and a pharmacy within walking distance. It's surrounded by expensive homes with beautiful flower gardens, and there are a lot of families with young children. However, I'm still worried about how Jim is going to get to work.

"There's a train that runs close enough to work; he would just have to get from here to the train station," his workmate offers.

"I could get me a bike," Jim suggests, and it's settled. We move in.

Sewing is out of the question now, as the factory won't deliver way out here. I buy a push mower for the grass and start digging up the weeds to prepare for the vegetable garden. Jim is reluctant to mow because, he says, he likes the "natural" look.

"We need a place for the children to be able to run around, Jim," I tell him, so he half-heartedly mows a small patch. He prefers digging, so he does some of that for me on the weekends, and we take turns with the mowing. Soon, the ground is ready, and we're excited to get plants into the rich soil.

The owner was right. The soil is so rich here that everything we plant grows bigger and better than any garden I've ever had. The corn is tall enough for the children to play hide-and-seek in. We have so many lettuces, cucumbers, and tomatoes that we're giving them away to everyone we know.

Late that summer, the customs office sends a letter to say a box has arrived from the U.S., and I need to come down to claim it. All the way into town on the bus, I'm wondering if this will be worth the time and effort. The box is huge and heavy. Now I'm wondering how I'll get it home.

"What's in it?" I ask the guy with the clipboard.

"The declaration says it's a rocking horse. There's a £22 duty payment, madam."

"No way! I can't afford that," I protest.

"Well, you must pay it, or we'll send it back," he threatens.

"Then send it back."

"Come on, lady. A rocking horse from America is worth a lot more than £22."

"How do you know that?" I ask.

"Well, if someone is sending a gift from America, it's bound to be the best. The stuff from there is worth a lot," he reasons.

"Have you ever been to America? They have cheap stuff there too, you know. May I open the box and see what's inside?"

"No. You can't open it until you pay the duty," he informs me.

"Look," I explain, tired and frustrated. "This is a gift from my ex-husband. He has never sent his children a present like this before. I have worked and supported his children all their lives, and now that he finally sends them something, you make the duty beyond my ability to pay. It will have to go back, and that's that." I begin to walk away.

"One minute," he says, holding up his hand. He goes into a back room and returns a few moments later. "All right. You may take it— duty free."

"Thank you!"

Well, that's nice, but how do I get this thing home? There is no alternative but to get a taxi. This is turning into an expensive present. I hope it's worth it. At home, I rip the crate apart and find a beautiful play horse made of molded rubber, with "Wonder Horse" embossed on the saddle. It is supported by a tubular metal frame with springs on each corner so the horse can move up and down or back and forth. It's a terrific gift, and I'm glad it wasn't returned. The children will have hours of fun on this, and it is good exercise too.

Now that I'm receiving child support from Nick, I'm able to save enough money for a down payment on a washing machine. With three children in cloth diapers, I need it. The only place where it can be connected to a water supply is in the kitchen, so that is where it sits. It has a large tub that I fill with water, soap, and clothes before setting the timer to agitate them. Once they are clean, I wring out each item by feeding it through the moving rollers at the top. I empty the tub of the dirty, soapy water, add clean water to rinse the clothes, then squeeze them through the rollers again before hanging them outside to dry. It's a lot of work, but it sure is easier than doing it all while leaning over the bathtub.

Three houses down lives the Blomfield family, with two daughters the same ages as our two girls. Their mother, Audrey, and I become instant friends. She is logical and clever, always willing to listen, and helpful as I think through decisions I need to make. Being in her company becomes my refuge. When I turn up on her doorstep, I'm always welcomed in as the kettle goes on for tea and the sandwiches are made. We natter for hours while the children play in the spacious backyard, and we solve the problems of our lives, of our neighborhood, and of the whole world! Our families go to parties together and spend vacations camping at the beach. We celebrate birthdays in their home and decorate our girls' rooms with the same pictures. Whatever is going on, we have each other's backs.

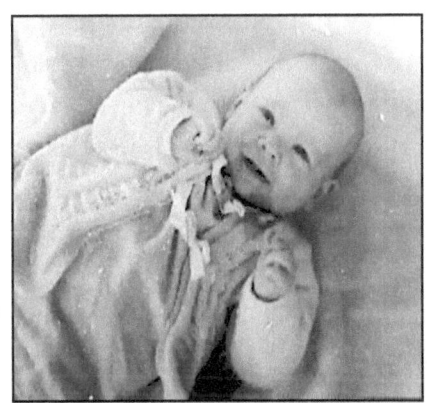

James (Jamie) Reason,
two months old.
Born May 9, 1959.

Diane (two), Jamie (one), and Celeste (three), May 1960.

chapter thirteen

A Place to Call Home

I want to have my own home. I've been saving up as much money as I can, but Jim thinks we should just get a state house.

"I don't like the neighborhoods where the state houses are. I want the children to grow up somewhere safe," I insist.

When a real estate agent shows us a house on Rangeview Road in Sunnyvale, I know this is it. Set on a steep hill overlooking the railway line, it's a split-level house with the bedrooms downstairs and the living room and kitchen upstairs. It's nothing grand, a box really, but it is affordable, with no down payment and a monthly mortgage not much more than our rent. I am happy to move out of the chicken coop but will miss my regular heart-to-heart talks with Audrey. We will have to find new ways to get together.

Not long after we move in, Mother asks if we can move back into her house to take care of Pop and my nephew, Robert, while she has hand surgery.

"It will probably take me about three months to recover," she informs me.

I don't want to do it—we're just getting settled into our own place, and I like it here. There's room for all of us in this house, and it feels like we're finally making headway on the bills. But I agree to do it. We rent out the house, pack our clothes, and move back in with her.

Robert, Daphne's son, is fourteen now and living with Mother because he's too much for Daphne to handle. He's immature and unreliable but keeps begging Mother for a lawn mower so he can earn money cutting grass for the neighbors.

"Don't be ridiculous, Mother. He's not capable of doing that yet. He'll end up hurting someone or running over his own foot. Wait until he's older," I plead with her. She buys him one anyway.

Jamie is eighteen months old and toddling around after his sisters, who are now three and four years old. It's a warm summer day about a month since we moved back into the old stucco house. I'm back at the sewing machine, trying to make a little extra money while we're living in town. I just found out I'm pregnant again. When I hear Robert mowing the grass in front of the house, something tells me to go outside and see what he's doing. *I'll just sew this seam and then I'll go.* But before I finish, I hear Robert yelling for me. He comes running into the house, carrying Jamie in his arms, blood pouring from Jamie's foot. My screams bring Pop running. He quickly ties a rag tourniquet around Jamie's leg and washes his foot under the bathroom faucet. The whole width of his foot from the base of his toes to the middle has a deep strip that has been cut off, leaving raw flesh and a lot of blood.

I fumble with the phone book, trying to call an ambulance, but I'm shaking too much to find the number. I call my doctor instead because I have that number memorized, and they send a taxi. Hastily wrapping my now-unconscious baby in a towel, I leave for the hospital. I wait forty-five excruciatingly long minutes in the emergency waiting area before finally being escorted into an examination room. I have been faithfully undoing the tourniquet every few minutes as Pop instructed, and Jamie has obviously lost a lot of blood. He is quickly taken into surgery. An hour later, he is stitched up and handed back to me. I'm given the instructions to take him to our doctor for antibiotic shots every day but not to remove the bandages under any circumstances.

I am so angry at Robert that I can't bear the thought of facing him when I get back to the house. I don't trust myself not to hurt him. I needn't have worried. He keeps well away from me, always eating his meals in his room and not even asking how Jamie is doing. I know I can't stay in this house a minute longer. I talk to a lawyer about how we can get our renters out so we can move home.

The fifth day after the accident, the doctor is concerned about Jamie's foot. He smells it and asks for permission to remove the bandage.

"Go ahead. I don't like the smell of it either. I've been walking around outside with him, trying to get rid of the horrible odor."

He takes a swab of the poorly healing area and sends us to the hospital laboratory with it. The next day, we're back in the doctor's office for the results.

"Is it gangrene?" I ask, terrified that my suspicions will be confirmed.

"No, but it's close. Jamie will need to be admitted to the hospital for surgery. They will open this wound, clean it out, and do a skin graft from the thigh area to cover it. He will be in there for several weeks until we know it's healing properly."

"Is his foot okay? Can you tell if the tendons are cut?"

"I can't tell yet. We'll have to wait until he's walking again to be able to see what function he still has."

It's so hard leaving my little boy crying in that white hospital crib. Memories of my own time in the hospital flood back. I wasn't much older than he is when I was lying in a busy ward just like this. I know how he feels. I wish I could stay with him. At least I get to visit for an hour every day, and the mother of the injured child next to him assures me that Jamie doesn't cry for long after I leave. We can't move out of Mother's house until Jamie is out of the hospital, because it's too far to travel daily, and I have other children to take care of.

Remembering the agony of my own time in the hospital, I ask Mother why she never visited me when I was in there all those years ago.

"They didn't allow parents to visit then," she says matter-of-factly. "They thought it would upset the children too much."

I wish I had understood that back then. It would have saved me such a lot of heartache. Maybe I wouldn't feel so unwanted and unlovable, even to this day. I don't ever want my children to feel this way.

During this time, I get the opportunity to ask our doctor about Jim's epilepsy, especially as it relates to Jamie.

"It's hard to say what the cause was, probably shock during the war. If you can keep Jim from worrying and make sure he is not stressed, he will probably not have any more seizures."

"That's what I've been doing. I take responsibility for all the decisions, and he is happy to let me do it."

"As for Jamie, it's hard to tell. He may have inherited his father's predisposition to some form of seizures. We'll have to see as he grows up."

Pop is in tears. I've never seen a man cry before, and it really upsets me.

"What's wrong?" I ask him.

"I can't take the way my tools for my repair work are being messed up by Robert. Every Tuesday night when I go to play cards, your mother allows him to go down to my workshop. He gets into the glue and uses my good camel-hair brushes to paint it on things, then leaves them covered in glue. They're ruined, and I can't afford to keep replacing them," he complains.

"Why don't you lock the door?"

"I do, but your mother gives him the key. I can't take the way she treats me anymore. Can I come and live with you when you move out?" he begs.

"I'll have to ask Jim."

It's okay with Jim, so Pop leaves with us when we move back home the following day. I'm not sure about this. He's never helpful around the house, and I remember all too well the severe beatings he gave me as a child. I'll have to keep an eye on him around my kids.

Back home, my first job is to scrub all the floors with kerosene to get rid of the flea infestation the renters left behind. With that taken care of, we move into a happy routine of caring for the children and working. Pop is organizing a workshop for himself under the front part of the house, and Jim is looking into a new job at Fletcher Construction, making plaster acoustic ceiling tiles.

"Be an independent contractor: Work your own hours, be paid by the piece," the ad says. He takes the job. It's a while before he gets the hang of it, but with practice, he becomes one of their best workers and begins to bring home a decent paycheck, all of which he hands over to his wife. *Very different from my last marriage.*

I finally have time to think about this new baby I'm carrying. Life has been so crazy for the last few months, and time has slipped by without my noticing. I'm due soon, so I start pulling out the old baby clothes and figuring out what else I'll need to get. Jamie's foot is healing well, and he walks normally. There's a bright red scar across the top of his little foot and another one on his thigh where they took the skin graft, but the doctor assures me that they will both fade as time passes.

———————

We are so fortunate to have wonderful neighbors next door. They are the ones who take me to the hospital when I go into labor early one evening in June. I have arranged for a woman to come and help with the children and make meals while I'm gone. Pop refuses to watch the children for even a few minutes, Jim is working long hours, and Mother won't come here because of Pop. So here I am at the hospital for the fourth time, alone and facing my worst delivery yet. Baby is presenting face-first, with no anesthetic and no doctor present, just an inexperienced nurse. After hours of impossibly painful labor, I'm not expecting the baby to be born alive, so I push as hard as I can to get it out as quickly as possible. When the labor is finally over, I wait to be told the grave news. Instead, I hear a robust cry, and I take a deep breath of relief. Trudy Margaret is a healthy 7 pounds, 14 ounces, but as I look at her, I notice her neck is badly swollen from her rough entrance into the world.

"Her delivery is rarer than triplets," the nurses tell me as they congratulate my determination. After a careful check to make sure she has all the required fingers and toes, I note the date, June 28, 1961, hand her back, and fall into an exhausted sleep.

I'm not sure how much time has passed, but it feels like several hours. I force myself to open my eyes despite the grogginess and immediately notice the bassinet next to me is empty.

"Nurse! Where's my baby? Is she dead?" I yell.

"Oh gosh, no! She was screaming so loudly, she was disturbing the whole ward! When we saw you were too worn out to wake up to that racket, we decided to let you sleep and took her to the nursery. I'll go and get her for you."

My hospital stay is a full two weeks, and I need every minute of it to recover. It's wonderful to have some one-on-one time with my new daughter before we return home to be a family of seven. As soon as we walk through the door, the older children gather around Trudy to touch her and to make her smile. Jim holds her for a few minutes, and Pop's only comment is, "What have we here?" as he looks over. He never was a man of many words.

Pop spends most of his days puttering around in his workshop. Guitars and violins hang from the rafters, and his tools are neatly organized in drawers or on wall hangers. As I pass by his open door on my way back from the mailbox, I see two-year-old Jamie standing near Pop with a pebble in his hand, looking up at his smiling grandfather. Thinking there is some kind of game going on between them, I smile at Pop and walk up the steps to go in and open the mail.

A moment later, a movement catches my eye, and I turn to see Jamie collapsing in the doorway, having a seizure. I carefully pick him up and hold him until he is conscious again.

"What happened?" I ask gently.

"Pop hit me with a hose," he cries.

"He did what?" I am furious. After asking Celeste to keep an eye on her brother, I storm downstairs.

"Why did you hit Jamie?" I yell at Pop.

"He was throwing stones at my guitars," he explains defensively.

"So you hit him with a hose?"

"He nearly hit one of my instruments," he says, as if that justifies hitting a two-year-old so violently.

"Get out of my house! I will *not* have you hitting my children the way you hit me," I yell and turn to hurry back upstairs.

It's several weeks before he can move to Gena's home, but relief settles in when he finally leaves. I keep an eye on Jamie, knowing now that he can have seizures too. Jim is having fewer seizures now that I know not to stress him about anything. He won't do much around the house, but he does go to work each day and comes home afterward. I know where he is and what he's doing. All the responsibility for running our home falls on me, but at least that way I know what's going on.

———————

We don't have a phone, so if people want to talk to me, they just turn up at the door. And a couple of surprises do just that. The first one is Nick. *Will I ever get away from this man?* He is back in the country, telling me he's trying to avoid having to be involved in the Vietnam War. Like most American men, he is worried he will be forced to go. With him back in New Zealand, the child support stops, so my lawyer draws up papers for a court battle. When the day of the hearing finally arrives, Nick is conveniently out of the country, so the judge asks me how much I want in monthly support. I give him a figure, and he awards it to us.

"If he ever sets foot in this country again, he'll be arrested," my lawyer assures me after I tell him I'm still not receiving any support money.

My other surprise visitor is my mother. She has sold her house in Mt. Eden and is living alone on Seccombes Road in Newmarket.

"I need you to come and take care of me again. I'm having an operation for cancer. Will you come? Robert isn't living with me anymore, and there's nobody to take care of me when I get home from the hospital," she explains.

"How long this time, Mother?" I ask wearily.

"Months."

"Why don't you come and stay with us?" I suggest.

"No. I have to be in my own home," she replies.

It's not easy to move a family of six, and I wish we didn't have to go, but I can never say no to her. I don't want to rent this house out again. Who knows how long we'll stay there or what crisis will develop this time. Finally, I decide to sell the house, and we move back in with Mother again.

Because we're back in the city, I can take in sewing, which helps us build up a better deposit for our second house purchase.

By the end of the year, I have found our next home. It is outside the city limits, past Titirangi, in a little semi-rural community called Woodlands Park. The house is quite new and spacious, with three bedrooms, a separate dining room, and a big yard. The property backs onto the open bushland of the Waitakere Ranges, so the children can play and explore to their hearts' content. The house is one of the nicer homes on the street. Growing up in the poorest house in the neighborhood and going through that again when we lived in the Te Atatu hut, I don't want my children to know the feeling of being poor while everyone else is doing well. I want them to feel equal to their peers and not embarrassed about how they live. I'm really glad that Mother is finally independent again so we can get out of her house and into our own space.

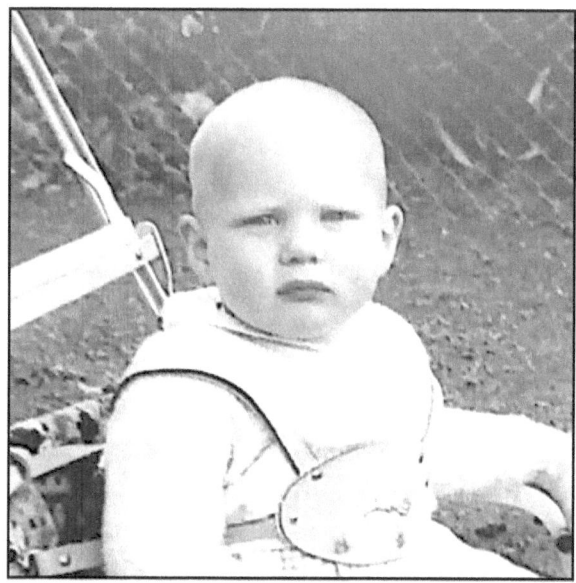

Trudy Margaret Reason,
ten months old.
Born June 28, 1961.

Jamie with the cup he
won at the beautiful
baby contest,
one year old.

Jim with Diane (four), Jamie (three),
Celeste (five), and Trudy (one), 1962.

Eunice, twenty-eight years old.   Eunice with the snapper she caught.

chapter fourteen

Yes, Your Honor

Jim and I are happy with our transition to Woodlands Park in May 1963, and we're both glad we didn't settle for a state house. Jim gets a motor scooter so he can get to and from work easily. He often falls off the scooter as he's learning to ride it and comes limping home to get patched up before trying again. He seems to constantly have a flat tire on the bike. When I realize it's because he doesn't patch the holes well, I buy a spare wheel for him so he can put that on while I get the other one fixed properly at the garage down the road. That works out better for both of us.

Celeste is now in her third primary school since beginning a year ago, and Diane started this year too. They walk to and from school together, and I only have two at home during the day. I'm still sewing and have started a new business as well, raising goldfish for the local pet shops. I have five large concrete watering troughs placed along the side of the house, and with chicken wire over metal frames to cover them, they are great ponds for hundreds of fish. We buy our first car, and now we can go to the beach, into town, or to visit Audrey in Te Atatu. It's such a lovely feeling of freedom. Our house is near the cul-de-sac of our street, and we're getting to know our neighbors. They are lovely families with nice children the same ages as ours, so everyone has a friend.

There is a large hall down the road which gets used for all kinds of events. I love going to indoor bowling on Tuesday nights with lots of my friends. I send the children to Sunday school there every week too. My family didn't go to church, but I remember how much I loved going to Sunday school with a neighbor. I want my children to have this opportunity to learn from the Bible so they can decide later in life if they want to go to church or not. It is a close community where everyone knows everyone else's business—not always a good thing—but it also means people are there to help you when you need it.

A year after moving to Woodlands Park, I'm visiting a neighbor when I notice a large American car driving down our little unsealed country road. Nick is back. Obviously, the assurance that he would be arrested if he set foot in the country wasn't true. Despite the court order, he hasn't been paying child support. When he wants to leave the country a few months later, he talks me into accepting his latest Buick in lieu of child support. I leave the car with a friend of Nick's, who is supposed to be converting it to right-hand drive. I explain my situation to this man, and he advises me that if I hear Nick has returned, I should let him know immediately.

"He could come and demand this car back from me if you have not taken possession of it. So if you know he's here, contact me, and I'll bring it around to your house. Whatever happens, don't let him sit in the car, or it will legally become his again."

When I hear Nick is back in the country, I call the guy with the car, who immediately drives it to my house and parks it in the driveway. When Nick arrives, he is angry that things are not going his way. "Give me the keys. I just want to check the glove box for something," he demands.

"No, Nick. No keys." He wants the car back without paying the child support he owes me. He is furious now and leaves swearing vengeance.

A summons to appear in court to determine the custody of my daughters arrives soon after. I cannot believe that our court system would even allow this ridiculous case. This man who hardly acknowledges his daughters, who avoids all responsibility as a parent, and who only paid child support for a short time so he could get U.S. citizenship, can waltz in here and try to take my children just because he's angry that he can't get his way. I'm beside myself and don't know what to do. Jim is no help to me, as he can't deal with any stress. I have never won an argument in my life, I'm terrified of courtrooms, and I hate being questioned. If the court is stupid enough to hear this case, then they could be stupid enough to award him custody. I am petrified. I turn to the only person I know who regularly creates court cases, often represents herself, and always wins—Gena. But unknown to me, Gena is working with Nick. It's a while before I realize this, and it's my lawyer who eventually points it out during one of the court appearances. I go back to trying to figure it out for myself.

I don't know why they keep postponing the hearings, but the fear and worry are like a huge weight I am crumbling under. I have to stop working, and I'm barely functioning at home. I eventually give in and return the Buick to Nick. He promises to pay the owed child support, but I haven't had a payment yet. What's worse, the court has awarded him visitation rights for every other weekend. He turns up when it's convenient for him, not on time and not even on the day he's supposed to come. The girls don't want to go with him, and it breaks my heart to make them go. I am so frantic for them, asking them questions as soon as they walk in the door after a visit, trying to find out if they are okay. Then what I have been fearing happens. Late one Saturday evening, they arrive home very upset.

"Where did he take you today?" I ask cautiously.

"We walked for miles, across the Grafton Bridge to the Domain," Celeste reports.

"My legs were so tired and my feet were hurting so much that he picked me up and carried me on his shoulders. And he touched me between my legs."

I call my lawyer, but with no adults to corroborate the story, it's pointless to call the police.

"You can have a doctor examine her, and in the meantime, I'll work on a summons to charge him in court."

Every time the summons is taken to his apartment, the door goes unanswered. Weeks go by, and he's still picking up the girls on the weekends. I'm beside myself. There's nothing I can do to stop this without risking being in contempt of court and losing them to him completely. I call my lawyer for the fifth time this week. He's sick of me calling.

"Has the summons been delivered yet?" I ask, exasperated with the whole situation.

"No," he replies with a sigh.

"Then give it to me, and I'll deliver it myself," I demand.

Summons in hand, I go to Nick's work and tell his boss that I have a summons I need to deliver to Nick.

"I can't do that," his boss says protectively.

"This summons is for sexual abuse of his daughter," I explain impatiently.

"I'll get him," he mumbles before heading back to the work area.

When Nick arrives in the lobby, I hand him the document. His look of absolute hatred makes me shudder as I make a quick exit.

"You're just saying this to stop my client from having visitation rights," his lawyer accuses me when we finally make it into court. There is no way to prove otherwise, so the visitations continue.

A few days later, I'm handed a summons of my own. I open it and read that my mother is accusing me of stealing money from her bank account. It is signed by Gena's lawyer, and I know Nick is involved because he's living with Mother. Tit for tat. I see how it is.

Years ago, when Nick and I were leaving for America, I gave my mother a passbook to my local bank account so she could deposit money in it from the sale of a button-covering machine I didn't want to keep. After I returned, I got the passbook back and was surprised to see the balance was more than I expected.

"I added some extra money in for your children," she told me, and I thanked her for her kindness.

Now she wants that money back, and I refuse since it belongs to the children. Our day in court for this situation arrives, and Mother takes the stand while Nick waits outside in the corridor.

"Did your daughter Eunice ever come to look after you when you were sick?" my lawyer asks her.

"She is the only one who would ever come to look after me," she replies quietly.

"Has she come to care for you more than once?"

"Yes, several times."

"Are you a single woman, Mrs. Johnston?" my lawyer continues.

"She took my husband away from me."

"What did you say?" the judge asks, leaning forward to look at her.

"She took my husband away from me."

"Do you have any assets, Mrs. Johnston?" my lawyer asks, ignoring her previous answer.

"No," she replies.

"Do you have a house?"

"Well, yes," she admits.

"Do you have a car?" he continues.

"Yes."

"Aren't those assets?" he challenges.

The judge can see that she is very confused and asks the lawyers to approach the bench. He talks with them briefly before addressing the courtroom.

"I don't like to see a mother and daughter fighting in court. I am calling a recess, during which time I would like to see this matter settled." Our lawyers talk, the decision is made to split the money, and we all go home.

"Please come and see me," Mother pleads on the phone after having yet another operation. Reluctantly, I go. I'm sitting in a chair next to her bed, chatting about what's going on, when in walks Nick with a wide grin on his face. He leans over me and runs his hand up my pant leg.

"Nice slacks you're wearing," he says salaciously. I stare at him until he finally leaves the room, then I turn to my mother.

"You have a choice to make, Mother. Surely you realize how hard it is for me to visit you while Nick is living here. Either he goes, or I won't come to see you again until you are dying," I say firmly. Nick stays, and I promise myself that I will keep my word.

Life rolls slowly along until we're sitting in another courtroom at last. It's as terrifying as the first time I was in court as a young child. Nick takes the stand and explains that he is engaged to a seventeen-year-old girl who is prepared to be the mother of the children.

"Has she met the children?" my lawyer asks him.

"No," Nick admits calmly.

"Then how do you know she will want to be their mother after she's met them?"

"Well, if she doesn't, I have several other candidates," he replies, smiling.

The judge wants a social worker to visit our home to assess how well the children are being cared for. The case cannot be settled until this report is done. Nothing is said about Nick having to pay the child support he owes me or about any assessment being done of how he lives and would provide for the children. It is all so unfair and one-sided.

Months go by, and Nick continues to play his games. His abusive phone calls are relentless, so I finally have the phone disconnected. The whole neighborhood knows our story by now, and it's embarrassing to meet neighbors at the store or see them on the street. The girls are still going on visitation weekends. It has been almost two years of this torture.

When a telegram arrives telling me we finally have a court date for the custody hearing, I am so terrified about how this is going to turn out, I feel like I just can't go. My doctor prescribes some tablets to help me relax, so as I'm trying to get dressed for the hearing, I take one. A little while later, I take a second one. They don't seem to be working at all, so I take a third. I remember taking these when Jamie was injured, and they were better than this. *Why are they not working?* I wish Jim were more help. I'm completely alone in trying to deal with this. I take one more.

By the time we enter the courtroom, I am unintentionally high on the pills that have finally kicked in. All inhibitions are gone and all sense of propriety as well. Nick arrives with a different girl on his arm—must be one of the alternative candidates—and seems very sure of himself. I start my speech as soon as they acknowledge I'm in the room during the opening formalities.

"I have no desire to be in this courtroom, Your Honor, and I don't believe my ex-husband does either. The only people gaining anything from this are the lawyers." I'm on a roll and enjoying this newfound confidence, albeit drug induced.

"No one has ever come to my house to see if the children are being properly cared for, as you, yourself, ordered the last time we were here. You say this is all about the welfare of the children, but I disagree. This is not benefiting the children in any way."

"Madam, I need to warn you that you will be charged with contempt of court if you continue with this tirade," a now very annoyed judge informs me. But years of pent-up emotions are on the move, and I cannot stem the flow. It doesn't help my situation, but I say my piece and feel better for getting it all out.

The judge finds me guilty of contempt of court and says he will decide on the matter in three months. Court adjourned. I can't believe this idiot! With all his wisdom and training, is this the best he can do? We really need better judges than this in our system. Three more months of this torment? No way! I'm going to call Nick's bluff.

I walk straight over to his lawyer and tell him that the children are at school and Nick can go and get them. I'm washing my hands of the whole mess, and he can take the children. He can be the one who gets up in the middle of the night when they have the nightmares he has caused, and he can pay for everything they need, including braces in the future. Nick overhears and hurries from the courtroom.

"You can't do that," his lawyer protests. So I go over to my lawyer.

"If Nick doesn't pick up those girls from school, then I will get them myself and take them to your office, sit them on your desk, and leave them there."

"You can't do that; I'm a bachelor. I don't know what to do with kids," my lawyer splutters.

"Poor kids!" some woman sitting nearby whispers loudly to the man next to her, while staring right at us. Nick's lawyer marches across the aisle to where I am standing.

"What do you want, madam? My client has paid you everything he owes you."

"Oh no, he hasn't!" I tell him. "I have not received one penny from him. Not one penny."

"He told me he paid you in full."

"Well, he's lying to you as well, then. I have not received any money from him since the court ordered him to pay it more than six years ago," I assure him.

His lawyer loans Nick the money he owes me, and it's done. Over, just like that. I am awarded full custody, and Nick is free of us. Jim and I apply to adopt the girls. It is ridiculous that I must adopt my own children, but the law says a man cannot adopt children alone. In the process, the girls have the choice to change their names if they want to. After much poring over name books, Celeste chooses to change "Pearl" to "Cheri," and Diane decides to be "Letitia" instead. So at ages eleven and ten, they become Celeste Cheri Reason and Letitia Lynn Reason. It takes us all a while to adjust to the name changes, but it is such a relief to know their father can never hurt them again.

Eunice, Jim, Jamie, and Trudy at the river, 1964.

Jamie (eight), Letitia (nine), Trudy (six), and Celeste (ten).
Woodlands Park School photo, 1967.

chapter fifteen

Who Do You Say I Am?

It's time to move again. I love living out of the city, and we have certainly made good friends during our six years here, but the high school options are not great, and Celeste will be thirteen soon. I find a beautiful, old Victorian home on a corner lot in Greenlane, not far from where I grew up. It is eighty-one years old, with twelve-foot-high, embossed-tin ceilings and a six-foot-wide hallway separating two bedrooms from the living room and dining room. Two enclosed sunporches serve as extra bedroom space, and big bay windows enlarge the living room and master bedroom. The original, pure-wool carpets cover solid wooden floors, and the old scrim wallpaper still decorates the walls—there's some work to do, but this new house has a comfortable, happy feel. We're close to shops and have paved roads with sidewalks for the first time. All the houses in the neighborhood are similar, and it finally feels like we're home.

The spacious yard is surrounded by tall hedges and has a large orange tree that smells divine when it's in blossom. It yields so many oranges every year that I can sell them to a juicing company. We pay to move the concrete water troughs over here. I dig sizeable holes to set them into the ground for an attractive pond area so I can keep raising and selling goldfish. Celeste and Letitia begin school at Remuera Intermediate, and Jamie and Trudy are at Cornwall Park Primary. Everyone is doing well, making new friends, and staying healthy. Jim's job is close, only ten minutes away, and he's glad that his lengthy commute has been eliminated. I continue a little side job I started at the last house, making Māori carvings for the tourist trade. I'm also doing sewing alterations at home and building a good clientele. Nick is out of the picture, and life settles into a comfortable routine.

Even though I knew it was coming, it is still a shock when I get word that Mother is in a nursing home, dying of cancer. It started as bowel cancer and has invaded her whole body, including her brain. She looks so small and frail in the white bed when I go see her.

"I'm glad you came to see me," she says as we chat for a little while. I leave, promising to return soon. When I walk in a week later, I can immediately tell something is different—she can't see me! The doctor had warned me that, once in her brain, the cancer would cause her to either go blind or die quickly.

"Who is it?" she asks as I approach.

"It's Eunice."

"I thought I recognized your voice." I stand at the foot of her bed, my hands on the iron railing, looking at her. It feels as if I'm staring into her very soul. I could never have looked at her this way when she could see. Suddenly, a strange coldness engulfs me, so deep it seeps into my bones and causes me to shiver. *How could you live so long, Mother, and be so empty?*

Out of nowhere, I clearly hear a voice in my head say, "This woman is not your mother." I look around, even though I know it's not coming from someone in the room. *What utter nonsense!*

"This woman is not your mother," the voice insists. "Your mother was kind and very beautiful. This woman is *not* your mother; she is evil."

I'm not sure what I said to Mother or how I got back to the car, but I find myself sitting there for a long time before the trembling stops and I can slowly drive home.

"What's wrong?" Jim asks as soon as he sees me that evening. "You're as white as a sheet."

After I tell him my story of the visit to Mother, he suggests we go to a Spiritualist church to see if they have any answers. I'm not sure that's a good idea, so I call my counselor at the Church of Christ that we have been attending for several months.

"That's the Devil talking to you," she tells me. I hang up the phone. I can't explain what happened, but I feel sure it's not the Devil. During my teenage years, I went to several different churches with my friends—Seventh Day Adventist, Presbyterian, and Anglican. I enjoyed them all but always left feeling as if something was missing. Now I don't know where to turn for answers.

Maybe I'm going insane. But I don't feel very upset about Mother's dying, so I don't think it's stress. What if the voice is right, and she's not my mother? Then who is my mother, and who does that make me? What nationality am I, and how did I end up with this woman taking care of me? A deep sense of disconnection settles over me. I feel like I'm floating alone without a mooring rope of past history or identity. I go through my daily routine as if in a fog while my brain tries to process this dilemma. I can't go on like this. I must get some answers. I have to know whose daughter I am.

I can't bring myself to go back to that room, and Mother dies several weeks later. All the funeral arrangements are made by Gena, without her consulting the rest of the family. Gena is the only one who rides in the funeral car and the only family member who gets to sit in the front row at the service and place a wreath on the coffin. Daphne is at the service with her husband, Alex, so I sit with them. She seems to be taking it better than I thought she would. We don't talk for long afterward, and I'm glad to head home and put this chapter of my life away. Except, it won't go away. There's something I'm supposed to be finding out, but I don't know how, and I'm afraid to know what it is.

Unable to put this to rest and mentally move on, I look up Spiritualist churches in our area and find one not far away. We go the following week. No stained glass, no altar, no crosses with Jesus dripping blood in this place, just a plain room with seating and a podium. A man gives a reading then introduces a woman who goes forward and gives "messages" to people in the audience. There's nothing particularly scary, and Jim likes it, so we go back the following week.

"I have a message for you," says the medium, looking straight at me. "There is a woman here with me. You knew her. She used to sit and sew small pieces of fabric together to make things. She is here now, and she is placing a bouquet of red roses into your arms."

I immediately think of the woman who lived next door to us out in Woodlands Park. She was always quilting. It brings tears to my eyes, and I can't wait to go again. I have no idea what's going on here, but maybe I can find answers to my questions. I get several vague "messages" in other services we attend, and as I learn the names of the clairvoyants who see clients privately, I make appointments with them.

"Who is my mother?" is my favorite question.

One old Scottish woman, staring into a crystal vase, tells me, "I see a young girl sitting by a river. She has long brown hair that she wears in a braid down her back. She is sitting on the riverbank, watching little paper boats floating along. That girl is your mother."

That sounds like my sister Daphne, but why is there a river and paper boats? I don't want Daphne to be my mother. The voice at Mother's bedside said my mother "was kind and beautiful," as if she were dead, but Daphne isn't dead. *This is so confusing. Maybe I heard wrong.*

———————

Even though I try to put all this behind me, my mind often ponders the meaning of all these bits and pieces. Slowly, like a jigsaw puzzle, they start to come together. I send off for birth, death, and marriage certificates. I find out that Daphne was out of school the year she turned fifteen, the year I was born. She would have been fourteen when she got pregnant. While examining the dates, I discover that Daphne was born out of wedlock, and Gena was born seven months after her parents married. I'm seeing a pattern. I remember sharing a room with Daphne as a small child, but as the youngest, you would think I would have been in Mother's room. Was I in there because she was my mother and was supposed to care for me? Was Mother's callous attitude about my having rickets because I wasn't her responsibility? Now that I think about it, rickets is caused by a lack of exposure to sunlight. Was she the reason I had rickets in the first place? Was I hidden inside because she was embarrassed about the whole situation?

I think about the train trip to Whangarei when I was ten and how much Daphne spoiled me there. Was it a trial to see if she wanted to take care of me? I remember hearing my parents arguing and Mother saying, "She's not entitled to it," when they were planning wedding gifts for me and Gena. Was that because I wasn't their child but their grandchild?

Eventually, I come to terms with the fact that I must be Daphne's child. I plan to go and ask her directly. I've asked Gena what she knows, but she won't say anything. Obviously, Pop knows, but Gena won't tell me where he is either. I'm finally beginning to understand why I always felt like I didn't belong and wasn't wanted. Of course Daphne wouldn't want to have a baby at fourteen!

It takes some time to find out where Daphne is living, but when I do, I drive out to see her. It is late afternoon, and she is wearing her dressing gown and slippers as she pushes food around in a frying pan. A cigarette dangles from the corner of her mouth. Her unkempt hair is beginning to gray, and her overweight body reflects the five pregnancies and years of neglect she has suffered. *Where is the "kind and very beautiful" the voice mentioned?* This is not the picture I want to have of my mother.

We chat for a while, then I ask her directly, "Were you sick when I was born?"

Without thinking, she emphatically replies, "No, I wasn't." She then raves on about how horrible nurse Cooper was and what a long exhausting labor she had.

That is enough for me. I have to accept the fact that Daphne is my mother and move on. That means Ethel and George are my grandparents, and Lorraine was my half sister—no wonder I loved her so much. Robert is my half brother, and Gena is my aunt, not my sister! This is all too much. We don't discuss it further, and I don't see Daphne again.

chapter sixteen

Soapsuds and Sales

As 1972 begins, I'm so happy that all my children are doing well in school. Celeste and Letitia are going to high school together, Jamie is in intermediate school, and Trudy is finishing up primary school. Jamie gets himself a job at the local family grocery store, delivering food on a big bike with a basket up front. He stocks shelves and tidies up when needed, and I'm very proud of him. He saves up his money and buys me a beautiful vase from the local antique store. It reminds me of when I bought the little silver pitcher for my mother, and I know I will treasure it all my life.

Jim tells me he is unhappy at work. His friend Albert wants to leave for another position, and Jim wants to go with him, even though it pays less. He asks me how much money I need to manage the house on. I work it out conservatively and let him know. From then on, his paycheck is always that exact amount. I can't figure out what he is up to, but I suspect he has another bank account that the rest of the money is going into and that Albert is in on the arrangement. Something doesn't smell right, but I can't quite put my finger on it.

A few months later, a friend from the Spiritualist church calls us out of the blue.

"There's a wonderful new opportunity surging through the country," he tells us. "It's a way to make money fast—a lot of money. It's an American-based company that sells soap and cleaning products, and they are looking for distributors. I've already joined, and I'd like you to be my guests tonight. Would you like to come?"

Jim is excited about the idea of making fast money, and it's great to see him enthusiastic for a change, so we go.

Several speakers demonstrate the products and rave about the wonderful difference that belonging to Golden Products has made in their lives. Jim wants to join, but I'm sure it will be me doing all the selling, and I'm not sure it's a good idea.

"It takes a lot of sales to make a dollar," I point out, but he's not listening. "I don't think we should join," I tell him again. "It costs $1,200, Jim. I just paid $1,000 on the house after saving up for ages. We only have another $1,000 to pay off the house completely."

"You call them and get that money back," he demands. He's so excited and determined that this is what he wants to do.

The next day, he takes the day off work and insists we go to the mortgage company to ask for the money to be returned.

"We're gonna be rich," he tells the clerk. "We're in on a scheme that is gonna make us a lot of money."

She looks at us dubiously but arranges for the money to be returned.

By that night, we have paid the $1,200 that entitles us to be "Generals" in Golden Products and to take a trip to Hawaii for training. I have been working at a rest home just down the street, helping to take care of residents and prepare meals, so I need to ask for time off to make this week-long trip happen.

I arrange for a friend from work to take care of the children while we fly to Hawaii two months later. The last time we were visiting this tropical paradise was in 1958 on my final trip from San Francisco to Auckland. I remember how beautiful it was the first time I saw it and can't wait to visit again. This time we will stay for a whole week.

What a difference fourteen years can make! Oahu is unrecognizable, and the beautiful Royal Hawaiian Hotel is now lost among row after row of the huge multi-story hotels that line Waikiki Beach. No longer an island paradise, Honolulu is like any other large

American city, with gift shops and cafes, tourist markets and shows, all vying for every visitor dollar they can get. It's so disappointing. I feel like I've been tricked and robbed of my beautiful memories of this place. I also suspect we've been robbed of our money by joining this scheme.

We spend hours each day in meetings to learn how to introduce this company and its plan to revolutionize soap sales around the world. We have to know all about each product and how to demonstrate its amazing qualities. We learn how to find potential customers and, of course, how to sell, sell, sell! But the big money is not in sales, we're told. It's in signing up other people under us, as we will get a percentage of whatever they sell and whatever the people under them sell. Building a team is key to making this work to bring in the big money quickly.

Jim is sure this will be easy and we'll be millionaires before long, but he only attempts to sell the products once. The weekend after we get home, he walks down to the apartments around the corner from our house and goes door to door. A group of girls living there ask if he can demonstrate the product used for cleaning sofas, so he runs home to get the necessary equipment and spends a good amount of time cleaning their sofa. They are impressed with their now lovely, clean sofa and laugh at him as they send him on his way with no sale. He is dejected when he realizes he has been used and won't try selling again.

I enjoy the Golden Products meetings and go several times a week. The people are positive and fun to be around, unlike Jim, who never talks except to complain about how hard his life is. Whenever I'm not working at the rest home, I travel long distances to visit dairy processing plants up north that use cleaning products. I have one that has taken some samples to try and will get back to me in a few weeks. It's exhausting, but I want to at least give this a go. I'm forcing myself to talk to people and promote these products, even though it is way outside my comfort zone.

———

During one of the evening meetings, we are introduced to Laurie Scott, an experienced salesman who offers to teach Jim how to sell. He is short and overweight, smokes a pipe, and seems to take an interest in helping people in general. There is usually a group gathered around him, asking his advice and listening to his experiences. A few days later, he turns up at our house. He tells us that the president of Golden Products has sent him to try to help me because, although I'm trying hard, I'm not making much headway. He thinks I could do with some one-on-one training. Jim is supportive of this idea and has no objection when Laurie wants to go with me to watch how I approach prospective clients and introduce the products.

In early September, Laurie tells us that he has arranged to give a product demonstration to a large company in Wellington, five hundred miles away, and he asks Jim to go along.

"Nah. Take Eunice," Jim insists.

"I'm too tired to make a long trip like that, and I don't want to go," I reply emphatically.

"This is a good opportunity ta make some money. You should go," he pushes.

"I'll only go if one of the kids comes with me."

"I don't care as long as you go."

I'm beginning to suspect he wants me to get involved with Laurie, and Laurie is making it known that he would welcome the idea. There's never been much for me in this marriage. I have to take responsibility for all the big decisions and family life so Jim doesn't get stressed and have a seizure. He's passive and uninvolved with our children. But I resent being thrown away again. I hate this.

On the other hand, Laurie is supportive, kind, and helpful. He talks about Jesus, so he must be a God-fearing man. I wonder if I would be better off being with him. This trip should be interesting—a good opportunity to get to know this man better. I ask the two oldest girls if they like him and if they would want to go with me if I were to leave Jim. They don't seem keen on the idea.

We are supposed to leave Thursday night so we can be down in Wellington for a Friday meeting. Laurie tells me he needs to fix the gearbox in his old VW van before we can go. It's after 3 a.m. on Friday before he finally turns up and we get on the road.

The back seats of the van have been converted into a bed so one of us can rest while the other drives. Laurie's eighteen-year-old son, Leon, and Celeste are in the back.

We get as far as Wanganui, which is about two thirds of the way to Wellington, when we stop because the gears are acting up. Laurie knows some people who live here, so we visit them while a repair shop looks at the van. They can fix it but will have to order parts. We make it to a small run-down motel nearby to spend the night. Leon and Celeste are asleep in the back of the van, so we fall into bed in a tiny room with one queen-size bed. Laurie sleeps for several hours, but I'm awake most of the night. When I do finally doze off, I'm woken by Laurie's advances. Is that what this trip is about? There doesn't seem to actually be a meeting in Wellington. I haven't seen Laurie make any phone call to Wellington explaining our delay. It can't just be a coincidence that the van broke down right here where Laurie knows people.

It takes all of Saturday to fix the van. I pay the bill, and we head back to the motel for another sleepless night.

After breakfast with Laurie's friends, we are on the road, heading home. We stop in Hawera to see some of my extended family and to visit the statue of my great-grandfather Arthur Albert Fantham in a park there. We drive on until the early hours of Monday morning.

"I can't drive any farther," Laurie says, pulling into a driveway. "We'll sleep here for a few hours. I know these people; they won't mind."

The good-natured friends provide beds for the night, make us a pot of tea, and go off to their own bedroom. I can't sleep. Something is very wrong, but I feel too confused and too tired to figure it out.

We're on the road again before dawn, and Laurie drops me off at my rest home job by 7 a.m. when my shift begins. Over the past three days, I've slept fewer than three hours. I know I look terrible, and I can hardly function. Laurie takes Celeste home and drops my suitcase off there.

Around 11 a.m., the matron calls me to the phone.

"It's your husband," she says happily.

"I 'ave ya right where I wantcha now!" yells Jim.

"What are you talking about?" I ask wearily.

"You're outta 'ere!"

"I'll see you later, Jim. I don't know what you're talking about, but I'm working and I'm exhausted. I can't follow what you're saying. We'll talk about this when I get home," I explain.

I call Laurie.

"How was Jim when you saw him?" I ask.

"He was okay. He said he was leaving for work soon and was glad you were back safely. I didn't have time to explain the breakdown, but you can do that when you get home," he replies calmly.

"He just called me, and he was livid. He was saying something about having me where he wants me. What do you think he meant by that?"

"I'll come with you tonight when you finish work, and I'll explain it all to him," Laurie assures me.

At 8:30 that night, Laurie is waiting in his van outside the house when I walk home from work. We go in together to find Jim irate and yelling obscenities at me like nothing I've ever heard before. I get the children out of the room, and he continues to yell as he orders me out of his house.

"This is it, Girl. And you ain't takin' me kids."

I know I don't want to go through some drawn-out court battle again. Jim has never been involved in any of the children's care or been to even one of their school performances, games, or parent/teacher meetings. I want him to have help raising them. I insist that he takes them back to England to raise them with his family. He ignores me. I remind him that the house is almost paid for, so they could sell it if necessary. I get Celeste and Letitia and head toward the door.

What happens next is a blur, but we go down to the rest home where I work and stay a few days in a small guesthouse in the back. When I try to get money out of the bank the next day, Jim has already frozen my account. I go back to the house to get our clothes and the girls' school uniforms and find that the doors are all locked.

We have never locked our doors in the past. I ask the minister who works at the rest home to come with me as a witness, and we go back there. I break in and begin to pile our clothes into bags. Realizing I may not get another chance to retrieve anything from the house, I also take some things of sentimental value and artwork I paid for from my wages. In the chaos, I forget to take the girls' possessions, and I don't even remember to pack any photographs. Here I am again, leaving with Celeste and Letitia, no idea what's next or where we will be living. It all happened so fast that I can't even get my head around it.

chapter seventeen

No Rest in the Rest Home

I'm in the process of finding a place for the girls to stay while I get life sorted out when I get fired from my rest home job. Someone has told them about me.

"This is a church home, you know. We don't want your type working here," I'm told.

The mother of a school friend of Letitia's agrees to take care of my daughters until the end of the year. Depression, exhaustion, confusion, and a sense of hopelessness envelop me. I don't know what to do and can't think clearly enough to make a plan. But Laurie is there to pick up the pieces and whisk me away to a life of happiness, security, love, and compassion beyond my wildest dreams—or so he says. I find myself at his house.

"Rest. You'll be fine now," he tells me. I spend my days and nights on a mattress on the floor, Laurie bringing me food and drinks and attempting to make love whenever he feels like it. He's impotent, but that doesn't stop him from trying. I suspect he may be drugging me, but I can't think straight enough to figure it out. I'm not sure how much time passes, but I receive a divorce summons from Jim, and he's complaining that I haven't finished paying off the new carpet. *Take it all. I don't care. Just please take care of my children.*

Laurie's house is old and falling apart. It's one in a group of homes that have been condemned and are due to be demolished. Mice and fleas happily live here among the piles of papers and junk. As I come out of my stupor, I begin to look around as much as Laurie allows.

He has lived here for a while with his two sons. He explains that he took them away from their mother when they were young and has raised them alone. Larry is twenty years old, and although he is physically very fit, he cannot read or write. He can drive well but does not have a driver's license, because he can't complete the written test. Each week, he hands his paycheck to the teller at the bank so she can fill out the deposit slip for him. He is outgoing and friendly but tells lies that are beyond plausibility. His younger brother, Leon, is also personable but scrawny and conniving. He lives by his wits and is uneducated, dishonest, and probably doing drugs. Both seem happy to have a woman in the house and immediately help me with the needed cleanup around the place before the girls move in.

Laurie wants to buy a rest home for the elderly because he knows I could run it and we could make some money while having a place to live. I beg him not to, but he insists that it would be a good way to finance a house for us.

"We'll just do it for three years," he assures me. So three months later, we buy Carolene Rest Home and move in to the rambling older home. It has a big veranda, wide hallways, and seven large rooms for the residents. There are fifteen people already living here, ten women and five men. A woman who was employed by the last owner stays to help with cleaning, but I do all the cooking and care of our residents. Two wings have been added to the original house for staff quarters, and we use one for our bedroom, living room, and bathroom. In the second wing, we keep one room for the boys to use when they're in town, and we use the other room for an elderly married couple who need care and want to stay together. Under the back half of the house is an apartment with two bedrooms, a living room, and a bathroom. Celeste and Letitia get moved in there.

I have seen Trudy a few times, but Jamie refuses to visit. Jim didn't take them to England as I hoped he would. Trudy doesn't do well in school, but we discover she's very good at playing the accordion. Just like her father, she can play by ear, without ever learning to read music. We sign her up for lessons and buy her a nice accordion. When I decide to try to get custody of Trudy, my lawyer suggests I would have more success if Laurie and I were married. So a month later, we have a quick private ceremony at our local Anglican church. It doesn't make any difference, because Trudy decides to stay with her father.

It is a lot of work being on duty twenty-four hours a day, seven days a week, and I often feel like a prisoner in this place. Laurie's true colors are beginning to show as his controlling nature seeps into every aspect of my life. The girls' apartment downstairs cannot be accessed from inside the house, and Laurie locks the outside entrance door with a padlock every night. All the windows are padlocked, so they can only open a few inches. Even the mailbox is locked. The three of us really are captives here. I can't do anything without Laurie being present. He's there when I take a bath and when I try on clothes in a store dressing room. He decides what I'm going to wear and eat and who my friends will be. He gets upset if he thinks any man is looking at me and accuses me of being unfaithful to him if I talk to any visitor. I can never go out alone, even for a walk around the block. I can't watch a TV show or read a book he doesn't approve of first. I've gone from having a husband who was completely dependent on me to having one that controls every breath I take. *What have I done?*

Celeste decides to study occupational therapy in Wellington, so in early 1975, we drive her down there and get her settled into a youth hostel near the school in Lower Hutt. I know I'll miss having her help at home, and I'm already anxious to receive letters from her saying she's doing well and enjoying her studies.

Letitia left high school at the same time as Celeste, and soon after we get back from our trip, we find a note saying she has run away, with no explanation about where she's going or what she is planning to do. I'm beside myself with worry as all kinds of horrible scenarios play out in my dazed mind.

Laurie says she is probably with Leon and seems to like that idea. He doesn't want to go looking for them.

I wonder if there is a baby involved, as I know those two have been sleeping together.

That night, I can't sleep. Overwhelming sadness and worry flood my thoughts as I toss and turn. As dawn finally begins to lighten the sky, I get up to begin the morning routine of resident baths and dressing before breakfast. But something isn't right—the whole right side of my body is painful and uncooperative. I can't bend my right knee, and my right arm is hanging limply by my side. *I must have had a stroke in the night.* Going up and down stairs is difficult and slow. Dishes fall out of my hand no matter how hard I try to hold on to them. My mind isn't clear, and it's not easy to speak. It takes about three weeks before I feel better, but it seems I've lost the ability to reason quickly or learn new things easily.

It's more than a year before I hear from Letitia. When I tell her how worried I have been, she says she wrote to me several times explaining things. Obviously, Laurie got those letters and never passed them along to me. *How could he do that, knowing how worried I have been, to the point of having a stroke!* I ask her about the baby.

"What baby?" she wonders.

"I thought you must be pregnant and that's why you ran away," I explain.

"No, there was never a baby. I just couldn't stand living there with Laurie," she assures me.

She is still living with Leon but has been working, bought a car, and started school. I ask her what she thinks about going to America to study in a university there. She's not sure she wants to do that, but when she asks a teacher at her night school about it, he thinks it's a wonderful opportunity and she should go. When I ask Celeste if she would go with her, she says she's not sure either. *I hope the girls can see what a great plan this is. They are Americans and can easily get into the country. They should go.*

At the same time, I'm developing an escape plan of my own. The first step is to convince Laurie to make plans to move to the U.S. as well.

"Let's get the girls there and then have them sponsor us," I tell him. "We should start packing up stuff we want to take." I'm counting on the fact that he could never get a passport, so there's no danger of him actually going. But I can't just start packing up my belongings without him noticing, so I have to act as if he's included. He gets large wooden tea boxes, paints the outsides pink, and we begin packing them.

I persist in my efforts to persuade the girls to go to America, and they both finally agree. The next hurdle is renewing their passports. They were both babies when they got them, and I haven't renewed them over the years. Letitia has had one name change and Celeste has had two name changes since then. We get together all the necessary documents to prove that these adults are the same people as the babies in their passport photos, send the applications in, and wait.

Six weeks later, they have new American passports! They won't need visas; they can go whenever they are ready. Celeste has finished school, but Letitia needs to decide which school she wants to go to in the U.S. I have been checking into universities around the country and writing to them for information. We settle on Oklahoma State University, as it is the only one to refer to my daughter by name and include a letter assuring me she will be taken care of. As we know nothing about any state except California, it seems like a good option, and Letitia soon gets an acceptance letter. If she can arrive by June, she can begin with some introductory summer classes.

Celebrating your twenty-first birthday is a big deal in New Zealand, and I don't want my girls to miss out like I did all those years ago when Nick didn't even give me a gift. So we arrange a fabulous trip to Pakatoa Island and travel out by boat with all our guests, to celebrate them both. Celeste turned twenty-one a couple of months ago, and Letitia will be twenty-one in ten months. We have an accordionist, who delights us with all kinds of old and modern music while we eat and dance the day away. As I hope for a better future for my daughters, I also dread the emptiness I know I will feel when they are gone.

May 17, 1978, arrives quickly. The girls are packed, and we're heading to the Auckland airport. Several of their friends have come to see them off, but the flight is delayed for hours, making the parting even more painful. After many hugs and tears, I watch the plane fly away for as long as I can. It's more than a day before we receive a telegram from them saying they have arrived safely. They are staying with old friends, our first landlords, John and Joyce Carroll. They will be there for two weeks before going on to Oklahoma to get Letitia settled into school. Celeste will then return to Oklahoma City to find somewhere to live and get a job. I am so relieved and wish I could be there with them.

With the girls settled and Trudy working, I secretly begin the process for my own visa application. A friend of Celeste's helps me to get the application materials where they need to go, and I have the return documents sent to Audrey's house for safekeeping. She and I have maintained our special friendship all these years, and she's still the only one I really trust.

Laurie and I have now been running this rest home for six years. Walking past our stack of packed tea boxes one afternoon, I notice several of my personal items have been removed, and I can't find them anywhere. I don't say anything, but that evening, I suggest it's time to ship the boxes to Celeste so they can be waiting for us when we arrive. Miraculously, Laurie agrees, and we get them sent off the following week.

When the phone rings around noon as I'm getting lunch ready for our residents, I'm surprised to hear Trudy's voice. She hasn't been to see us for a while.

"Mum, I'm pregnant. Larry is the father," she tells me between sobs. "Dad wants me to get an abortion, but I want to keep the baby. What should I do?"

"If you want to keep the baby, don't let anyone talk you out of it," I tell her, my own experience still weighing heavily on my heart. We talk for a while about some options and say goodbye with the understanding that she will keep the baby. At dinner that night, I tell Laurie.

"Trudy is pregnant, and it's Larry's baby," I announce.

"No, it's not!" he insists.

"How do you know that? I'm going to ask him about it when he gets here tonight," I say.

But Laurie talks to him before I can, and Larry denies it all.

When we go to bed, Laurie won't let me sleep. He's going on and on about Trudy and the pregnancy until I finally tell him to be quiet and let me sleep.

"Jesus says to obey your husband," he tells me. I'm so tired of hearing this line. He has threatened me with having to do this or that because "Jesus says so" for years. His "godly man" act is just a lie he uses to try to impress people and control me.

"I have to sleep. I'm going to the sitting room to sleep on the sofa," I tell him as I go to get up.

"You will do as I say," he says, and he holds me down. As I struggle to get up, he grabs both my arms and twists them behind my back. He has one hand holding my arms, and his other arm is across my chest. I bite down on it as hard as I can. He lets go, yelling obscenities. As he examines his arm, I jump out of bed and scramble across the room. I unlock one door, dive across the narrow hall, unlock another door, open a window, and call for Larry to come and help me. Laurie is already beside me as Larry wakes up and comes running, unlocking doors as he comes.

"What's wrong?" he asks.

"Larry, this is all over Trudy being pregnant. Your father is going on and on about it and won't let me sleep. I'm on duty again in three hours, and I need some sleep." Larry stays until he thinks his father has calmed down then goes back to his own room.

I lie down on the sofa. Laurie comes in and sits beside me, flicking the tip of my nose with his finger.

"You're not going to sleep, Eunice. This is not your bed, Eunice. Your bed is beside your husband. Jesus says you have to do what your husband says. This is not your place. Your place is beside me in our bed, not on this sofa. What are the Ten Commandments, Eunice? Say the Ten Commandments. Say them. I want to hear them." He keeps flicking the end of my nose. "You will not sleep, Eunice, unless you go to bed in the bedroom."

I am too scared to go to bed, so I stay on the sofa for the rest of the night, and so does he. When I see Larry the next morning, I whisper to him, "I have to get out of here."

"I agree," he whispers back.

"I'll have to arrange for somewhere to go while he's not watching me. Can you take me there tonight?" I ask.

"Get your bags packed. You can jump the wall, and I'll have the car running," he says.

I hope I can trust him not to tell his father any of this, or I'll be in big trouble. I call a friend and set up to stay with her that night. I also call the doctor for the rest home residents to explain the situation.

"Don't let him stop you from leaving," he tells me. "And don't worry about the residents there. They are all capable of leaving any time they wish. Just go!"

Miraculously, for the first time since we moved here six years ago, Laurie has not locked the bedroom door. During the day, as I have the opportunity, I sneak back there and pack some clothes into a box. I take a few minutes to break the lock on the window nearest to the street.

Later that night, as Laurie is going downstairs to the laundry room, and I'm already locked in the bedroom, Larry runs outside and starts his car. I grab the box of clothes, make my way out of the unlocked bedroom window, and climb over the nearby wall to the street below. I shove the box into the back seat, climb in beside Larry, and we speed away. I have never been more terrified in my life and keep looking around, expecting to see Laurie coming after us at any minute. Once I'm safely at my friend's house, I grab my stuff and say thank you to Larry. I remind him not to tell his father anything and to deny helping me if he asks. It's several hours before I can take a real breath.

After a few days there, I call Audrey and ask if I can come and stay with her.

"Do you need a ride?" she asks without hesitation.

"Yes, I do."

"Give me the address, and I'll come right now." Soon I'm settling into Audrey's home. She makes me comfortable and resists questioning me about what happened. She knows I'll talk about it when I'm ready. In the meantime, she's there to lean on, with a cup of tea and her loving support, just like always. *What would I do without her?*

I rest for several days then walk into town to look for work. A factory that makes men's jackets and outerwear tests my skills and gives me a job, starting immediately. I enjoy the daily walk, especially after sitting at a sewing machine all day. Six months go by before my visa is granted and I'm ready to leave the country. I'm excited to see Celeste and Letitia again after eighteen months, but I'll miss everyone here, especially Audrey. Trudy has been moving around, trying to find a place to live, and is currently with her father. I have had no contact with Jamie since we left, but Trudy tells me he's training to be a police officer. I decide to quit smoking and throw what's left of my last pack into a trash bin at the airport. I call Laurie and tell him I'm leaving the country. After hugs and tears with Audrey and Neil, I walk down the gangway into the belly of the plane.

As soon as we take off, I begin to cry. It's as if all the years of pain and fear, doubt and self-loathing, hurt and anger just pour out. I can't stop. The poor man next to me never looks over. He adjusts his pillow and sleeps for most of the thirteen-hour flight. I envy him. I would love to be able to sleep. I finally run out of tears by the last hour and wearily look out at the palm trees, freeway traffic, and stucco houses of Los Angeles. We taxi to the terminal, and I'm back in America. Twenty-one years have gone by, and everything looks different here. I take some time to wash my face and change into a fresh dress. It's a four-hour layover before my flight to Oklahoma. I wonder what it will be like and if I will ever get back to New Zealand. I wish I hadn't decided to give up smoking—I could do with a cigarette about now.

Twenty-first birthday party at
Pakatoa Island, Auckland.
Trudy, Letitia, Eunice,
and Celeste, 1978.

At Auckland Airport saying goodbye to Letitia and Celeste, May 1978.
Laurie, Letitia, Leon, Celeste, and Eunice.

Letitia and Celeste at the
Auckland Airport, heading
for the U.S.A., May 1978.

Celeste and Donna, May 1978.

160

chapter eighteen

Beginning Again

It has been nearly thirty-six hours since I left Auckland. I'm exhausted, but adrenaline keeps me going as we finally land in Oklahoma. Celeste will be here. I've finally made it. We find each other on the pavement outside the airport. I'm so relieved. She loads my bags into her huge old car. I eagerly watch the passing landscape as we drive to her apartment. My heart drops a little more with each mile of flat brown earth. It's so ugly, and it isn't getting any better, no matter how far we drive.

"Why didn't you tell me it was like this?" I ask Celeste.

"I know it's not much to look at, but the people are really nice here. They make up for the lack of beautiful scenery," she tries to reassure me.

I get settled into her tiny one-bedroom apartment and meet Mr. and Mrs. Atlee, who have helped her so much over the last year and a half. They are her landlords and live in the house next to the apartment block she's in. There's a two-bedroom place that is going to be available soon, so we plan to move there as soon as it's open. This will take some getting used to. It's not at all like New Zealand. The next day, we make the one-hour drive to Stillwater to visit Letitia. She tells me she goes by "Teesha" now and proudly shows us around her campus. I'm so happy to see that both my girls are doing well and are happy here. Now to get myself settled.

Celeste is working as an occupational therapist at a nearby hospital, and I decide to look for a job there so we can travel to work together. There doesn't seem to be much of a public transportation system here. I take the unit-clerk course, get my certificate, and begin working on the pediatric floor. It takes a while to get used to being in the center of all the crazy activity on a hospital floor, but I like it. When I see a job advertised that involves living with an elderly woman to care for her during the week, I move in with her and continue working at the hospital on the weekends. My bank account is beginning to look healthier, and I'm feeling happy that I am supporting myself, getting to know some interesting people here, and spending time with my daughters.

We have all been waiting for Teesha to graduate, as we have been making plans to move up to Oregon when she does. No one is prouder than I am that day as I watch Teesha receive her bachelor's degree in zoology. She has completed the four-year program in three years, and we are ready to head north. I purchase a three-quarter-ton pickup from our neighbor and put a camper on the back. Now we can travel cheaply and pull a U-Haul for our belongings. Celeste drives her new little car that is loaded down with essentials for the trip, and we drive west. Although our goal is to get to Oregon, we plan to see as much as possible along the way, so we make stops in places like Mesa Verde, the Grand Canyon, and the Hoover Dam. We wander around Santa Fe, ride on the Durango-Silverton railway, stay in a parking lot in Las Vegas, and make sure we see Death Valley and Yosemite. We save money by staying in campgrounds or rest areas and by cooking for ourselves in the camper. Finally, we cross into Oregon and find it as beautiful as we had imagined, with forests of tall green trees, beautiful beaches, mountain views, and rainy skies.

We stay in a campground just outside Portland while Teesha and I find places to live. She finds a group of young people on the west side of the city looking for a roommate, and I get a caregiving position for an elderly man. We unload the U-Haul into a storage unit, and Celeste takes the truck and camper to meet a friend from New Zealand so they can travel around the U.S. for two months.

I decide to study business-related subjects at a small school in the city while I work, but as I'm graduating, Oregon's economy takes a downturn. The struggling housing industry reduces the need for lumber and causes many timber mills to close. I apply for an office job with 326 other women, but I know I won't get it. When my old boss from Oklahoma calls and offers to pay my airfare if I will go back there to take care of her mother-in-law, it seems like a good idea.

Back in Oklahoma, I work in an office during the day and return each evening to the old lady's house to cook and care for her. Someone else is with her during the day, as she needs full-time care. Two years go happily by. When I realize my charge is dying, I start to see the pattern in caregiving for the elderly—you work yourself out of a job. I decide to try being a nanny instead, as the ages of the ones needing my care might guarantee me more time in the position. I find a live-in position with a family in Oklahoma City, not far from where I have been living. They have two young children and live in a large modern house, expensively decorated with off-white carpets, sculptures, paintings, and exquisite china.

I have my own room and bathroom, and I drive their van. They pay for gas and my insurance while also giving me a nice paycheck every two weeks. I teach the four-year-old boy how to swim and help him learn the alphabet and numbers. I cook meals and transport both children to various activities and school. I'm enjoying my time here, living the rich lifestyle, but it feels like something is missing. I try going to several churches, but I still have a longing I can't explain. Maybe if I owned a rental house, I would feel more settled.

I love looking at houses and go regularly with an agent to find something in my price range in Oklahoma City. Eventually, I fall in love with a small older home that has three bedrooms, one bathroom, and an open kitchen/dining/living area. It has a nice big backyard and is in a quiet established neighborhood with a post office and stores nearby. It doesn't need any work before I rent it out, and I quickly find good tenants.

About this time, Celeste returns from two years overseas. She has been in Calcutta, India, working with a woman who was starting a home for destitute children. She also went to Malaysia to work with Vietnamese refugees. I am so proud of her for being willing to go to these places alone and for working in such poor areas to help others. Not long after she returns, she meets Chris, a tall, good-looking man with a wonderful smile. When they decide to get married, I make her dress, and Teesha and I travel up to Oregon to be part of their happy day. The wedding is so beautiful, as the people in their small church work together to do the flowers, food, photos, and cake. I'm happy to see they are part of such a loving community.

Back in 1984, Teesha took a trip to New Zealand to attend Trudy and Roger's wedding. On the way home, she met the man of her dreams while visiting Fiji. Jens is from Denmark, and she soon moves there to live with him on his family's farm. Their wedding is scheduled for August 1986, but a week before I am set to leave, the family I'm working for tells me they are declaring bankruptcy and no longer need my services. When I wake up the next morning, I am partially paralyzed down one side again, and it takes me several weeks to feel better. The trip to Denmark for the wedding comes in the middle of my recovery. I make Teesha's dress and am excited for this trip, even though I'm not feeling well. Before I leave, I move my clothes to the home of an elderly friend, say goodbye to the children I have grown so fond of, and sign up for classes to become a certified nanny when I return. I have no idea where I'll be living or working when I get back here, but I set my mind to enjoy this time.

It's Danish tradition to fly their country's flag for all celebrations, so the first activity on the morning of the wedding is the raising of the flag in front of their home. All the neighbors do the same as a way of sending good wishes to the happy couple. At the church the family has attended for generations, we file past the gravesite of Jens's grandparents as a way to include them in the day's activities. The gold ring Jens places on Teesha's finger is the same one his grandfather had placed on his bride's finger in this same church, many years before.

The driveway to the house where the reception will be held is lined with Danish and American flags. Jens carries his bride over the threshold to the reception area. A seven-course meal follows, all prepared by Jens's mother, interspersed with speeches and jokes. Then there's dancing, which goes on well into the night. Such an amazing day! I'm so glad to meet Jens's family, see where Teesha is living, and share in this special day with them all. I wish them well and look forward to visiting again in the future.

Teesha graduating from OSU with a
bachelor's degree in zoology, 1981.

Celeste and Chris Delaney.
Married August 3, 1985.

Eunice and Teesha at her wedding to Jens,
August 9, 1986.

Trudy and her father, Jim,
at her wedding to Roger, 1984.

chapter nineteen

Answers

Back in Oklahoma, I stay in the home of an elderly lady as her companion while I do the nanny training. With my certificate in hand, I quickly find a nannying position.

"What do you mean you don't know how to swim? You have a swimming pool in your backyard," I ask the five-year-old boy I now care for. He looks up at me with big eyes.

"But, Eunice, I'm scared of the water," he admits.

"I'll help you. I know how to swim very well. I started swimming when I was only three," I assure him.

We begin spending time in the pool every day, and he quickly gains confidence and skill. Although his parents both work, I am not well paid. This is not a live-in position, so I have to pay rent for an apartment near their house. I take on extra jobs on the weekends, caring for a retired couple and babysitting twin girls. When the lease is up for the people renting my house, I happily move in there and fix it up just the way I want it. I *love* having my own place. This is the first time in my life that I've owned my own home and lived alone. It feels so good to be independent and free to make decisions without having to compromise with anyone. I'm still caring for my little swimmer, but I start making shortbread to sell as well. I buy a big pizza oven and have it installed in the garage. I have special tools made so I can shape the pieces evenly, and I design the boxes for Grandma Eunice's shortbread.

Teesha comes to help me promote my new venture at the Ethnic Food Show. We wear tartan skirts with white blouses and have a great time handing out samples and selling boxes of shortbread. A distributor begins selling for me, but I'm getting worn out. I need to look for another solution. I'm so busy just trying to survive that I can't enjoy life. If I want better wages, I'm going to have to get out of Oklahoma. I send my resume to two nanny agencies, one on each coast. My second interview is with a family in Los Angeles who hasn't had their baby yet, and they offer me the job. I hire a property manager to take care of renting out my little house, close down the shortbread business, and go west, back to California.

Yes, I think I can be very comfortable here. I'm unpacking in my newly decorated room. It has a pretty green and pink comforter on a queen-size bed, matching lamps on the rattan nightstands, and pictures of flowers in gilt frames all around the walls. My room is on the first floor of a large French Riviera-style home that overlooks the ocean from its perch on a steep hill in Santa Monica. The baby's room is also on this floor. Our rooms are on either side of the main entrance, which includes a winding staircase that leads up to the rest of the house.

The anxious parents are friendly and kind to me as we await the arrival of their first child. When the day finally comes in October 1990, I'm amazed to be included in the birthing room and watch in awe as this new life comes into the world. Even though I've had four children of my own, I am overwhelmed by this miracle and envy the medical staff who get to do this every day. The sweet baby girl is healthy and strong. She is showered with love and attention from us all and gets the finest of everything. As she grows, lessons begin early with ballet, Kumon math, music, and gymnastics before she's even in kindergarten. She has birthday productions of outrageous proportions, each bigger and better than the last, and every month,

I'm asked to make a cake for her "unbirthday" as well. We travel all around the U.S. and Europe together and rub shoulders with famous people whose children go to the same events. It's all very exciting and glamorous at first, but after a few years, I begin to see the emptiness and pain behind the facade of wealth. Something is still missing, even with everything I could possibly want in material things. I need answers.

I begin to attend the Church of Religious Science that's just down the road from me. Here, I am taught about the power of thought and creating your own destiny. It takes time to understand the concepts and to wash away all the other teachings about jealous gods and vengeful punishments. Coming to terms with being truthful in all things and learning to take responsibility for my own life is a challenge. When this group moves to another location that I can't get to by bus, I start going to the Unitarian Universalist Church. There, I find a group of people interested in helping their community and growing personally, while allowing the freedom to worship whomever or whatever you want.

As I grow in self-confidence, I find the courage to write to Daphne and ask her to admit she is my biological mother. It is a difficult letter to write, as I try to be honest but not judgmental, hoping she will understand my need to clearly know the truth. I also write to a cousin for some information about another cousin, Alison, who I think may be my identical twin. Although Daphne never mentioned my being one of twins when I visited her, I have wondered about this for years. Alison was born around the same time I was, and Mother described her as being "your twin" once when we were young. I feel a deep need to know if this is true. If it is, it would give me a sense of belonging with someone, something I have never had.

Replies to both letters arrive on the same day. Alex, Daphne's second husband, replies for her, saying that Daphne died five years ago from a stroke and that he knows nothing about my birth. My cousin's letter says there is no possible way that Alison is my twin, as she was born a year after me and two hundred miles away from where I lived. She also died five years ago, although in her case, it was in a car crash. After weeks of anticipation, I'm disappointed, and so much still feels unresolved.

In the fall of 1996, I know it's time to return to New Zealand to face the children I left behind seventeen years ago. Trudy has kept in touch, but I have had no contact with Jamie since our family split up twenty-four years ago. This is not going to be easy, but I have to do it. I know we all need to mend the rift between us. I write to Jamie, hoping for a reply. A nice letter arrives from his wife, Jane. It gives me hope and the courage to book my tickets, pack my bags, and get on a plane heading south across the Pacific, just before Christmas. During the long flight, I wonder about how things will be in the homeland I haven't seen for so long.

Flying into Auckland is not the grand entrance I've enjoyed on a cruise ship, but I'm just as excited. After clearing customs and immigration, I find Audrey and Neil sitting together in the terminal, scanning the passing arrivals. They don't recognize me until I walk up to them with a cheery, "Hi! Yes, it's me. You didn't know who I was, did you?"

I fall into their arms, so relieved to be surrounded by their love and warmth again. It's as if the years melt away and we have never been apart. Back at the same house I left from all those years ago, I know I'm home, I'm safe, and I'm loved. We visit some of the old haunts, and I'm amazed at how much the new highways and downtown development have changed the once familiar landscape. I definitely couldn't find my way around here anymore.

"Hello?" I hear Jamie's voice for the first time in far too long.

"This is your mother," I reply tentatively, breaking into a sweat.

"Who?" he asks.

"Your mother."

"Oh yeah. How are you?" he says somewhat formally.

"I'm fine. I'm here in Auckland, visiting for a week. I would like to see you," I manage to say.

"Why don't you come on over now?" he offers.

"I will. Tell me how to get there."

I'm still shaking with fear. I really wasn't sure what would happen when I called. He didn't say he didn't want to see me. He didn't start yelling about how much he hated me.

"Audrey, can you drive me over to Jamie's right now?"

"Absolutely! Let's go," says Audrey as she grabs her car keys and purse on her way out the door. Before I have time to change my mind, I'm standing in front of his door, knocking timidly. It opens, and I look up into his eyes. His arms come around me, and I know it's going to be all right.

It's awkward at first. Years of pain stand between us as we try to chat casually about his work and the children and Jane's job. He shows me around his house and makes a cup of tea. Jane arrives home a little later—such a sweet, caring girl, sensible and hardworking. I give the grandchildren, Sam and Sarah, their gifts to unwrap. The ice is broken. Healing can begin. *Coming back was a very good idea.*

The next day, I'm standing in front of another door. Alex, Daphne's second husband, has a little apartment of his own now. All the children are grown and have moved away. We chat through the pleasantries before I ask about my birth.

"I don't understand why you want to know," Alex says.

"Well, for medical purposes, for one thing. When my doctor asks me what my mother died from, I have to say I don't know. But apart from that, it's important to me to know. As my mother lay dying, I was told she wasn't my mother, and others have hinted that it was Daphne. I've got documents to support the fact that it could have been her, and she didn't deny it when I spoke to her that day. You were there; you remember. Alex, was Daphne my mother?"

"Yes, she was," he replies, turning his body away from me as he speaks, an expression of secrecy across his face. "But I don't know anything else." He pauses for a few seconds. "Would you like a copy of her death certificate, Eunice?"

"Yes, please," I mumble, still taking in the fact that I now have a clear answer. He just said Daphne was my mother. I still don't really want it to be her, but I guess I have to finally accept that it's true.

I read over the document in my hand, noticing that it lists the ages of her seven living children, and I'm not included. Daphne has taken her secret to the grave.

"These are my half brothers and sisters," I process aloud.

"Would you like to meet them?" Alex offers.

"No. There's no point now, Alex. I'm planning to go back to America, so they don't need to know about me." I can see Alex has said all he's going to say, and although I'm sure he knows more, there is no way I can make him share whatever information he's hiding. I got what I came for. I'm sixty-two years old and just now finding out who my mother was for sure. She's gone, and I'll never be able to talk to her about it or ask why she didn't raise me. What happened that she got pregnant at fourteen, and who was my father? So many questions that will just have to be left unanswered. I cry about it all the way back to Audrey's home.

The Christmas festivities with Audrey and Neil have been spectacular. I have enjoyed meeting their children as adults and playing with their grandchildren. Audrey has made sure I've had all my favorite foods, and we have loved our long talks every night. One evening, we are talking about a friend who visited earlier that day.

"I can't get over how much she's aged. She's so wrinkled. She looks seventy," I remark.

"Eunice, she *is* seventy!" Audrey replies.

172

"Oh well, I guess that explains it, then," I say, and we burst into school-girl laughter. Best friends—they get you. The closeness and understanding don't change with the years.

Audrey and Neil are packing up their boat, tent, sleeping bags, fishing tackle, and camping equipment for their annual pilgrimage to the beach. I'm heading to the South Island for the first time in my life. Trudy is living down there now with her four children, and I'm going to do a bus tour on the way down so I can see some of this country I call home. Audrey takes me to the bus station, and suddenly, I don't want to leave. We hug and reassure each other that we'll get together again soon as I climb up into the fancy tour bus. We wave goodbye as the bus pulls away, and I can't seem to stop the tears.

The bus trip south takes us through some familiar towns, like Hamilton, Rotorua, Taupo, and Wellington, but they have changed so much since I was travelling this way in the 1950s that it all feels new to me. In Wellington, we board a ferry that takes us across to Picton on the South Island, a three-hour journey through one of the most spectacular waterways in the world. On this island, the rolling green hills give way to open acres of honey-colored grasslands, with the snow-covered Southern Alps to the west and steep cliffs going down to rugged beaches to the east. We visit all the cultural sites and take endless photos. Each night, we sleep in a comfortable hotel and wake up ready to enjoy another day of catered meals and constantly informative talks by our driver. I reach Christchurch ready to see Trudy and her children, who are waiting at the bus station when we arrive.

They live in a small state house with very little money, but Michelle loves to bake, and there are always cookies or a cake in the oven. Clare, Shawn, and Hayley keep me entertained with their laughter and stories, and I enjoy being the center of attention. Trudy has a big job making ends meet and taking care of her children as a single mum. We promise to keep in touch as, all too soon, I'm back at the airport, boarding another plane for the long journey back to America. I'm so glad I came. Reconnecting with my children was so special after all this time, and I finally established that Daphne really was my mother. I'll have to be content with that.

———————

Change is part of life, and I've certainly had my share of it over the years. When my position with the family on the hillside ends after eight years, it's a hard adjustment, like leaving one of my own children. My next family lives in an even larger, more expensive house, but it's not a home. The parents fight continuously, and the atmosphere is cold and unfriendly. They are distant and suspicious of others. It seems like money is their god, and they reap constant illness as a result of their greed. I don't stay long. I've come to the point where I realize I don't need an expensive lifestyle or lots of people around me to feel okay about myself. I know I can live alone, and I trust in my ability to make a good life.

When my attorney calls to tell me that there has been a fire at my home in Oklahoma and the house needs to be demolished, I don't go to see it. I ask him to take care of the details and sell the property for me. I move into a one-bedroom apartment in a retirement community in Santa Monica. I'm sixty-five years old when I enroll in a course to learn computerized accounting and business-related skills. It is seven months of intense work, and although I'm easily the oldest in the class, I do better than most and graduate with straight A's. I soon have my first office job, and I'm ecstatic. What a feeling of pride and accomplishment I have as I walk into the lavish office building that first morning. I go up the elevator and through the big double doors that bear the gold-lettered names of the executives working there. *You've come a long way, Eunice, from that shy little girl who couldn't speak up for herself and that young woman who let others run her life. You have the job you've always wanted, where you're treated with respect for the skills you offer. You have a sweet place to live, and you're making it on your own. Good on you!*

174

In the evening, I return to my home on the fifth floor, open the sliding glass door to the balcony to enjoy the view, and give thanks to God for having brought me so far.

Eunice traveling in Europe with a family she worked for in the 1990s.

Note from the author:

Eunice's story continues in Part Two as part of Celeste's story.

Eunice learning kayaking,
horseback riding, and sailing.

PART TWO

Celeste's Story: You and Me, Lord

Celeste C. Delaney

Dedication

For my wonderful children, Mikeah, Joseph, and Erin: You have given my life new meaning and taught me so much. I love each of you even more than tea and crumpets!

For my grandchildren, so far, Naomi, Joshua, Nora, Saraia, Rhett, and Gabriel: What a joy it is to watch you grow into the next generation of God's faithful ones.

For my husband, Chris: Thank you for taking this hazardous journey with me and staying in the river, even at those times when we both wanted to bail out. My heart is always yours.

After looking through the grimy airport window toward the empty expanse of concrete runway, I turn and take a seat. It has been quite an ordeal to get this far, with all the packing and goodbyes and the airport rigmarole. A minute to wait and collect my thoughts and scattered feelings should be helpful.

The one plane that goes to Thailand each day is late, as usual. I glance at the boarding pass in my hand—Celeste Scott, Calcutta to Bangkok, May 5, 1983. This struggling Indian city has been home for almost a year. I have helped establish a home and school for children who live in indescribable poverty, and I have worked with Mother Teresa's ministry on my days off.

Now it is time to move on to the unknown again, a new country, new people, and new work to do. As the Thai Airways plane finally taxis into the space near the terminal entrance, two men push the mobile stairway toward the front door of the Airbus A300. A few minutes later, a weary gate attendant unlocks the double glass doors near my seat, and the thirty or so people with me form a queue. I pick up my worn overnight bag and follow the line of passengers across the hot cement to an unknown future. *I'm not sure I want to do this. I'm leaving behind so many people I know and care about. I have no idea what's next, but it looks like it's just You and me again, Lord.*

---

chapter twenty
Beginnings—Four Years Old

There's blood everywhere. Jamie is screaming, and the adults are all yelling. I stand near the bathroom sink as Pop holds Jamie's bleeding foot under the running water. He uses a rag as a tourniquet and tries to comfort him. *What happened?* A few minutes ago, we children were all playing outside at the front of the house, running around and yelling, "Can't mow me over! Can't mow me over!" to our cousin Robert as he mowed the grass. Diane and I went to the backyard to play, but I guess Jamie didn't come with us. *He's only eighteen months old. I just turned four. I should have taken better care of him.*

Mum is beyond distraught. She quickly checks in with her doctor by phone, and a taxi is on the way. She grabs Jamie from Pop, wraps his mangled foot in a towel, and rushes out. We all wait to see what will happen next.

December 1960 is the beginning of a hot, humid summer in Auckland, New Zealand. We are living with Nan in her old house in the city, because she just had surgery and has convinced Mum she needs help while she recovers. Nan is a large woman with curly gray hair that is usually tied back in a bun. She is very strict and rarely smiles. Her favorite stories, when she's in the mood for such things, are about being part of the Macrae family from Scotland and how they have a place there called Eilean Donan Castle. It sounds wonderfully exotic to me, and I'd love to visit someday, but Scotland is very far away, and I'll probably never leave here.

Jamie and Mum finally return as we're sitting down for dinner. He has stitches and a huge bandage on his foot and doesn't want anyone to hold him but Mum. A week later, he's back at the hospital for a skin graft and stays there for several weeks. It takes him time to relearn how to walk when he is finally back home, and as soon as Mum can arrange it, we pack up and move back to our own house.

Our square green house sits up on a steep hill, surrounded by grass and trees. It looks out across a narrow gravel road to a railway line and an orchard beyond that. I like to listen to the rattling sound of the train at night and imagine where it might be going. My three-year-old sister, Diane, and I share a small bedroom downstairs. We have twin beds with fluffy pink candlewick bedspreads and a white wooden nightstand between us. Jamie sleeps in a crib in our parents' room down the hall, but he's getting too big for it—he often stands, holding the side rail, and rocks it back and forth to move it around the room! There is no air conditioning or central heating here because it doesn't get extremely hot or cold. In winter, we have a small space heater in the living room and hot water bottles under the warm wool blankets on our beds.

Because I'm the oldest, I help Mum around the house and make breakfast for us most days. I'm not a great cook, but I can make toast and cereal with milk. I'm also pretty good at sweeping the floors and making beds. Ever since we moved back home, our grandfather, Pop, has been living with us. He begged Mum to let him come, because he was tired of the way he was treated at Nan's. He is a short, heavy man with a balding head, who often seems to be grumpy. He smokes a smelly pipe, which is always in his mouth, and most of the time he's in his workshop under the house, making instruments or fixing something. He is also from Scotland, and before the war, he was an engineer. He doesn't talk much and never plays with us. Honestly, I'm scared of him, but I like to see the violins and guitars he has hanging from the rafters downstairs.

———————————

We're finishing up dinner one evening, and I'm hoping I have eaten enough vegetables to be allowed to have dessert, when Mum announces that she's going to have another baby. She tells us that she will be at the hospital for two weeks, and while she is away, a lady will come to help with cooking meals and washing clothes. When the long-awaited day finally arrives, a neighbor takes Mum to the hospital. Dad isn't allowed to be in the delivery room with her, so he might as well wait at home. The caregiver we were told about arrives the next day to make dinner and get us ready for bed. She's a very stern older lady, and I don't like her. She's strict beyond all reason and won't even let us talk at the table.

"Children are to be seen and not heard," she announces firmly.

It's really hard to survive a whole meal without saying a single word, especially if you're a chatterbox like me. I wonder if I can make it through two weeks of this torture.

It's June 1961 when we get to welcome tiny Trudy into the family, wrapped in a pink blanket and watching all our faces as we pass her around for cuddles. A Karitane nurse[14] comes to check on mum and baby every week to make sure they are doing all right. She checks Trudy's weight and length and asks about breastfeeding. Mum is having some trouble with nursing, so the nurse recommends bottle feeding.

"There's baby formula you can buy, or you can add water and sugar to regular cow's milk," she says. She also checks that Mum is healing well after the birth and recommends she get more rest.

———————————

14 Karitane nurses provide in-home postnatal care for mother and baby.

"Not likely with four kids in the house and no help!" Mum tells her with a sarcastic laugh. The nurse leaves, shaking her head as she looks around at all of us.

"Rather you than me!" she mutters.

———————

I'm standing in the kitchen as Mum walks in from getting the mail around lunchtime one day. Suddenly, Jamie is at the door, wailing uncontrollably before falling to the floor, shaking violently. Mum scoops him up as he recovers from a seizure, and he tells her that Pop hit him with a hose. She is obviously angry but holds Jamie until he has fully recovered. She tells me to take care of him while she talks to Pop. From where we're sitting, I can hear her desperate yelling.

"Get out of my house! I will not have you hitting my children the way you hit me."

A week or two later, Pop is gone.

———————

I'm trying to be brave. My fifth birthday was in December, and now that it's January, I have to go to school. I like my routine at home and am not at all sure this school thing is a good idea.

On the first day, Mum takes us all down our long driveway, along the gravel road, across the main street, and up a couple of blocks to the little school. I stand close to Mum while she talks to my teacher at the door of my first classroom. There are wooden tables with chairs around them and brightly colored pictures on the walls. Children are sitting at the tables, coloring pictures. I think I'd like to do that, but when Mum says it's time for her to leave, I start to cry and so does she.

After that first day, I do the long walk to school by myself each morning. My teacher is very kind, and I enjoy drawing pictures and playing outside. Mum seems worried the day I show her I can write my name all by myself. She says the letters are all backward, and she's not sure I should be using my left hand when I write. I don't know what to think, but I soon learn how to write it correctly.

"Line up everyone. We are going down to the lunchroom together," our teacher announces when we arrive one rainy Monday morning. Mum told us about the time she had four months off school because of a polio outbreak back when she was only twelve years old. This year, 1962, is the first time they are going to give all the school children in New Zealand a polio vaccine. We line up by classes, and they give us each a tiny tube of liquid to drink. It tastes okay.

Just as I get used to this school business, Mum says we're moving back in with Nan, because she is having *another* surgery. Nan has assured her that Robert isn't living there anymore. I wish we didn't have to go. Mum has decided to sell this house and tells me we will buy a bigger one when our time with Nan is over. But I like this house.

———————

Living in town means a new school for me. Newmarket Primary School is close to Nan's home. Every day, I walk down the busy city street and around the corner to the big old brick buildings surrounded by ancient Pohutukawa trees and bordered by a huge rugby field. My favorite part of the day is playing "doctors and nurses" at lunch time. One of us lies down on the stone wall under the big tree in the yard while the others use sticks and leaves to do "surgery." We play it every day, and my sister Diane joins in when she starts school here too.

I'm thinking about school as I try to pick out clothes to wear, but it has been hard to swallow since I woke up this morning.

"My throat hurts, Mum." I say as we stand in front of the bathroom mirror while she does my hair in two little ponytails.

"Let me see," she says, tilting my head back and pushing a spoon handle down on top of my tongue.

"Hmm. Guess we'll have to go to the doctor."

The next day, our doctor takes a quick look in my mouth and confirms it is tonsillitis. Before I know it, I'm in a *real* hospital, seeing *real* doctors and nurses, and I'm about to have a *real* surgery!

After the operation, I wake up in the children's ward. My bed is in the far corner of a big room, next to a window with a view of the rolling green lawns outside. There are lots of metal-framed beds in here with sick children in them, and everything from floor to ceiling is white. It smells like medicine, but I love to watch the nurses working. They seem to know exactly what to do to help people, and I'm impressed by their tidy starched uniforms. Most of them are too busy to spend any time with me, but there is a cleaning lady who comes to talk to me for a few minutes as she's mopping the floors and taking away dirty linens. Mum comes each day, and yesterday she brought me some books. My throat still hurts a little bit, and they only give me soft foods to eat, like Jello and ice cream.

A week after the surgery, a nurse is standing next to my bed when I wake up.

"You're going home today," she whispers.

I can't think of anything to say, but I smile up at her.

"We will miss you, Celeste. You have been such a good patient."

I'm glad she likes me, but I'm really happy to be heading home. Within a few days, Diane and Jamie get sick too, and they take turns going to the same hospital. Mum spends a lot of time going back and forth, because she doesn't want us to feel sad or alone like she did when she was in the hospital as a child.

On the first Sunday after Diane gets back from the hospital, Mum sends us to Sunday school with a neighbor who attends a little church down the road. I love singing "I'm in the Lord's Army" and doing the arm actions while we sing. I earn stars for learning verses from the Bible, and it's fun to put them in my memory book. Everyone is so nice here, and I wish our whole family could come, but Mum says Nan doesn't like church, and Jamie and Trudy aren't old enough to go yet. When Nan is finally better, it's time to move to our new house out in the country. Mum says it's a big house with all kinds of fruit trees and acres of bush to play in. I can't wait to see it!

At the beach in New Zealand.
Diane (three) and Celeste (four), 1961.

Eunice with Diane (four), Jamie (three),
Celeste (five), and Trudy (one), 1962.

chapter twenty-one

Life in the Bush

"Stay out of the way, you lot. Celeste, keep an eye on the others." An enormous truck moves slowly up our steep driveway, and men in overalls quickly start unloading the furniture as Mum shouts directions about what goes where. She showed us around our new house before the movers got here. Diane, Trudy, and I will be sharing the biggest bedroom, and Jamie has his own room down the hall, across from our parents' room. There's a bathroom with a separate toilet in its own little room, pretty French doors between the living room and dining room, and floral carpet throughout.

In the back, a path beside the garage leads down into the bush. There are no fences down here, because it's all part of the Waitakere Ranges, which go on for miles. This will be a great place to play. The front yard is really an orchard, with apples, oranges, lemons, grapefruit, and mandarins growing next to roses and an arch of sweet-smelling jasmine. This brick house with its green corrugated iron roof is bigger than our old home and much newer than Nan's house. We have met our new neighbors and are excited that they have children our ages.

It's very different living here than in the city. Most weekends, we children spend hours playing down in the bush behind our house. We know the trail down to the creek so well we can run through it and make it to the water in ten minutes. There, we build little dams and try to catch the tiny crayfish that hide among the rocks. The giant kauri and rimu trees tower above us, and the branches of the tall ponga ferns are great for making huts. It is damp and quiet except for the twittering calls of the fantail birds as they follow us around. The only critters down here are possums, and they don't come out during the day. There are no snakes or poisonous bugs to hurt us like we've heard live in other countries.

I'm a shy, skinny six-year-old when Diane and I begin walking the quarter of a mile to Woodlands Park Primary School each morning. We make friends with the other children who take the same route along our gravel road to the two small wooden buildings that house four classrooms and seventy children. During recess and on sports days, we stay active in a small grass area, a tennis court, and a large field that's used for rugby, soccer, and cricket. As I become one of the older children in the school, I'm honored to take a turn filling the coveted "milk monitor" role. Fresh milk is delivered in half-pint bottles every day. I'm one of two appointees who get to put the straws through the paper cap on the top of each glass bottle before they are handed out to the children during morning recess.

I like school and usually do well in every subject except the torturous reading aloud we have to do every morning. I can read well on my own. The problem comes when I'm standing at my desk with everyone watching me. I stumble through the words, blushing with embarrassment and wishing for it to be over. I don't write things backwards anymore, but my scrawly left-handed writing is the bane of my poor teacher's existence. Even with these challenges, I'm one of the top two in my class. My best friend, Moana, and I go back and forth getting the top mark in most tests. Our teacher is very strict and sometimes uses a leather strap on the boys if they misbehave. Fortunately, he's not allowed to strap the girls, but then, it's not usually the girls who are getting in trouble.

"Celeste, Celeste, come quickly! Malcolm is hurt!"

I stop playing hopscotch on the square concrete pavers next to my classroom and follow my yelling friend to where Malcolm is lying on the tennis court. I pick him up and carry him to his father, who is also the headmaster of our school and my teacher. He makes sure his son's wounds are cleaned up and bandages are applied before Malcolm is quickly back outside, running around with the rest of us.

Malcolm has special needs—I'm not really sure what his condition is called, but he's only about two-and-a-half feet tall and has club feet, curves in his spine, and floppy arms and legs. He can walk and talk and loves to be included in everything, but he's also inclined to get knocked over when the bigger kids speed around without noticing him. I don't remember how we became friends, but we frequently play together, and if anything ever happens to him, which it often does, it's me everyone knows to call.

On most weekends, Mum takes us to the Tepid Baths in downtown Auckland to go swimming. This is where she learned to swim when she was only three years old. We all know the story of her having rickets and needing to strengthen her legs after being in casts for a year. She teaches us to swim in the very same pool where she was the first in her class to swim the width and had her photo taken for the newspaper. After swimming, we're always starving, so Mum buys fresh fish and bread at the fish market on the wharves, and we hurry home for our favorite feast.

My friends always say how pretty Mum is when they come over. Eunice Fantham Bruce Johnston was her maiden name, and she is tall and slim. People say she looks younger than thirty-two years old, and some think she looks like Grace Kelly. She is very good at knitting and sewing and is always busy with projects at home as well as working at a factory, making dishes. She earns extra money by raising goldfish that live in huge concrete tanks along the side of the house, and for a while, she makes Māori carvings to sell to tourists.

Jim Reason is my stepdad, and he works long hours at Fletchers, a construction company in town, making plaster tiles. When he is home, he eats dinner, watches TV, and sleeps. I have never had a conversation with him, but I've been yelled at by him and spanked a few times. He comes from a big family in England and has seven brothers and sisters. We have never met any of them. Quite often, we get parcels from England with clothes and old toys, and he sends them letters and photos back. He never includes Diane or me in those photos, because he doesn't want his family to know he married a woman with two children. He is very good at playing any musical instrument by ear, and he was in a band on the ship where he and Mum met a long time ago.

"Off you go!" Mum says as we each walk past her on our way out the front door. Her sharp eye checks over each of us to make sure our clothes are in order and our shoes are clean and buckled. We join the neighborhood children walking down the road to the Sunday school that is held in the old community hall near us. Most of the children from the neighborhood go each week, and four adults come from a Brethren Church in town to teach us. We sing songs, learn Bible verses, have a little snack, and play games. Every week, my favorite part is the Bible story with the flannel board pictures, but I don't believe the stories are true. I think they're made up by adults to make children behave. During the week, we go to regular school to learn to read and do math, and then on Sundays, we're sent to learn these moral lessons so we will behave properly. My parents don't seem to believe it, but it does give them a nice break to have us gone on a Sunday morning for a couple of hours.

Tonight, like every night, I lie in my bed, and I pray the Lord's prayer like the Sunday school teacher taught me to do. I think about what will happen when I die and how no one will ever, ever, ever, ever know me again. I'm not frightened by that, just sad. It feels lonely. I lie awake, waiting for Mum to come in to check on Trudy. She does this every night on her way to bed, because Trudy tends to kick the blankets off, and Mum wants to make sure she's warm. I really, really want her to do that for me too. It seems like Mum takes care of us because she has to, not because she loves us. I have never heard "I love you" from anyone, and even this small gesture would feel like I am loved. So I push the blankets off and lie still with my eyes closed, waiting for her to come in. She gently opens the door, and as the light from the hallway streams in, she looks over at Trudy, who is in the bed next to me, and comes in to pull the blankets back on her. She leaves, as always, without seeing me lying there waiting, so I cover myself up and go to sleep. *I'll try again tomorrow night.*

It's 1963, and we're finally joining the modern world. Earlier this year, we got a telephone for the first time. It's a party line, which means five households share the same line. The ring tone is different for each home so you can tell if the incoming call is for you. Of course, this does not stop other people from listening to your call if they want to, so privacy is a rare thing in our small community.

We also have a television set now. It is in a large wooden cabinet, similar in size to our radio/record player that sits next to it in the living room, and the screen is about eighteen inches across. We have one black and white channel, with programming from 5 p.m. until 10 p.m. The first half hour is children's shows, so we youngsters all eagerly gather on the floor in front of the set to watch the test pattern for five minutes before *Torchy, Gumby, Bill and Ben the Flowerpot Men, and Fireball XL5* come on. These shows were made in England and America, and although they're from the 1950s, they are new here in New Zealand. Like with most things, we're several years behind the rest of the world. There are also local news programs as well as *Coronation Street* from England and *Bonanza* from America. One evening, I watch in shocked silence as the coverage of the assassination of President Kennedy is shown on the evening news. Even though it has happened in faraway America, the tragedy is not lost on this sad seven-year-old.

Christmas falls in summer down here in the Southern Hemisphere, so every December, we go to Smith's Holiday Camp in the Bay of Islands for two weeks to camp and play in the sun. We have a large green canvas tent where our parents sleep on cots, while we children sleep in our VW van. Every day, Mum cleans the bathrooms here so we can get a cheaper rate. It's not much of a break for her, but this has been our routine for several years. We eat crayfish for Christmas dinner at the table outside our tent, and there's always a decorated fruitcake that a friend makes for our dessert.

The Smiths, who own the camp, have four boys, and we four often play hide-and-seek with them up among the tea trees behind the campground. I'm nine years old when I find myself alone with the oldest boy, probably in his early teens, as we run away from the others to hide. Suddenly, he pushes me to the ground and lies on top of me, holding my arms down as he moves and moans. I'm terrified, and I can't get away. I look around to see if any of the others are coming, but there's no one in sight. When he finally gets off me and runs away, I sit there wondering what to do next. I wander back to our campsite and don't tell anyone. A day or two later, everyone is getting ready to head up there for another game, and I don't want to go.

"Oh, go on. It will be fun," Mum pushes me. She knows I'm very shy and tend to not want to play with the others. I can tell I'm not going to get out of it.

"I'll only go if Diane stays with me," I say.

"She will. Won't you, Diane?" Mum assures me as she looks at Diane, who nods quickly. But once we get up into the bush, the boy convinces her to go with someone else, and the whole assault happens again. I feel betrayed and hurt. I never play with the group again, and I don't tell anyone what happened. I'm not sure why, but

I feel ashamed and scared, even though I know it is not my fault and I don't really understand it.

"Do we *have* to go?" Diane and I cry as Mum gets us ready on Saturday morning.

"I know you don't like it. I don't either. But we have to do this for a little while longer," Mum tries to explain.

"But we want to go to the wedding. It's at one o'clock, and we won't be back in time. Can't you tell him we'll go next week?" I beg.

"I tried that, but he insists on it being this week. You can ask if he'll take you to the wedding then bring you back here when it's done."

"He won't do that," I say sadly.

For almost two years, Diane and I have had to go on visits with our father—Jim is Jamie and Trudy's real dad but not ours. We didn't know Cyril Nichols before this started, and we're not sure why all this is going on now. Mum says he wants us to live with him, but why would he? He doesn't even know us. He drives a big American convertible car, and there's usually some girl with him when he picks us up. It's embarrassing driving down our road with him. Everyone knows what is going on and watches from their windows.

We usually spend the day at his little apartment, drawing pictures, but sometimes we go to the zoo or to the beach. It's boring, and we're always glad to get back home. One day, he holds me up by putting his hand between my legs. When I tell Mum about it, she is very angry, and that night, she has a talk with me about sex. She goes through all the details in a book she keeps in her bedroom. She's worried something might happen on one of these weekends with him. Now what happened among the trees at the camp makes more sense, and I feel a renewed sense of disgust and shame.

So here we are, on this visitation day, trying to get out of going. Two of our teachers from Sunday school are getting married, and all the children in our class have been invited. We really, really want to go to the wedding, but now we're stuck going on this annoying visitation day instead. On the way to his apartment, we explain to Nick that we want to go to this special wedding. He doesn't say we can or can't go; he just ignores us. So after we get to his place, the two of us quietly make a plan. We tell him we want to color pictures outside on the front step, and he agrees to let us do that. While he's inside getting something ready to eat, we pack up the colored pencils, place them on the doorstep, and quickly run toward the street, terrified he will see us leaving.

It's a really long way home, and we're worried he will come looking for us and be angry, then we'll never get to go to the wedding. We walk and run and walk some more, always looking back to see if he's found us yet. It's about twelve miles through city streets and along country roads to our house. Eventually, we realize we're never going to make it in time, so we stop at a small store, explain our situation to the nice man behind the counter, and ask if we can call someone for help. We don't have a phone at home now because Mum got tired of Nick harassing her with nasty calls, but our neighbor has one, so we call them. They pass the message along to Mum about what we have done and where we are. She happily comes to get us, and we get to the wedding just in time. Nick never says anything about it, so we don't know if he went looking for us or not.

A while later, dressed in our Sunday best with big bows in our hair, Diane and I go to court with Mum for the second time. The marble hallways of this massive old building echo as people wearing white wigs and long black robes hurry up and down, talking in hushed tones and darting into courtrooms through ornate doorways. She tells us we may have to say who we want to live with if the judge can't decide. We wait in the busy waiting room, listening to Mum yelling somewhere down the long corridor. I'm worrying about having to say something in front of all those people when, suddenly, Mum returns, looking exhausted, and tells us it's done. They have finally decided we can stay with her. Within a few days, we are choosing new names and being adopted by Dad. I change my middle name to "Cheri" and Diane changes her first name to "Letitia," so now we have matching initials—CC and LL. I'm so glad that is over, and we never have to see Nick again. We're moving into the city soon so I can go to a good high school. I have loved living here and will miss my friends.

Glen Eden Intermediate School.
Celeste (eleven), 1968.

Woodlands Park Primary School: Standard 3 and 4, 1966.
Mr. McMillan—teacher/headmaster.
Celeste seated third from the left with Moana second from the left.

Woodlands Park Primary School.
Jamie (nine), Letitia (ten), and Trudy (seven), 1968.

chapter twenty-two

I Have Chosen You

I love everything about our new house in the city. It is an eighty-one-year-old Victorian-style home with big bay windows and a beautiful garden. The manicured lawns have high trimmed hedges that are edged with cineraria flowers. There's a massive orange tree in the front yard and guava bushes near the gate. The concrete troughs are now buried in the ground to form fish ponds so Mum can continue selling goldfish to the pet stores. Inside the house, there are twelve-foot-high ceilings covered with embossed tin, the original old scrim wallpaper, floral wool carpets, and a central fireplace. Letitia and I share a room, and Jamie and Trudy each have their own rooms in the enclosed porches. It feels comfortable and cozy here.

Soon after my family moves into the city, Mum starts looking for a church to go to. We visit a few and then begin going regularly to the Church of Christ in Mt. Albert. They always have an evening service on Sundays that includes a Moody Bible Institute movie. It is at one of these services, right after the movie, that they ask us to go forward if we want to have our sins forgiven and receive Jesus into our hearts. I have heard a lot of Bible stories and learned a lot of verses over the years and never thought it was actually true, but sitting here tonight, something deep inside me changes, and I *know* it is all true. Jesus really *is* the Son of God, and I can be forgiven for all the wrong things I have done. Although I feel like I am the shyest child on the planet, I know I have to walk up to the front. We are sitting in the middle of a row near the back of the church. It won't be easy, but I stand up as they sing "Just as I Am" to make my way forward.

Quite a few people are heading that way with me, including my mother and all my siblings, who got up after I passed them in the row. Near the front, there are people meeting each one of us, and a lady takes me over to a seat in the front pew on the right side. We sit down as she re-explains what the pastor has said. She checks to see if I want to pray with her to ask God to forgive my sins and to come live inside me. I *really* want to do that, so we pray together, and I immediately know something wonderful has happened. I am forgiven! As a twelve-year-old, I know I have lied to my mother, been unkind to my brother and sisters, and even stolen some chewing gum from a store once. It is such a relief to know I am forgiven that I start to cry, not something I ever do in front of others if I can avoid it. We walk over to where my mother is standing, and the lady with me remarks about my tears.

"Oh, she's just tired," Mum replies, but I know it is not that. I know something deep and important has just happened, and a new sense of joy and peace fills my soul.

I'm not sure why, but we don't stay at that church for long after that. We go to a Spiritualist assembly for a while, but then Mum stops taking us there. I decide to go down the road to the Presbyterian church. My new friend Donna meets me there, and I'm glad to have someone with me. They give me a Bible, and I have a whole new understanding of how the lessons apply to me and the choices I make. I want to know God more and to please Him. I don't feel as alone, because I know He's always with me, no matter what's happening in my messy family. Prayer becomes a conversation with Him, not just rote words I say to not feel bad. I'm glad to know for certain that I'm going to heaven when I die, and I no longer lie awake at night contemplating death.

It's 1972, and Donna is my best friend. We met when we were twelve years old in intermediate school, and now we go to high school together. She is smart and outgoing, not at all afraid to talk to adults like I am, and always wins the annual speech competition. We are in the commercial class, which means we do bookkeeping, shorthand, and typing classes along with the usual math, language arts, and science. Because we are the top two students in our class, we are asked to run the stationery room together. We hang out there every recess and lunchtime, selling books and supplies to students.

At fifteen, I'm always happy to get out of the house. Even though things are reasonably peaceful these days, it doesn't feel like a family to me, more like six people who happen to live in the same house. I love to go to Donna's house, where everyone talks to each other and they laugh and joke around all the time. And it's great to be together every day at school.

"Did you finish the book?" I ask when we meet one morning.

"Yep," Donna replies as she pulls our book out of her bag and hands it to me. I eagerly open it to read what she has added. We started writing stories together during our first year in high school. We have filled nearly seven notebooks so far. We write romances and mysteries as well as doing comic strips and "how to" pages. It's always exciting to see what the other one has added to our latest edition of "Yours, Mine, and Ours."

"Oh! I like the way you changed this one into a movie script. I'll have to add to it this weekend," I say after a quick glance over Donna's most recent addition to our story.

"Barney is running at Ellerslie on Saturday. Do you want to come with us to watch him?" she asks. Donna's father trains racehorses, and they live near the Ellerslie Racetrack. Barney is one of five horses that live in the stables on their property.

"Sure. I'll have to ask Mum first, but I don't think she'll mind."

When I get home, I ask Mum about going to Donna's, but she has a much less agreeable alternative for me. She asks me to go away with her this weekend on a business trip with a man she and Dad met through the new business they are in. It's hard for me to say no to her, so my plans get put aside. Laurie has a dilapidated old VW van and has made the back of it into a bed. Mum and Laurie ride up front, and I'm trapped in the back with Leon, Laurie's eighteen-year-old son. I'm fifteen, and he's obviously flirting with me. We talk a lot during the trip, but it's very uncomfortable, because he's constantly suggesting I could sleep with him in his bed that's up over the engine at the back of the van. Of course, I know he's wanting to have sex, so I keep saying no, but I'm not sure if he is going to force me to or not. *Why did Mum put me in this situation?*

Wellington is five hundred miles away. We drive for hours then get stuck in Wanganui and have to stay overnight while they fix the van. Laurie and Mum are in a small hotel room, while I'm left in the van with Leon. After a full day and another night there, the plan for the business meeting is dropped, and we head back north. We spend the night in Hawera before arriving home in the early hours of Monday morning. Laurie drops Mum off at her job and takes me home. Even though I'm exhausted, I hurry to get dressed in my uniform, make a lunch, grab my books, and run to the bus to try to make it in time. Before we left for this trip, Mum pulled Letitia and me aside to ask how we felt about going to live with Laurie. We both said, "Absolutely not." I'm hoping Mum has seen that living with Laurie is not a good idea.

That evening, Laurie is with Mum when she arrives home from work. We children are sent out of the room, but we can hear the distraught yelling between the adults a wall away. An agreement is eventually made that Letitia and I will go with Mum, while Jamie and Trudy will stay with Dad. Everyone is upset, and several of us are crying. I'm confused and sad and scared. In an instant, my world has been turned upside down. As Mum, Letitia, and I are going out the door, Dad says to Laurie, "Oh, your boys will have a good time with her," pointing to Letitia, "but you won't get anything out of that one," pointing at me.

It is crude and mean, and I know exactly what he is implying. Was that what this weekend in the van with Leon was supposed to be about? I shudder and want to run away. Instead, Mum takes us down the road to spend a couple of nights in the guesthouse behind the rest home where she works. Soon after that, we are moved in with a family whose daughter goes to school with Letitia, while Mum moves in with Laurie and his sons. We will stay here until the school year ends in December.

I do my best to study in the middle of this chaos, and I somehow pass the school certificate exams in all five subjects, as we must do to move on to the next year in school. Just before Christmas, we move into the flea-infested, garbage-filled, condemned pigsty that Laurie calls home. I miss our beautiful home in Greenlane, and I often wonder how Jamie and Trudy are doing. Several months later, Mum and Laurie buy a rest home, which gives them an income and all of us a decent place to live.

Fifteen elderly residents live here, and Letitia and I work after school and on weekends doing dishes, cleaning, and taking care of the residents. We're not paid, and every night, Laurie locks the door to our apartment downstairs, trapping us inside. He has padlocks on every window and door in the building; there's even one on the mailbox. We can't do anything without his permission.

Laurie Scott is an intelligent man, which makes his need to control everyone very scary. He tells us his father died when he was young. He had to go to work to support his family, which ended his plans to become a lawyer. He says his brother died in a motorcycle accident as he rode away from an argument they were having, and he has always blamed himself for his brother's death. Laurie also claims to have served in the military during WWII and says he was in a Japanese prisoner-of-war camp, though he won't tell us what happened there. I'm not sure if any of this is true. He and his sons lie a lot, so it's hard to know. We have no idea why Mum is living with this disturbed man, but we also have no escape until we're older.

———————

My last year in high school is an extremely lonely one. Donna has left school to work as a newspaper reporter, and although we see each other on the weekends sometimes, I really miss her. I stay for a fifth year in high school because Laurie wants me to go to medical school and this year is required to get the needed scholarships. I am struggling with the classes, and life in lockup has taken its toll emotionally. I am always tired, and I have difficulty focusing. I can see that God revealed Himself to me when I was twelve so I could make it through these hard years, but I'm very alone with my faith. At school, I meet Peter. He's in my class, the youngest of four boys in a Christian family, and soon he's taking me to and from school in his old Morris Minor van. I meet his family, and we go to the school ball together at the end of the year. He's the first boy I kiss.

I have loved the idea of working in a hospital since I had my tonsils out at age five, so when a school guidance counselor suggests occupational therapy as a career, I'm all in. I'm also excited about the prospect of moving five hundred miles away from here. I feel bad about leaving Mum to deal with the rest home without me, but she seems happy for me to go. Peter is heading to Australia to do military training. It's hard to say goodbye, and I will miss him. I'm so grateful for his loving support that got me through the hardest year of my life so far. Leaving Donna is just as hard. I wish she could come with me.

In January 1975, Mum and Laurie drive me down to Lower Hutt near Wellington to get me settled into the Central Institute of Technology. I'm eighteen and away from home at last. Now the adventure begins.

Celeste and
Donna visiting her
parents' stables.
Fifteen years
old, 1972.

At home in the garden.
Trudy (ten),
Celeste (fourteen),
Jamie (twelve), and
Letitia (thirteen), 1971.

chapter twenty-three

In Quietness and Confidence Shall Be Your Strength

On my way to mail a letter home, I meet Alice, and we quickly discover we're both here to study occupational therapy. It turns out, a lot of women doing our course are living at the Woburn Youth Hostel with us, and within a week, we know most of them. One is my roommate, Sue. She is an energetic morning person from Christchurch. She is also a Christian and a gifted guitarist with a beautiful singing voice.

After hearing my story about coming to know Jesus six years ago, she invites me to go with her to the local Baptist church. Being part of a loving church family is a wonderful, new experience for me, and my faith grows in leaps and bounds as I get to know the Bible and God's people. We have an enthusiastic college group that meets every week in different homes. I watch believers sharing what they are learning in God's Word and praying for each other. I learn to worship God through song—people closing their eyes or raising their hands while singing is all new to me. *This isn't a sing-along; it's worship of the one true God, our Creator, the One who sustains all life.* I'm excited to get baptized as an expression of my gratitude to God for saving me and my commitment to serve Him. After so many years of loneliness, I revel in the joy of being part of God's loving family.

As I spend time with the college group, I see friends who are outgoing and confident in front of a group and wish I was like that. I'd like to be able to say how I feel and what I'm learning, but I'm too shy. When I find the verse, "In quietness and confidence shall be your strength," in the book of Isaiah,[15] I hear God's reassurance that it's okay to be quiet. I want to give my whole life to God and do whatever He says. I sense I will be a missionary one day. I have no idea when that will be, but I'm trusting God's timing and direction. I have so much to learn, but God is patiently leading me along as I heal and gain confidence in Him.

After four months away, I can't wait to fly back to Auckland to tell Mum about all the things I'm learning. I stay and work at the rest home to help Mum have a break. I'm shocked to hear Letitia ran away soon after I left and Mum still doesn't know where she is. I wish Mum had told me, but she didn't want me to be worried. Trudy has come and gone several times. She's fourteen now and doesn't like living with her dad, so she comes here when she needs a break. I'm excited to spend time with Donna, who's doing well as a newspaper reporter, and we enjoy hours of catching up on all the details of our new lives.

Soon after I return to Wellington, a group of us move into a big old Tudor-style house out in Eastbourne, a beach community around the bay from Lower Hutt. This lovely home has been divided into two apartments. Five guys live downstairs, while Sue, Jill, Jenni, and I live upstairs. We are all believers, so we often meet for prayer, Bible study, and meals together.

I watch the various relationships of my roommates and daydream about a possible relationship of my own one day. I see men who love God and care for the women in their lives with respect and kindness. I haven't seen that in my family. Three men have been married to my mother, but none of them were really a father to me. I haven't seen how men and women should treat each other and work together to

---

15   Isaiah 30:15 (ASV).

raise their children. *Lord, I've got a lot to learn. Show me Your ways and heal my heart.*

―――――――――

Just before the Christmas break, Bob, one of the guys downstairs, asks if any of us wants to go to Beach Mission with him for a week in January. It's a summer outreach to campers and bikers at a Oakura Beach near New Plymouth. Alice and I talk it over and decide to go together. A month later, we're driving south from Auckland and talking about what to expect. I've never shared my faith with anyone outside our group, and I'm not good at talking to strangers. *Lord, was this a good idea? I'm not sure I want to do it after all.* During the day, we have teams who do programs with children and teens. I am part of the evening program team, organizing singing, testimonies, and a movie. Afterward, we have time to talk with visitors one-on-one. This is *so* out of my comfort zone. I start off by listening to Bob and his friend Charlie talk to whoever will listen, and I eventually get into some conversations of my own.

Even as I'm recognizing that I can't debate people into the kingdom of God, I'm amazed to see God reaching into people's hearts with His words of love and eternal life spoken through us. We can't do this on our own, but with God, eyes are being opened. We have time as a team each day to talk about what happened the evening before and pray for specific people. *I love being part of a team like this, and I can't wait to come back again next year.*

I have been praying for Letitia and finally hear she is living with our stepbrother Leon, not far from the rest home. Mum is, of course, very upset by this but glad to at least know where she is and that she's all right. Apparently, Letitia had written to Mum several times, but Laurie hid the letters from her. *How cruel!*

―――――――――

Years of strenuous study and clinical rotations in hospitals all over the country finally come to an end in December of 1977 as I complete the national examinations. I move back to Auckland and take a government-assigned job at a geriatric rehabilitation hospital. Mum is talking about Letitia and me going to America. She wants Letitia to finish her education there, and she wants me to go with her. I need to seek God's will for this decision, and as I'm waiting on Him for that, Mum's impatient for an answer.

I am walking downstairs one evening after a long day of working at both the hospital and the rest home, and I'm thinking about this decision I need to make. A thought comes into my head that I know is not something I came up with.

You are thinking about this as a New Zealander going to live in America, but you are an American who has been living in New Zealand for twenty years. It's time to go back. I would never have thought of it like that. I know I have just heard the quiet voice of God for the first time, and now I have my answer. I'm going to America with Letitia! *Thank You, Lord.* With this answer comes a deep peace that this is God's leading and timing.

I tell Mum that I will go with Letitia, and she is relieved to finally be making definite plans for us to leave. It's only a few months away, and we have a lot to do between now and then, including my graduation in April.

Letitia and I travel down to Wellington for the formal ceremony and sumptuous celebration dinner that night. *Thank You, Lord, for getting me through this incredible training. I have no idea what I'll be doing in America, but the last three years have shown me that I can trust You to have a plan and to take care of me.*

Celeste and her first occupational
therapy friend, Alice.

Celeste graduating with a Diploma in
Occupational Therapy, April 1978.

Fellow occupational therapy students and roommates.
Jenni, Celeste, Sue, and Jill, 1975.

chapter twenty-four

I Know the Plans I Have for You

"It will be okay," I try to reassure Letitia as we walk away from our family and friends at the Auckland airport on May 17, 1978. She is still crying as we make our way slowly through the last checkpoint.

"Looks like you're being deported!" the uniformed officer jokes when he sees her tears.

"We might as well be," she sobs, collecting her documents and trudging onto the plane. She cries on and off as we make our way slowly toward our new lives in America. The past three months have been a whirlwind of preparation, and as we sit on the cramped plane, we finally have time to contemplate our decision. We had to renew the passports Mum got us as babies, proving name changes and identities. We both had jobs to finish and endless decisions to make about what to take. We had a shared twenty-first birthday party on Pakatoa Island and said goodbye to all our friends. It has been hard for me not to worry about what's next. Letitia has arrangements to study at Oklahoma State University, so she has a dorm room and classes already set up and paid for. I have no idea where I will be living or if I can find a job. It is difficult to arrange things like that ahead of time.

So here we are, twenty and twenty-one years old as we fly across the Pacific Ocean. It has been twenty years since we moved to New

Zealand with Mum in 1958. This is what she hoped we would do all those years ago as she traveled on the *S.S. Orcades* with two small American daughters, unsure of what the future would hold for her or for us. *Thank you, Mum, for all the sacrifices you made to make this happen.*

The culture shock is immediate—the light switches work the opposite way from what we're used to, the toilets are different, and we can't figure out how the lamp works at all. We have never seen this "Life" cereal before, and no, we have never eaten an artichoke. Driving on the other side of the road is hard to deal with, and I can never remember which side of the car to get into. We are staying in San Francisco with John and Joyce Carroll, our parents' first landlords. John shares the story of Nick dismantling the piano to haul it upstairs and reconstruct it—I've heard the story before, and I'm surprised to see he's still talking about it so many years later. We visit Calaveras State Park with their daughter Terry, who has been my pen pal for many years. We're delighted to see squirrels and raccoons for the first time and take photos to send home.

Mum's friend Joyce Bickel is still working at Koret's and takes us out for a day to see Sausalito, Fisherman's Wharf, the Ghirardelli Chocolate Factory, and Chinatown. There are so many incredible places in this fascinating city, and we're grateful for her kindness to Eunice's daughters after all these years.

Everyone we talk to wonders why on earth we're going to Oklahoma when San Francisco is so much more beautiful. We found Oklahoma on a map before we left home, but there wasn't much information about it in the encyclopedia. Mum and Letitia chose OSU because they sent a few photos of the campus and reassured Mum that they would take good care of her daughter. The Californians make it sound dreadful as they talk about tornadoes and dust storms. I'm beginning to wonder what we've gotten ourselves into.

"You tip the cabbie!" the driver demands after I hand him the fare. Letitia and I look at each other. We have never had to tip anyone before in our lives, as there is no tipping in New Zealand, and we have no idea how much is appropriate. We have just arrived in Oklahoma City after a long flight from California, and we are making our way from the airport to a local motel. I pull out the change in my purse, look it over, and hand the expectant man a quarter.

"Is this all right?" I ask.

"Ugh!" he moans and throws it back at me as he walks back to his cab. I shrug, put the money away, and start hauling my bags into the motel lobby.

"We'll have to figure out this tipping thing some other time." I smile at Letitia.

That evening, we get some food from a nearby restaurant and sit on the bed, going through the phone book, trying to find a local youth hostel. *There aren't any? This has to be the only country in the world that doesn't have youth hostels.* We had no idea. We find something called "Travelers Aid" that sounds good. After all, we're traveling, and we need aid. We call and explain that we just arrived from New Zealand and need somewhere to stay while we get organized. The lady on the phone gives us directions to get to their place downtown, so the next morning, we find another taxi and set off. It turns out to be a homeless shelter! We have nowhere else to go, so we leave our suitcases in the main office and spend the night with the other homeless people of Oklahoma City, eating a simple meal and nervously trying to sleep on dorm room bunk beds. *Welcome to America!*

Letitia is due on campus the next day. We get directions to the bus station, load up her belongings, and enjoy the one-hour bus ride to Stillwater. Through the bus windows, everything we see is flat, brown, and dry. There are no mountains or beaches and not many trees. In stark contrast, we're delighted to see that Oklahoma State

University is nestled in the beautiful tree-lined town of Stillwater, and we feel welcomed with the flow of other new students looking for directions. We get her signed in and find our way to her dormitory. No one had mentioned we needed to bring bedding. Many of our campuses in New Zealand don't have dormitories, and we both lived off campus while studying, so we didn't even think to ask. We spend the first night sleeping on the bare mattresses, using our clothes as pillows and covers.

Letitia's roommate arrives the next day, and we are convinced she comes from a very wealthy family, as she fills the room with designer bedding, a refrigerator, a rug, a coffee maker, decorations for the walls, and all kinds of bathroom appliances. She also has a car, so she takes us to a local store to shop for bedding. Once Letitia is settled in, I'm back on the bus, going toward Oklahoma City, wondering what I'm going to do next. *Lord, please find me a place to stay so I don't have to spend another night in that shelter alone.*

"Well, I thought I would stay in a youth hostel, but apparently, there aren't any," I explain to the man in charge of Travelers Aid when he asks what my plan was before coming to the U.S.

"I'm an occupational therapist, so I will be looking for work in a hospital around here."

"How much money do you have with you?" he asks.

"Fifteen hundred dollars."

"That's not much. It won't last very long here."

Staring at the floor, I'm trying not to panic or cry in front of this very blunt man.

"Let me talk to someone who might be able to help us out. I'll be right back." He leaves me sitting alone in the tiny office and goes off to make the phone call. He returns a few minutes later.

"I just talked with a lady who often houses foreign exchange students, and I asked if you could stay with her. She's on her way to pick you up." Relief floods my heart. Someone nice is coming. I don't have to spend another night in this shelter. I have never been so grateful in my whole life! *Thank You, Lord. You are so good to me.*

Sweet Mrs. Atlee arrives in her huge Cadillac fifteen minutes later and bundles me off to her lovely home on the outskirts of Oklahoma City. It's an older two-story farmhouse with several acres of land around it. There are apartments that they own directly behind the house and a baseball field next door. Their son and his wife live in a triplex on the far corner of the property, and huge pecan trees surround each house. She gets me settled into a comfortable upstairs room and tells me to take my time as she hurries away to get dinner ready. I plop down on the quilt-covered bed, finally able to breathe a huge sigh of relief. *I don't know how You did this, Lord. I'm safe. I have a place to be. It's beyond anything I could have hoped for. Thank You.*

Mr. Atlee arrives home in time to eat, and we talk about where I might work.

"Our niece works in a hospital near here. We could ask her to check if there are any occupational therapy openings there."

"Thank you. That would be great," is all I can manage to say. Two days later, I'm sitting in the OT office of Baptist Medical Center, talking to the department head. She is from Denmark, so she understands how I feel looking for work here.

"I do have one opening, and you could start immediately with a temporary license. You will need to sit the American national board exam as soon as possible to get your state license. You will be working with the oncology rehabilitation team and helping out with general rehabilitation and the burn unit when we need it. The pay is good, and you will have health insurance benefits."

My head is spinning from all these sudden changes, but I'm so happy to have a job lined up. Over dinner that evening, Mr. Atlee has another idea for me.

"A lady who lives in one of our apartments just bought a new car, so she has her old car for sale. I think you should buy it. It's been well cared for and has lots of miles left on it." By the next evening, I own a 1969 Ford LTD—a giant green boat of a car that will definitely keep me safe in a crash. I'm so happy to be able to write to Mum and tell her how God has provided. I have gone from being homeless to having a place to stay, a job, and a car in less than a week. Mum writes back with obvious relief. She has been worrying about how this would all work out. *Lord, I don't know how You did this, but I'm so glad You did. Thank You, thank You, thank You.*

————————

Oklahoma is devoid of decent scenery and is instead blessed with tornadoes, dust storms, giant hail, killer lightning, and snowstorms, just as we were warned. There are deadly water moccasin snakes, tarantulas, and scorpions, none of which are in New Zealand. But despite all these negatives, the people here are the nicest, most down-to-earth and caring humans I've ever met. So many have gone out of their way to help me and make sure I feel welcome, even when they can't understand a word I'm saying because of my accent!

Mr. and Mrs. Atlee head north to Alaska during the summer, so I take care of their home until one of their apartments opens up. I love my job, and honestly, I'd do it even if they didn't pay me. Working on the state's first oncology rehabilitation team is challenging and fast paced. I attend doctor's rounds, make splints for patients in the burn unit, see trauma patients in the ICU, and visit homes of patients who are ready for discharge to make sure they have the equipment they need to function safely. I make lots of new friends on the staff and love being part of this busy hospital.

Teesha, as Letitia is now called, visits from time to time and seems to be doing well in school. Mum writes to say she hopes to be coming soon—without Laurie. Large packing crates of her belongings arrive, and I have to pick them up from the customs department at the airport. I don't know how she is escaping, but I can see now that this was her plan all along—get us over here so I could sponsor her. I'm glad she's getting away from that awful, controlling man and pray she gets here safely.

———————

I'm going to a local Southern Baptist Church, as here in the "Bible Belt" there seems to be one on every corner. I teach Sunday school for the first time and join an evangelism training group. One Sunday morning, there is a particularly loud thunderstorm raging around us as the pastor struggles to be heard over the noise of the heavy rain. Bright flashes of lightning and long rolls of thunder keep distracting the congregation. Suddenly, lightning hits the roof with a loud crack. We all look up in time to see smoke billowing from a high beam in the ceiling as a piece of wood comes hurtling down and hits a man sitting in a back pew on the head. He falls into the aisle as others rush over to help him. We are all stunned. The pastor stops his sermon to take time to pray for the man then finishes up quickly. An unusually large number of people go forward during the altar call a few minutes later.

One lady sums it up for everyone. "I have been singing in the choir here for years. When that lightning struck and Fred got hit on the head, I suddenly realized that I didn't really know God. I knew I had to make a decision to follow Christ right then. None of us know how long we have."

I realize for the first time that people can be serving in church their whole lives and not actually know God. There's a big difference between knowing about God and actually having a relationship with Him.

———————

Mum arrives in October 1979, a year and a half after us, and moves in with me for a while before getting a caregiving position with an elderly lady. She also works as a unit clerk at the hospital on the weekends, busy as always. She is so relieved to be away from Laurie and is amazed at how different the U.S. is from the 1950s when she was last here. She is not impressed with Oklahoma and prefers California.

Just after Mum joins us, I travel to the U.S.S.R. with the American Occupational Therapy Association. We visit a hospital in Moscow and talk about rehabilitation in the U.S. They share how they work with similar patients and show us around their facility. We also fly to Georgia, Ukraine, Armenia, and Azerbaijan, which are all part of the Soviet Union. We are particularly interested in their extensive support of new mothers and young children, but everywhere we go, conditions are poor, equipment is years behind what we're used to, and there is very little rehabilitation for the injured or care for the handicapped. The stores often have empty shelves, and we are aware of being followed when we go sightseeing without our guides. Life under communism certainly seems hard.

Two more years slide by, and as Teesha's graduation nears, the three of us begin making plans to move up to Oregon. It is the part of the country that is the most like New Zealand in climate and scenery. I'm wondering if, with this new start, I should be looking at going overseas with a missions organization. *Is it finally time for this, Lord?* I've known for more than five years that this is what I'm being called to do. I discover an organization called World Concern that is based in Seattle, just three hours north of where we will be. I'm excited to even be thinking about this next step.

Another round of sad goodbyes precedes an amazing ten-day road trip to the gorgeous Pacific Northwest. I drive my newly purchased Chevette, while Mum and Teesha handle a pickup truck weighed down with a camper and pulling a U-Haul trailer loaded with our belongings. We get a real sense of how big this country is and the diversity of cultures that make up the population as we visit

Albuquerque, Santa Fe, Colorado, Four Corners, the Grand Canyon, the Hoover Dam, Death Valley, Las Vegas, Yosemite, the redwood forests, and finally, Oregon. We find a campground just outside Portland, and within three weeks, Mum and Teesha both find places to stay and work.

I leave my car for Teesha to drive while I'm on the road with my first OT friend, Alice. She is here visiting from New Zealand as part of her adventurous "gap year" travels. We drive the pickup truck with the camper on the back for our two-month journey through thirty-four states. We see everything, including deep snow on the Beartooth mountain pass near Yellowstone, rush-hour traffic in downtown New York City, and spectacular thunder storms in Texas. We visit parts of Canada and Mexico, climb around Mesa Verde, camp in the Circus-Circus Casino parking lot in Vegas, enjoy Disneyland, and eventually find our way back to Oregon. I join Alice on her return trip to New Zealand and have Christmas there, catching up with Donna and lots of other old friends. I'd forgotten how beautiful Auckland harbor is and how lovely people's gardens are here. I've been homesick for the smell of flowers and the sound of birds. I soak it all in and go to the beach as often as I can. *Thank You for this sweet time here, Lord. I love this country, and it will always be home.*

Back in the U.S. by January 1982, I stay with Mum for a few weeks until I move in with a family from my new church, Sunnyside Community Church, in Clackamas, Oregon. I visit World Concern in Seattle.[16] I am very impressed by the work they do getting people into countries as doctors, vets, or social workers to help in crisis situations. A few weeks later, I do their orientation training and get assigned to go to Calcutta, India to help start a home and school for

16 World Concern, 19303 Fremont Ave. N., Seattle, WA 98133; (800) 755-5022; email: info@worldconcern.org.

slum children. Vaccines, letters to raise financial and prayer support, and organizing what clothing and medicines to take fill my days. Mum and Teesha have both moved back to Oklahoma, as there's not much work in Oregon. I miss them, but we'll keep in touch.

Here we go, Lord! I have no idea what this will be like, but I'm trusting You with all the details of yet another new adventure, this time just You and me.

Harry and Colleen Atlee, 1980.

Celeste's first apartment (at the top of the stairs) and her first car, 1978.

Teesha and Celeste visiting in 1979.

Occupational therapy staff at Baptist
Medical Center, Oklahoma City.
Karen (dept. head), Barb (office),
Chuck and Celeste (occupational therapists), 1978.

Donna and Celeste catching
up in New Zealand,
December 1981.

Teesha, Eunice, and Celeste at Teesha's graduation from OSU
with a Bachelor of Science in Zoology, April 1981.

Traveling across the country, 1981.

chapter twenty-five

The Lord Will Guard Your Going Out and Your Coming In

August 18, 1982. As I walk out of the crowded Calcutta airport building into the intense heat and humidity, the new sights, sounds, and smells of India overwhelm my senses. I pause, looking for Mrs. Chandana Banerjee. I have flown across the ocean alone. I don't know anyone here and have no plan if she doesn't come. I wrote to her with my flight information, and the plane arrived on time, so I hope she's here. I *really* hope she's here. The expectant crowd in front of me searches the faces of emerging passengers, some looking for family or friends, others trying to persuade me to ride in their taxi, and many just begging. *I really hope she's here!* After a few minutes, a slim lady in a cotton sari moves forward, holding a sign with my name on it. *Thank You, Lord. That's her!* We introduce ourselves, and she indicates a taxi she has waiting.

I'm so glad she speaks English well. We talk about the flight, the work she has started, where I am from, and where she plans for me to stay for the first week I'm here. I'm only half listening as our car hurtles recklessly through traffic, dodging potholes, rickshaws, buses, wandering water buffalo, small children, and dead dogs. Barren poverty drenched in stifling humidity and the stench of open sewers surrounds us—desolate fields, mountainous garbage piles, dilapidated buildings, dust, and decay are everywhere. All the drivers keep their hands firmly on their car horns, and we're not even in the city yet. This is going to take some getting used to.

In addition to my one suitcase, World Concern has asked me to bring a trunk of supplies for the children and another box with a sewing machine in it for Chandana to use with the women she is helping. We take this luggage to her house, unload the donated items, quickly meet her family, and head downtown, where she has arranged for me to stay at the Fairlawn Hotel.

At first, it seems like an oasis of beauty. A long palm-lined driveway leads to an open foyer and dining area that has a black and white checkered floor and tables covered with crisp white linens. It's such a stark contrast to the chaotic streets. Pictures on the walls tell of the famous people who have happily stayed here. According to the plaque posted on the side of the building, it was built in 1783, giving it a long history of hospitality and service. The impression of opulence is somewhat dulled, however, when I see my room. Quite large, my ground-floor space has rusting metal-framed French doors that open to a very tiny concrete patio with an in-ground drain and a tall concrete wall obstructing the view. There are no screens, and the doors must be open to get any air. The wrought iron hospital bed looks like it has been here since the 1800s, and resting on top of it is a hard, thin straw mattress hidden beneath dirty linens. The bathroom door leads to a small tiled area with a shower head coming out of the peeling concrete ceiling, a badly stained toilet, and a small sink. But the most interesting feature of this deluxe room is a large cage-style rat trap placed near the bed. I put my suitcase on the floor, sit down on the bed, and stare at this contraption. I wonder which would be worse, to have a large rat wandering around my room or one trapped in this thing, screaming to get out. *Best not to think about it.*

It is not a good night's sleep with the twelve-hour time difference, new bed to adjust to, and thoughts of a rat invasion. I toss and turn. There is no lock for the door. The ceiling fan squeaks and looks like it might fall down at any minute, but it has to be on in this heat. Morning finally comes. No rats visited, and the fan continued its noisy job without collapsing. I wash quickly in the sink and get dressed. I have chosen to wear full-length skirts while I'm here, because the local women dress very modestly. It's going to take time to get used to the heat and humidity of this wet monsoon season. Breakfast is eggs, toast, fruit, and tea, and Chandana arrives on time at ten o'clock. I get my first rickshaw ride as we make our way through the crowded streets to her home. This seems like a very dangerous mode of transportation, but the barefoot young man is very good at dodging through traffic, pedestrians, and animals, ringing a small bell in his hand to ask for permission to pass. He skillfully avoids the tram lines in the cobblestone streets that would send him and us tumbling to the ground if a wheel accidently got caught.

Along the congested city streets, we see a portion of the one million people who live on the wide sidewalks. They bathe, eat, sleep, beg, and make items to sell while pedestrians step around them. Some people toss a coin, some yell at them to clean up their mess, but most just ignore them. Small stalls sell heated sweet corn, sugary snacks, leather goods, and hardware. Men squat at typewriters, ready to prepare needed documents. Ear-cleaning services are available from a man with long metal instruments, and the dentist has a chair open on the sidewalk in case you need help to get a tooth out.

It is a scene of continuous movement and noise. Smells of bus diesel and cooking food mix with the odor from the huge garbage piles that grace most street corners. These provide animals with a place to eat, while children clamber through the piles looking for metal, paper, or plastic items they can recycle into cash. Reusing trash is an art form here—the bag for the oranges I buy at the market turns out to be made from a page of someone's medical records. It's interesting reading.

We spend the first part of the morning visiting offices and banks to set up an account for me to receive funds from the U.S., and the second half we spend making plans for the new home. In the afternoon, we return to the house where Chandana lives with her husband, her new baby boy, and the sixteen destitute children that she has taken in. She is working with a Dutch sponsoring agency to get funding for each child. If she can find a bigger house to rent, she hopes to eventually have fifty children in her care. She also wants to set up a preschool to help children from a nearby slum prepare to go to the local schools next year. It's an ambitious plan, and she has hired ladies to help her with cooking, cleaning, teaching, and laundry.

Chandana also has a group of women that she's teaching to make crocheted items, which she plans to sell overseas. She hopes they will make enough money to help support themselves and the school programs. That way, the community would eventually be able to take responsibility for educating their own children. Having met the children, I can see why she feels so passionately about helping them. Shy smiles greet me as they gather around, wanting to touch my clothes and my hair. Many have been abandoned by families who just can't afford to feed them. Some are handicapped, and they are all desperate for love and attention.

I spend my first week in Calcutta living at the hotel while we look around for somewhere more permanent. Within two days of arriving, I begin to have stomach issues—frequent pain and diarrhea from amoebic dysentery. I learn to fast for a day when it's bad and slowly introduce solid food again over the next few days. I move into the YWCA hostel on Middleton Row and am delighted to be with people from all over the world who came to work with Mother Teresa. I plan to visit some of her homes on my days off. I learn that she was born in Albania and joined the Loreto nuns in Ireland at the age of eighteen. She came to Calcutta in 1929 and taught at St. Mary's School for girls, eventually becoming the principal. On a trip up to Darjeeling in 1946, she felt God calling her to start a work to help the poorest of the poor, who she saw living and dying on the streets. She started a home for the dying first, and now she also has a home for children, a home for handicapped women, a home for leprosy patients, and a feeding program that gives out thirty-five thousand meals every single day. It's an amazing ministry, but it still feels like a drop in the bucket compared to the overwhelming need in this ocean of poverty.

"Are the new children from the slum area healthy?" I ask as Chandana and I go over the list of fifteen new children expected to arrive for school this morning.

"Yes. They all have scabies and lice, and I think some may have TB, but they're healthy," she assures me.

Well, "healthy" is obviously a relative term!

"They will all be washed and have their heads shaved when they arrive today. Then we will give them new clothes, feed them, and start with some simple lessons. We don't want to overwhelm them on their first day of school," she explains. "We also have a medical worker coming later today to test the children for TB so we can start the ones who need it on medication."

"Who's going to be teaching?" I ask, not having seen any of the teachers yet.

"I have hired a couple of women from town to do the teaching."

"And what will the lessons include?"

"Bengali, Hindi, and English reading and writing, as well as mathematics and history," Chandana says.

"Sounds like a lot."

"It is, but that's what they will be expected to know if they're going to go to the local school next year. We also teach them about God and introduce them to the Bible. Those who live in this house come to church with my family each week too."

Right at the appointed time, we hear the sound of knocking at the front gate. Twelve of the fifteen children are here with two adults who have accompanied them for the quarter-mile walk to the house. Before they come inside, helpers bathe each one at the only water source for the house—a hose outside near the back door—and shave their heads. After quickly drying off, they are dressed in clean clothes and brought inside to wait for lunch. They quietly sit cross-legged on the concrete floor with their metal plates of dahl, rice, and vegetables in front of them. They have been told to wait until someone prays. The house children join them, and Shambu, one of the older boys, leads in prayer. The new children shyly look around and only start eating when they see the house children begin to talk and laugh while they eat. No utensils are needed here—everyone eats expertly with their right hand and cleans every piece of rice off their plate. After lunch, all the children head upstairs for their first day of school.

Later in the afternoon, the medical worker arrives to do the TB tests. He is casually dressed in a sarong and button-up shirt. He has no medical bag with him. As the children line up, he pulls a syringe from one shirt pocket and a vial from the other. He draws the liquid into the syringe then proceeds down the line of children, jabbing one after the other with the same needle and without cleaning any arms first. I watch in horror, convinced that if the children didn't have something wrong with them when they got here, they do now. But these kids are tough. No one gets sick, and only one tests positive for TB when the results are reviewed a few days later.

"Where are you going?" a messy little face asks me as I step out the hostel's front door and into the busy street on my way to Chandana's school for the day.

"To visit a friend. How are you doing today?" I reply.

"Very good. You see Miss Margaret?" he asks.

"Yes, she was at breakfast. I'm sure she'll be down soon."

"Very good," he says, giving me the customary greeting of a nod of the head with hands in a praying position to send me on my way.

We have all made friends with the three homeless boys who live on our front doorstep, giving them food, soap, and clothes when we can. They often sell the soap to have money to go to the movies, which they have plenty of time to see, as they don't go to school. We are shocked one morning to hear that one of the boys has been bitten by a large rat that snuggled in under his blanket as he slept on the step. Dr. Jack checks him out and insists he have painful rabies shots in case the rat was infected. He recovers without serious illness, and his dangerous life on the streets continues.

Dr. Jack Preger is a well-known local character here. He is an English doctor who lives at the hostel and has been running a sidewalk clinic for the local poor for several years. One or two volunteers help him out, and we all consult with him about the various illnesses we experience. He has prescribed a medication to help me with the dysentery, but as I keep getting reinfected, it hasn't helped much.

It's odd how so much that was strange in India three months ago has become "normal" to me now, like the critters that visit my small room at the hostel. There are no windows; instead, shuttered wooden doors open onto an outside balcony that runs the length of the building. Without screens, everything can fly in when the shutters are open, and the cockroaches and crows often do. The cockroaches come in looking for glue to eat from the labels on any container they can find, while the crows watch for pink bakery boxes to raid or shiny coat hangers to steal. Down the hall, the one bathroom the whole floor shares has old-fashioned toilets, three cold-water showers, and three sinks. Besides brushing our teeth and washing our hands, these sinks are also where we hand-wash our clothes before hanging them on the railing around the balcony.

Our daily plans are governed by the unpredictable availability of water and electricity and by our own health needs, as there's always someone sick with dysentery, TB, or malaria. Even so, I'm grateful to have the support of the volunteers who live here. There are about thirty to forty of us who have come from all over the world. Most work with Mother Teresa and stay anything from a week to two years. We take care of each other when someone is sick and have lively sing-along times on the balcony in the evenings. We share food parcels from home, go to church together, celebrate birthdays and holidays, and make regular visits to the local restaurants and bakeries. Some of us take a train trip north of Calcutta to visit the leper colony run by the male Missionaries of Charity. The permanent deformities this terrible disease causes are difficult to look at, but it is moving to see the residents being cared for with love and respect. *Thank You, Lord, for this amazing international family. I am learning so much from them and definitely need their love and encouragement every day.*

Some of Celeste's friends at the YWCA hostel, Middleton Row, Calcutta, 1982.

Ruthie, the youngest of the
house children and everyone's
favorite, fourteen months old.

Some of the house children and two
of the rickshaw drivers, 1982.

Chandana Banerjee (far left), two house workers,
and some of the house children, 1982.

Celeste at the picnic with Tutti,
who tested positive for TB, 1982.

Thank you card that volunteers
received for working with
Mother Teresa.

A crowded Calcutta market.
Photo by C. Paul, Chitrabani, Calcutta.

Life on the sidewalks of Calcutta that more than one million people call home.
Photo by C. Paul, Chitrabani, Calcutta.

chapter twenty-six

Trusting Him in Suffering

I've been here for three months when I have to leave India to renew my visa. World Concern has missionaries living in Bangkok, Thailand, so I'm going there for a short break. I hope to see a doctor about this amoebic dysentery, which has reduced me to a mere 98 pounds. I have never been sick like this before. I realize how much pride has been in my heart over the fact that I have been, until now, very healthy. I see how ridiculous this is—good health is a gift from God. *Forgive me, Lord.*

There's only one flight a day going to Bangkok, and I almost miss it, as the authorities at the airport take their time making me pay an importation tax on the sewing machine I brought in for Chandana. They had made a note of it in my passport when I arrived, so now that I don't have it with me, they assume I sold it without paying the necessary taxes. After running to the exit gate, I collapse into a seat near the window and ask the lady next to me if the plane to Bangkok has gone yet. She shakes her head "no" and is obviously wondering why I would ever think it would be on time. Don't I know this is India?

A few hours later, I make it to Bangkok to stay with the Mattson family. What a relief it is to be able to rest for a while and eat safe food in their lovely home. A doctor confirms I have amoebic dysentery and puts me on medication for a week. I visit the Indian embassy to renew my visa, but I can only do this once on an American passport. As I also have New Zealand citizenship because my mother was born there, I look into getting a New Zealand passport for reentry next time.

I'm feeling much better when I return to Calcutta two weeks later. Chandana's two daughters, nicknamed Pinky and Rinky, are about ten and twelve years old. They live and study at St. Mary's School for Girls, where Mother Teresa once worked. We pick them up from there so they can be home for the holidays and celebrate their birthdays with the family. When they find out my birthday is also in December, they add me to the combined birthday celebration.

When I have a day off, I go with some of the volunteers who work in Mother Teresa's children's home, Shishu Bhavan, to help with the handicapped children. While I'm there, I get invited to attend the initiation service where the sisters take their final vows to become Missionaries of Charity. These women have been serving with the ministry for ten years in various places all over the world. On the big night, each one wears a wedding dress and receives a ring as the "bride of Christ." They take vows of chastity, poverty, obedience, and wholehearted service to the poor in a solemn but joyful and very moving ceremony. Family and friends celebrate their commitment to this work with flower leis and a simple party afterward. I am excited to meet Mother Teresa as she quietly serves tea to her many guests. What an honor to be part of this unforgettable evening. *Thank You, Lord, for letting me see this amazing ministry up close and for being able to help in a small way.*

———————

Back at Chandana's house, we are busy with big plans for the house Christmas party coming up soon. We buy gifts for all the children and make lots of traditional small fruit cakes to be given to friends and family members. All around the city, many homes are decorated with a string of lights, and loud, happy processions make their way through the streets every night in anticipation of Christmas Day. Although the vast majority of Indians are Hindu, Christmas has become widely celebrated by more than just the small minority who are Christian, as western traditions and styles are now more popular.

The long-awaited house party is a boisterous celebration. Twenty-six children, some of the children's relatives, all the staff, and Chandana's family crowd into the small house. There's food, presents, singing, dancing, and loud music. Everyone gets a paper hat and a funny mask, and the party goes on for most of the day. No one wants to leave, but I can see that many of the little ones are exhausted. It has been quite a week. Last Sunday, all of them did a twenty-minute musical nativity play for the church Sunday school program. They had been practicing for weeks, and it was the first time on stage for all of them. With their costumes, make-up, and musical instruments ready, they were very nervous but so cute as they retold the ancient story from a night so long ago in Bethlehem. I felt like a proud parent watching them do so well.

As the new year begins, we're very excited that nine of our boys and five of our girls have been accepted into the local government school. They start classes tomorrow and are very pleased with their new uniforms, books, and school bags provided by World Concern. The mission will also pay for their school fees, lunches, transportation, medical costs, and extra tutoring. Our preschool will continue with five of last year's children and ten new slum children.

The craft production is slowly increasing too. We received a large order from the U.S. and hope to ship the first items to them this week. We are having problems keeping the white items clean as the ladies make them. Calcutta is such a dirty city, and with only bars and shutters on the windows, dirt blows into homes constantly. Many of the crocheted items must be washed before they can be bagged and sent, but we're getting this down.

Chandana has been very ill with a heart condition and is on bedrest for several weeks. While she is resting and the children are on a short break, I spend some time working in Mother Teresa's home for the dying. Kalighat was originally set up to take sick people off the streets and care for them so they wouldn't die alone on a cold city sidewalk. However, with a little hydration and food, many recover and return to life on the streets.

Some have more serious problems, like the young woman who was brought in last week with burns covering eighty-five percent of her body. She says it was a cooking fire that caught her sari alight, but we suspect it was probably her husband who did it to her, as local custom allows a dissatisfied husband to set fire to his wife. Although this horrible practice is against the law now, it still happens. Wives are also blamed if their husband dies before they do, and they are expected to throw themselves onto the burning funeral pyre. Those who don't, often become tortured slaves to their mothers-in-law. Our patient passes away several days after arriving, but we are at least able to help her be comfortable in her last hours, and several of us pray with her.

"You have a message here to go to police headquarters tomorrow morning at nine o'clock," the hostel supervisor tells me as I check my mailbox.

"Oh great!" I grumble. "I wondered how long it would be before they sent for me again." I have just returned to Calcutta from my second visa renewal trip to Thailand. Having used up the six months I'm allowed to be in India as an American citizen, I have reentered the country using my newly issued New Zealand passport. The local authorities have been regularly harassing all the foreign volunteers about getting the new visa they say has been created specifically for volunteers. Although many have applied, no one has been issued one yet.

The next morning, I make my way to the police headquarters and wait to be escorted into the all-too-familiar back office. As the gruff officer behind the messy desk scans my passport and looks back at me, I can see he's wondering what is going on. *I thought this girl was an American—so why is she here now with a New Zealand passport?* In hushed tones, he confers with the man next to him but never directly asks me anything. Silently, he hands me back my passport. I don't offer him any explanation, and I leave quietly, glad there wasn't some big confrontation. Sadly, all the foreign volunteers continue to deal with being followed, threatened, and questioned regularly by the local police. We never know when we will be asked to leave the country, even after applying for the "volunteer visa" they say we should have instead of our tourist visas. I wonder why they can't see that we're not only helping their people but also bringing money into the economy as we pay rent, eat in the restaurants, shop, and take public transportation. It doesn't make sense.

Several volunteers have already been forced to leave. I have made several phone calls to the leadership at World Concern in Seattle, explaining the situation. They are worried I won't be able to stay much longer and ask if I would consider going to Malaysia to work with Vietnamese refugees. They have a large team there, and I would be living and working in Kuala Lumpur. I'm torn. It feels like I'm giving up by leaving here sooner than I had anticipated, but the goal was for me to help the school get started, and that has been accomplished. There's not as much for me to do now. World Concern can send someone else if Chandana needs more help in the future. I agree to go to Malaysia and reluctantly make the decision to leave in a couple of weeks. *Lord, I know this is Your work, not mine. Please take care of the children and Chandana.*

Even though the constant sickness, filth, chaos, and poverty have been overwhelming here, I have had peace knowing I'm right where God wants me to be. I will miss the sweet smiles and hugs from the children the most. It has been inspiring to watch them grow and learn as they thrive on the stability of regular meals, a school routine, and affectionate love. Some have made decisions to follow God and are growing in their relationship with Him. Chandana will, of course, continue the work and is still looking for land to build a bigger home, somewhere on the outskirts of the city. World Concern is planning to continue supporting her now that the work is established and they have seen firsthand that it is doing well.

My leaving coincides with Raja's first birthday at the end of April, so Chandana sets up a wonderful party at the house for us both, with all the children from the home and school invited. They shower me with flower leis and gifts of local crafts. The children sing songs and line up to hug me goodbye. It is so hard to leave. God has shown me so much here in the desperate needs of the poor and the loving hearts of those who are willing to sacrifice to help them. I am grateful to have had a small part to play in this place and wish I could have done more. *Thank You, Lord, for being with me here and for teaching me to trust You in difficult times. Thank You for teaching me the value of good friends and for the unconditional love of children.*

The smiles always come out for a camera. These are some of the house cuties, 1983.

The cook preparing the Christmas meal in the tiny house kitchen, 1982.

Celeste and Mukul taking four of
the children to the picnic, 1982.

A farewell for Celeste and a birthday
celebration for Raja, May 1983.

Shamu (far left) and the other boys who lived in the Banerjees' home, 1983.

Chandana, Mukul (teacher), Celeste, and Chandana's father, holding Ruthie, 1983.

The boys ready for their first day in the public school, 1983.

I wanted to take the children back with me ...but then realized that wasn't the answer

by Celeste Scott
World Concern fieldworker
helping the Banerjee home

As I look back now, I remember two strong feelings from my first month in India.

The first was a mixture of guilt and anger as I compared the overabundance and waste at home with the desperate need I saw in Calcutta.

The second was a strong desire to take some of the children back with me to give

them the opportunities they could never have in India.

Both of those feelings mellowed with time as I overcame the initial shock of Cal-

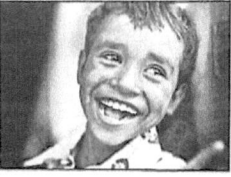

cutta and began to see things in perspective. There is no need for us to feel guilty about what we have . . . if we have an attitude of sharing, living simply and giving away our excess.

But just sending aid to countries such as India is not enough — people become dependent and lose their self-esteem with constant handouts. The best aid is to help people to help themselves. I was happy to see that this is what World Concern is do-

ing with Mrs. Banerjee.
As I began to see the need for India to

solve her own problems, I realized too that there is little to be gained by taking away her children. It is important that they all get an education and learn to accept responsibility for helping others. Mrs. Banerjee teaches them this as she tells them about Jesus and his love for them.

I've watched the children in the Banerjee home grow during my time in Calcutta, but I've grown too. I've learned through the difficulties to depend on the Lord more and more and to see him as the truly loving, gentle shepherd that he is.

My prayer for the children of the Baner-

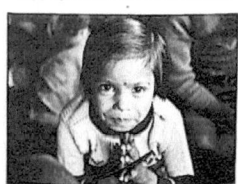

jee home is that they will come to know Jesus and serve him as the one true God. They have a lot to overcome growing up in Calcutta, but God's hand has already touched their lives in a beautiful way by bringing them to Mrs. Banerjee. **WC**

Celeste Scott, 27, was born in San Francisco and raised in New Zealand. She helped at the Banerjee home for 10 months. For the past year she has been working at World Concern's project in Malaysia aiding Vietnamese refugees.

14 May/June 1984

World Concern magazine article, 1984.

239

chapter twenty-seven

Just You and Me, Lord

Here I am, back at the Calcutta airport, waiting to leave for the last time. As I walk across the tarmac toward the waiting Thai Airways plane, I feel alone. I'm leaving people I know and care about, and I'm heading into something completely new. *Looks like it's just You and me again, Lord. Thank You for my time here. Please take care of everyone. I'm glad You go before me and are already preparing the way in this new place. Please give me the wisdom and strength I need to do this new work.*

After two weeks in Bangkok, I'm on another plane, flying south to Kuala Lumpur, Malaysia. Here, a large team of World Concern workers from the United States, South Korea, and the Philippines live in a modern high-rise building. Each day, they are taken by van to the refugee camp outside the city to work as doctors, dentists, nurses, and social workers with about thirty-three thousand Vietnamese refugees.

There is also a camp on an island along the east coast where many of the refugee "boat people" arrive in small overcrowded boats. They are processed there before being sent our way. Several of our team live and work on the island, which houses about six thousand refugees. I will be serving as a social worker for people who have chronic conditions like leprosy, polio, strokes, mental illness, TB, cerebral palsy, and amputations from landmines. It seems like a big challenge, and my first day in camp is intimidating.

Armed Malaysian guards provide security within the tall fence line that surrounds the large sprawling camp on the outskirts of Kuala Lumpur. We have to pass through the locked checkpoint each day. Dusty roads wind between makeshift buildings that act as sleeping quarters, bathrooms, and a medical clinic. Three simple meals a day are provided from the large kitchen, but there are also snack shops and a restaurant for those who can afford to purchase their own food. A tailor, hair salon, church, and school provide a sense of normality and community during the long stay here. Although it's not fancy, it's clean and adequate. There are some jobs in the camp, so people can earn a little money to buy additional food items, clothes, or toys. There are so many refugees, and they are all anxious to move on as quickly as possible. Two of them introduce themselves to me soon after I arrive in the camp.

"Hello. My name is Mr. Chau, and this is my friend Miss Hanh.[17] We are your interpreter and assistant."

"Hi! I'm Celeste. So nice to meet you both. I'm taking over from Duane with the handicapped-zone people."

"Yes, we worked with him also. Can we show you around and introduce you to some of the people you will be working with?"

"That would be great."

Over lunch, they share their story with me. Mr. Chau is thirty-three years old and trained for a year as a ship navigator in New York. When Saigon fell to the communists in 1975, he was put into a "reeducation camp" because of his involvement with the U.S. This overcrowded place with filthy living conditions, little food, and cruel treatment was supposed to convince previous leaders, the wealthy, and the educated to accept the communist philosophy. Mr. Chau was released after seven years of these torturous conditions, determined to escape the communist rule that had ruined his country. Because of his navigational skills, he gained free passage on a boat but was not allowed to take his mother or sisters. They could not afford

---

17 All names have been changed to protect privacy.

passage, so he reluctantly left at their insistence, knowing he would probably never see them again. On the boat, he met Miss Hanh, who is twenty-three. She was in high school when the war in Vietnam ended in 1975.

Growing up in a middle-class family, Miss Hanh had planned to go to college like her sisters, but despite her excellent academic record, she was not permitted to go, because her family was not communist. She secretly learned English by listening to the forbidden BBC and Voice of America radio broadcasts and eventually escaped with her sister and brother-in-law. Like Mr. Chau, she left family she will never see again. Chau and Hanh became engaged while in camp and are applying to go to Australia. This sweet couple speak English well and help me adjust to life in the camp. They teach me about the Vietnamese language, culture, and customs and act as my interpreters when I'm working with the refugees.

I have about one hundred people with medical conditions on my caseload and am responsible to make sure their special needs are met while in camp. I also help them to get through the application process as they meet with representatives from various countries. Acceptance can take two to three years for people with disabilities or mental illness, and there's always the possibility that they will be returned to Vietnam if no country accepts them for asylum. I take people into town to get fitted for prosthetic limbs or to purchase wheelchairs, the cost being covered by the UNHCR (United Nations High Commission for Refugees), which runs the camp.

All workers come under the Red Crescent here, which is the Islamic version of the Red Cross, so we wear white shirts with their red crescent moon logo every day. Malaysia has an elected king, who is also the leader of the Islamic faith for the country. It was once a British colony and is still part of the British Commonwealth. The population is made up of people of Malay, Chinese, and Indian decent. All Malays have to be Muslim by law, and it is against the law to try to convert them to other faiths. Everyone else, including visiting foreigners and the Vietnamese refugees, can practice any religion they choose. Because Vietnam was a French colony until 1954, many of the refugees are Catholic. The church building in camp is shared by Protestants and Catholics, and we are allowed to participate in weekly services if we want to. There is some tension in the camp during Islamic holidays, but generally, the wide variety of faiths coexist peacefully.

An overcrowded boat of refugees has arrived on shore after fifty-two days at sea. The journey typically takes about seven to ten days for a small boat to cover the seven hundred miles. They have long since run out of food and water. Twenty-one of them have died, and those who are helped ashore are severely dehydrated and malnourished. Most have watched relatives die while many boats passed by without helping them. Thai pirates often attack these boats, stealing valuables and killing, raping, or kidnapping the occupants. The survivors must go on to new countries without ever knowing what has happened to loved ones who were taken.

The stories of what can happen on these dangerous escapes have reached Vietnam, so some prepare in ingenious ways. My interpreter, Mr. Chau, took a gold wedding band, had it broken into three pieces, cut open his own skin on his upper arm to hide it underneath, and stitched it up himself. Another man went to our camp dentist and asked for a filling to be removed. When the dentist noted that the filling looked quite new and was in good repair, he was reluctant to remove it, but the man insisted. When it was finally taken out, three small diamonds appeared from underneath, and everyone applauded his clever smuggling trick.

Several patients with immediate needs have come across my path. Duong is a fifteen-year-old boy who was crippled by polio. He cannot walk and needs help to dress and eat. His father has carried him on his back his whole life. Giang is a quiet five-year-old boy, also suffering from polio because noncommunist families were not given the available vaccine. Tien is four years old and was born with several deformities that make movement and balance difficult for her. Anh is sixteen and suffered a head injury several years ago, resulting in arm weakness and poor coordination. Muy Linh is an elderly lady who had a stroke and is learning to walk with a cane. Hoa has unexplained leg weakness, but at twelve years old, he really wants to learn to ride a bike. I ask the camp leaders for permission to use a small unoccupied room near my office for a therapy room. They agree, so we clean it out, and I get an old exercise bike, some arm weights, a dowel, a few basic toys, a beach ball, and a tricycle together. Now we're in business.

I work with each one individually and teach them or their parents what exercises to do, as I have no way of knowing how long they will be in camp. We take Duong into town to get a wheelchair. The look on his face is priceless when he sits in it and is able to move himself along without being carried for the first time in his life. Giang's parents are excited that he is being helped. They risked escaping their homeland because they wanted better opportunities for their son. They have been accepted for resettlement in the U.S. and can't wait to get him into therapy there. Tien and Giang become friends and don't realize their playing together is therapeutic exercise. Muy Linh gets a quadruped cane, and her daughter learns how to help her walk with it. Anh and Hoa come daily to work out, and both are happy to be getting stronger. *Lord, You placed me here where my skills could be put to good use. I can see You had a plan all along. Thank You so much for showing me how to help.*

There has been something on my mind for a while, so I have started praying about it and have shared it with my Korean roommate, Young In, so she can pray with me. I'm twenty-six years old. I'd like to know if I'm going to get married or not. I don't mind either way, really, and I don't have to know when or to whom. I just don't want to keep wondering and looking and waiting and then get to sixty and realize the answer is no. If I know that now, I can go on with my life and not focus on that possibility at all. *Lord, maybe it's silly to make this request, but could You please let me know what the plan is?*

"What do you mean we don't have a reservation? I sent you a postcard more than a month ago! We need somewhere to stay tonight," Kim insists.

My friend Kim is an American nurse in the camp, and we have come to the beautiful island of Pulau Tioman, about twenty miles off the east coast of Malaysia, for a short vacation from the stresses of camp life. This hilly isle is covered in dense jungle inhabited by monkeys, large lizards, and snakes, and it is a popular tourist destination for spectacular snorkeling and jungle hikes. Kim had found this place in a tourist brochure and thought she made a reservation for one of the cute little A-frame huts a few feet from the water, but the owner of the resort doesn't seem so sure.

It has been quite the trip to get here—seven hours by bus, two hours by taxi, overnight in a coastal town, then four-and-a-half hours on a small fishing boat. There is no jetty at this beach, so we had to jump off the boat and wade ashore. It's now after 4 p.m., and this is the last stop the boat makes today. If we can't stay here, we'll have to go back along the island and find somewhere else to spend the night.

"Well, we're full. We don't have anything else," the owner explains again.

"There must be something!" Kim says, sounding desperate. "We just spent two days getting here, and it's late."

"Well, there is a room at the back of the kitchen here," our host replies as he walks to the back of the building.

"Oh good," Kim says, relieved.

He opens the old wooden door to a small dark room with two sets of bunk beds that take up the whole space. An intricate network of spider webs hangs from the ceiling and the bed frames. Everything is covered in a thick layer of dust. Stained, threadbare straw mattresses are rolled up on the rusty bunks, and there are no windows. Obviously, no one has been in this place for a very long time, except, I suspect, a lot of questionable critters we'd rather not encounter. We walk slowly into what looks like the setting of a horror movie. I don't want to stay here, but I've survived Calcutta, so I guess I can do this if we clean it up a little first.

"There is absolutely no way we can stay here!" exclaims Kim. "I wouldn't put a dead dog in this place." She walks straight out without any further conversation. The decision is made. I follow her back to the beach and into the water as she wades out to the boat while holding her luggage above her head. The patient fisherman helps us back aboard and takes us along the coastline to the one hotel on the island.

We spend a couple of days in luxury that we didn't plan on having to pay for, until we find a nice guest house a bay away that is simple but clean. Not used to the tropical sun, we're both badly sunburned by the end of the first day, but that doesn't stop us from snorkeling along the coral reefs full of tropical fish, moray eels, sea turtles, and sea urchins.

One afternoon, we go for a walk along the white-sand beach that stretches for miles and have a wonderful fish dinner near the water. Forgetting how quickly the sun goes down here near the equator, we suddenly find ourselves far from our lodging and standing on a dirt road in pitch blackness with no shoes on and no flashlight to help us navigate. Kim remembers a little pack of matches she has from the hotel. She lights one, and we move forward as quickly as possible before it goes out. We light another one and another and another until we finally see a streetlight up ahead. We have discovered a little police checkpoint where two young officers are relaxing for the evening. They are surprised to see tourists way out here in the dark, but when we explain we need help to get back to where we're staying, they are more than willing to rescue us. The problem is, the only transportation they have is an old scooter, so we can only go one at a time on the back.

It seems a little sketchy, but we don't have much choice. As I ride away into the darkness, holding on to the officer, I wonder if I'll ever see Kim again. *Will one or both of us end up dead in the surrounding jungle? How long should I wait before calling 911? Do they have 911 here? Are these the guys who would answer if I did call? Best not to overthink all this, Celeste. Just pray.* The helpful policeman respectfully leaves me near our guesthouse, and I wait outside, peering into the darkness, anxious to see my friend taking her turn on the scooter. When our rescuer returns a few minutes later with Kim, I am *so* glad to see her, and we spend the rest of the evening laughing about our crazy adventure.

Daily life at the camp continues. We go into town once a week to shop for the refugees. They give us money to buy clothes and shoes for them so they have something decent to wear when they arrive in their new countries. Stories of the horrors endured by the "boat people" are recounted to us daily. One man tells me about his wife, Phong, who visited him regularly in the reeducation camp in Vietnam to bring him food and clothes. When he was finally released, he found out she was pregnant by a guard who insisted she sleep with him or her husband would starve to death. He was angry and didn't want to keep the baby, but she insisted. During their escape by boat, they were stranded on a barren island with no food or water. Many died, and Phong ran out of breastmilk for the baby. In her desperation, she cut herself to give him blood to drink. She died the week before they were rescued, and her husband was left to care for her son. Grief mixed with mercy as he looked into the baby's face and saw Phong's eyes. She was still with him, and he could raise this baby to know what an amazingly selfless mother he had.

My time in Malaysia is nearly over. I am reluctant to leave a place and people I have grown to care about and enjoy, but at the same time, I'm excited to see what God has next. He has confirmed to me the answer to my question about marriage from a year ago. Through His quiet voice and the counsel of friends, I now feel confident I will be getting married one day. With that realization comes a contentment to wait and see what He is planning but also a sadness. It really has been just me and Jesus for so much of my journey since coming to know Him fifteen years ago. I'm worried that having a special man in my life will somehow take away from that relationship. I don't ever want to depend on someone more than I do Jesus. So while I am happy I will be getting married one day, I am already thinking about the possible loss of the deep spiritual focus that the single life allows.

After several fond farewells at camp and with my teammates, I'm alone again on a plane, this time heading north to Thailand. Paul and Mary, who led the Malaysia team, have now moved up here, so I stay with them for a few days. My next stop is Calcutta. Chandana has two homes now, with forty children in her care. She is well and happy to announce that she is expecting another baby early next year. The children all look so grown up and are excited to show me their new schoolbooks and uniforms. What a joy it is to see this work continuing to do well and the children all thriving.

The next leg of my journey is long and slow, with layovers in Karachi, Damascus, Istanbul, and Amsterdam before I make it to London, England. I stay with a volunteer friend from Calcutta days and visit others in Birmingham, Northern Ireland, and across the channel in France. It's October before I'm back in Seattle for debriefing at the World Concern headquarters. A medical checkup is required. I find out I have had amoebic dysentery and giardia for the last two years. Strong antibiotics and an antiparasitic mediation take care of those, and I soon feel much better. I'm so used to feeling tired and weak, I didn't even know I was still sick.

I'm so grateful, God, for these two years in Asia. I have learned to trust You through all kinds of difficulties, I have sought Your forgiveness as You revealed pride and judgement in my heart, and I have discovered what horrible circumstances so many people deal with every day. Amid all this suffering, those who find You have amazing hope and peace and love beyond their circumstances, something we all need to learn. I want to live every day thankful for Your love and Your patience with me. Living with You is such an adventure. I can't wait to see what You have planned next.

Celeste's assistant, Mr. Chau, and interpreter, Miss Hanh.

Celeste with Hien, one of several children who befriended her in the camp.

One of the longhouses where each family had a 12x12 foot space to live in.

249

Anh (sixteen) exercising to
strengthen his arms.

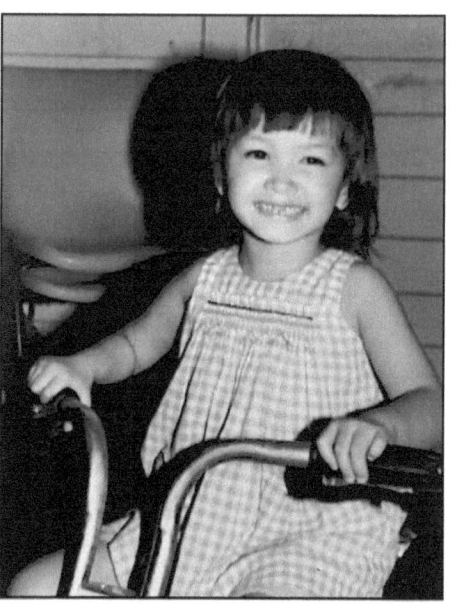

Tien (four) learning to ride a
tricycle as part of her therapy.

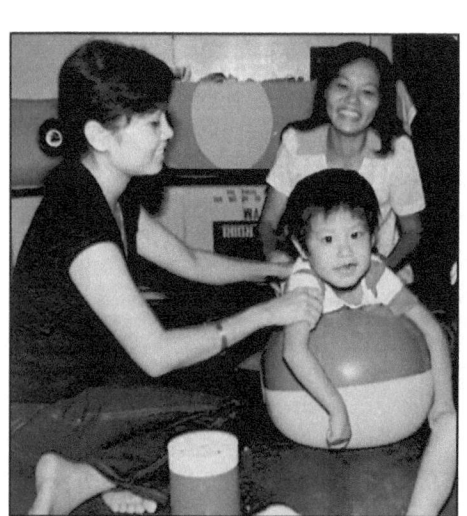

Celeste's assistant, Minh, helping Giang
and his mother in play therapy.

Young In and Celeste dressed
up for a farewell dinner.

Celeste and Kim enjoying Pulau Tioman, 1983.

The World Concern team in Malaysia from the U.S.A.,
the Philippines, and South Korea, 1984.
Celeste in the back row, far left.

chapter twenty-eight

Frisco (Chris) Delaney

"I have a young man I'd like to introduce you to," a man from my church announces.

"Ahh, no thanks, Dan. I'm still coping with getting used to being back here in Oregon. I really can't deal with that right now," I reply.

"But this one is special. I know you two are going to hit it off," he insists.

"Maybe in a couple of months, but thank you for thinking of me."

I had no idea how hard it would be coming home. I expected going to a new country to be strange and overwhelming, but coming back home has been difficult too. My first struggle was with the tremendous variety of products in the stores—a few days ago, I stood in the toiletries aisle, just looking up and down at the hundreds of different kinds of shampoo! In Calcutta, there were maybe two or three kinds in a small store where the guy behind the counter had to hand it to you after you pointed to the one you wanted. There were no big supermarkets to wander around, making your selections. Faced with so many choices, I felt so overwhelmed that I couldn't decide, so I walked out.

I have been thinking about getting my pilot's license for many years, so I'm very excited to finally get to take a test flight at a local aviation school. Even though I do well and absolutely love it, I decide it would be better to use the money I've saved doing the graduate course at Multnomah School of the Bible instead. It is a one-year intensive program that covers all the material usually done in three years. This allows people who know they are going into ministry to get the Bible training they need as quickly as possible. I have a part-time occupational therapy job and have arranged to get an apartment with Marilyn, one of the school librarians. People at church are going to lend me furniture, so after a week of classes and trying to adjust to working as an OT again, it's move-in day.

As the last of the boxes find a place to wait for unpacking, I'm exhausted and wondering why I agreed to go to dinner at Jeff and JoAnne's. I don't really know them, but they go to Sunnyside Community Church with me. Last Sunday, they asked if I'd like to come over for dinner tonight, and it seemed like a good idea at the time. I could call them and say I can't make it, but we don't have a phone connected here yet, so I guess I have to go.

Torrential rain makes the driving dangerous as I slowly make my way along unfamiliar country roads in the dark. Fog is hanging low in the surrounding forest of trees, and I'm having difficulty making out the house numbers. Guessing I might have found the right home, I cautiously make my way down a long driveway toward a house with lights on. There are a couple of cars parked near the garage. I hope this is it. If it's not, I'm going back home.

"You made it!" What a relief it is to see JoAnne at the door and not a confused stranger. "Come in out of the rain. What a night for visiting," she adds. Inside their warm home, I find that Jeff is putting their two-year-old to bed, and Pastor Dave and his wife, Marilyn, are already here.

We are finishing up a wonderful lasagna meal an hour later when there's a knock at the door. Jeff gives JoAnne a knowing look and bounces down the stairs to answer it. He returns, chatting with a tall dark-haired man I have seen at church but never met. The others obviously know who he is and greet him enthusiastically. Finally, Jeff turns to me.

"And this is Celeste. She has just returned from India and Malaysia, where she was working as a missionary. Celeste, this is Chris Delaney," he says.

Chris smiles as he shakes my hand, and I get the distinct feeling that I have known this gorgeous man my whole life.

We wait for dessert while Chris eats the main course. He was working a late shift in the jewelry department at Fred Meyer when Jeff called him and suggested he come over for dinner. All single males know not to pass up the offer of a free home-cooked meal, so he found his way to their house as soon as work finished. We talk into the night. Dave and Marilyn leave around ten o'clock since he will be preaching in the morning, but we stay until around one o'clock, answering the leading questions from our hosts, who are anxious for us to get to know each other.

We sit together at church the following morning and meet after work on Monday. Wednesday is the evening prayer meeting at church, and he is there too. The group has the tradition of going out for pie after the meeting, and the pastor asks me to go.

"I'm sorry. I have a ton of homework to get done. Maybe another time," I reply reluctantly.

But then Chris asks me to please come, and I can't say no. Thursday, he invites me over for dinner at his apartment, which turns out to be a warmed up can of stew with bread. We find ourselves once more talking late into the night. We meet at church again on Sunday and go out for lunch afterward.

When we can't get together, we talk on the phone. We're both at the next Wednesday prayer meeting, and then it's another Thursday night dinner at his place. We have seen each other nine times in the last twelve days. I have been praying, *Is this the one, Lord?* There's a deep familiarity and comfort with this man; conversation is easy, and I admire his love for the Lord. He wants to go on the mission field and is serious about serving and knowing God, qualities I have not found in many men. After dinner, I decide to ask the question my heart needs an answer to.

"Where do you see this relationship going?" By way of an answer, Chris gets up and retrieves a letter he has just written to his best friend, Keith.

"I just wrote this. Let me read part of it. 'I think I have found the woman I want to marry.'"

"That's what I was thinking too," I reply in amazement. We smile at each other and kiss for the first time.

"Does this mean we're engaged?" I ask.

"I guess so!" he says, staring at me.

It's a strange feeling. I wouldn't say we are "in love" yet, but we know God is bringing us together—almost like a marriage arranged by God Himself. *So this is what You had planned? I'm so excited! I can't wait to get to know this wonderful man. Thank You.*

I soon find out that the firstborn son of Paul and Juanita Delaney arrived April 30, 1952. He was named "Frisco" after his father's brother, who had died a few months earlier on a battlefield in Korea. He grew up the oldest of six children in a poor Mexican-American family living in the projects of Los Angeles, California. He never liked the name "Frisco," because it was different and others teased him about it constantly. In later years, he changed his name to "Chris" after a coworker began calling him that by mistake.

Chris had a famous uncle, James Delaney, a boxer who fought under the name Jimmy Doyle. Chris's dad, Paul, was also a boxer and managed the career of his younger brother. After taking many blows to the head while winning forty-three of fifty-two bouts, Jimmy was banned from boxing in California because of the high risk of further brain damage. This, however, did not stop him from going to Cleveland, Ohio, in 1947 to challenge Sugar Ray Robinson for the world welterweight title. He planned to buy his mother a house with his winnings. Sugar Ray had a dream the night before the fight that Jimmy died in the ring, so on the day of the fight, he refused to participate. Both a priest and a minister were called in to talk him into it, and he eventually agreed. Jimmy went down in the eighth round and was rushed to a local hospital, unconscious. He died a few hours later. Sugar Ray gave his winnings from his next four fights to Jimmy's mother so she could buy that home. He never got over the pain of taking a man's life in the ring.

As Chris turned four-and-a-half years old, his mother gave birth to her fifth child, and their father was taken to prison for abusing her. Juanita was left with five children under five years old to raise alone. She had lots of support from her family of eleven siblings, who all lived close, but it was not easy. Four years later, she met and married Jack Hawley, who was newly on shore after spending six years serving on a Navy submarine. Baby Tommy joined his siblings Chris, Marina, Paul, Zanita, and James a few months later, and the family was complete.

It was hard for Chris to accept his Mexican genetics growing up in Los Angeles in the 1960s. The Watts riots drew attention to the ugly racial issues bubbling to the surface in many communities. During one recess in grade school, he was chased around the playground while his classmates called him a "N-----." He was so angry that when he finally got into the classroom with some of his tormentors, he picked up a desk and threw it over. His surprised teacher asked what was going on, and he told her.

"Don't listen to them. You have beautiful skin and a wonderful smile," she reassured him, but that night, he went home and spent an hour trying to wash the color off his face.

Taking his role of being the oldest seriously, Chris taught the younger children how to play chess, but his truly competitive nature would never allow him to let them win. He made up games in the backyard for his siblings and visiting cousins. One favorite game was for Chris to lay on the ground, balance one of the younger children on his feet, then catapult them into the air. Sometimes they landed safely, but quite often they ended up stuck on a fence or flying into an innocent spectator. There was also the time his younger sister

Zanita was deliberately left outside in a large closed refrigerator box while her siblings went in for dinner. It was quite a while before mom realized someone was missing and went looking for her. Zanita was also the victim of a heated potato masher that left a permanent scar on her upper arm and gave her many opportunities to tell her sympathy-invoking story for years to come. Chris had a paper route and spent his earnings on comics and candy, some of which he shared with his siblings.

Chris's favorite memories from his childhood were of the huge extended family gatherings at Christmas with mountains of presents, pots full of freshly made tamales, and loud, happy laughter all around. But both his father and his stepfather were alcoholics, which meant anger, violence, and instability were part of their lives too. His earliest memory was of being left in a car while his father spent several hours in a bar, late into the night. As a teenager, he came home to find his drunk stepfather hurting his mother. Without thinking, Chris pulled him off of her and punched him as he yelled a warning to never touch his mother again. He left the house, shaken and angry, and drove across the city to his uncle's home in east Los Angeles.

Uncle Solomon, married to Juanita's sister Alice, had his own story. He and his brother Ruben had also been heavy drinkers. One evening, Ruben staggered out of a bar and found his way to a phone booth to call for a ride home. As he fumbled with the phone, he noticed a little booklet tucked behind the receiver. Curious to see what it said, he stuck it in his pocket. He found it the next day and realized it was a tract left there by a church. He read about how much God loved him and wanted a better life for him. It said God wanted to forgive him of his sins and give him eternal life. As he knelt in prayer, asking for those changes, he felt God's presence and knew his life would never be the same. He began attending the church named on the tract, the Church of the Open Door in Los Angeles, to learn more.

A short while later, he shared this tract with his brother Solomon. Alice and Solomon prayed the prayer of salvation together, and they began attending church with Ruben. Chris often spent time with them, going to church or on outings to the beach. He wanted the love and care he saw in that family. When he was seven years old, his uncle explained to him that Jesus was knocking at the door of his heart because He wanted to come in, forgive his sins, and live within him forever.[18] Chris said he wanted that, because he saw how his uncle's life had changed. He prayed and asked Jesus to forgive him and live inside him. After praying, he imagined taking a key, locking the door, and throwing the key out the window so Jesus could never leave him.

When Chris arrived at his uncle's house after the fight with his stepfather, Solomon could tell something was really bothering his teenage nephew. He let him stay the night without any questions, but in the morning, he took him aside and asked what had happened. After an emotional recollection of the events from the day before, Solomon asked what Chris was planning to do next. Chris wouldn't say, but his uncle knew.

"I know you're thinking about running away, but that is not the right thing to do. Go back home, submit to your stepfather, and be a light in that place. Your whole family needs to know Jesus." It took some time to convince him, but eventually, Chris did as his uncle asked. He learned a valuable lesson about choosing to do the hard thing when everything in you wants to give up and run. He shared his faith with everyone in his family, and one by one, many of them prayed to receive Jesus as well.

School was always difficult for Chris, partly because he mainly spoke Spanish before starting kindergarten but also because he had inherited some learning disabilities that made memory, focus, and understanding concepts difficult. He was twelve years old before a teacher put him in a remedial reading class so he could finally learn to read. His report cards consistently showed C's and D's in every subject except for PE, where he always got an A. Still, he loved learning and

---

18 Revelation 3:20.

always shared whatever he had newly discovered with others.

He excelled in baseball and wanted to play professionally, but he blew out his shoulder pitching too hard, so he moved on to football instead. Newspaper clippings from his high school days talk about how much stronger he became over a summer break and how his running speed made him a great tight end for his team. In track and field, he enjoyed competing in javelin, discus, and shotput.

At every sporting event, Chris was the one handing out tracts and talking to people about Jesus. He loved tracts because of Ruben's story, which had led to him being saved too. At the trial for the javelin nationals, a fellow contestant threw the tract back at him and told him he wasn't interested in his Jesus talk. Chris shrugged it off and moved on. When his turn came to compete, he fouled out in the first two tries. On his third and final attempt, he tried to throw the javelin as hard as he could, but his foot slipped in the mud, and he fell on his back, barely releasing the javelin before hitting the ground. Disappointed and embarrassed, he lay there a second until he heard someone call his name and tell him to look up. There was his javelin, sailing down the field just a few feet off the ground, moving forward as if some invisible person was carrying it! When it finally landed, it was his personal best, winning him the meet and a place in the national championship. As incredible as that was, it was the encounter he had a few moments later that he would talk about for years. The young man who had thrown the tract away found him in the crowd and asked to shake his hand. "I can see that your faith is real," he said.

In 1970, Chris turned eighteen, and two months later, he graduated from high school. With the Vietnam War raging, he knew he would soon be drafted, so he decided to enlist and signed up for the Air Force. Boot camp brought all kinds of new lessons as he lived with unbelievers who did drugs and partied all night. He found out that racism bred a whole new depth of depravity in Mississippi, where non-whites were not welcome in all places. By God's grace, he survived this first adventure into the world and spent two years of active duty working for the wing commander at March Air Force Base in Riverside, California. He then joined the Air Force Reserves so he could use his GI Bill to go to Biola College and work on his bachelor's degree in biblical studies, with the goal of becoming a youth pastor.

Chris worked in janitorial services and as a gas station attendant while also ministering in a local youth group and taking a full load of classes. It took him five years to graduate, but he was the first person in his family to earn a college degree. He loved learning, especially studying Greek, Hebrew, and Old Testament history. He continued to share whatever he knew with everyone he met. He enjoyed spending time with his college friend Keith, who was planning to continue his studies at Western Seminary in Oregon. Chris quickly decided that he would like to do the same, so in the summer of 1978, they each headed north to see what God had planned for them next.

Keith and Chris arrived in Oregon during a hot, dry summer and stayed with friends of Keith's while they found a place to live. Soon they moved into a duplex not far from Western Seminary, and before long, a young woman and her little girl moved into the other half of the divided old house. Martha and her daughter, Nadine, along with their dog, Seral, soon became good friends with Keith and Chris. They shared many happy meals and cups of tea together, which led to long discussions about the Bible and God and the purpose of life.

Keith began working at UPS, and Chris found a job as a delivery driver when they each realized they couldn't afford to keep on attending school. They both dropped out of Western Seminary but continued ministering as youth group leaders at a local church. Chris eventually led Martha to know Jesus, and Keith married her in June of 1981.

Over the next year, Chris moved back and forth between California and Oregon and in and out of various jobs. His first sales job was with Kenney Shoes near Los Angeles, but when he and his brother James moved up to Oregon, he found his way into jewelry sales at Gordon's and later, Zales. His competitive nature and outgoing personality made him a good fit for sales, and he was soon managing the stores he worked in.

Gradually, the focus on the world's desire for money and status led him away from his call to follow the Lord. He looked around the church and felt like he was the only one who cared about God, so he decided to go and see what the world had to offer. For three years, he lived the "party life" with a new sports car, money to spend, and women to help him spend it. Like the prodigal son in the Bible, he discovered it brought no long-term pleasure or peace, and his growing sense of having failed God plagued him day and night. It didn't seem possible that God would ever forgive him.

In the middle of a long afternoon, a young man walked into the busy jewelry department of the Fred Meyer store where Chris worked. They got into a discussion that led the visitor to ask Chris if he knew God. Shame and sadness filled his heart as he had to admit that he had once known Him but had chosen to walk away. The youth pastor assured him it was never too late to return to God and invited him to attend his church on Sunnyside Road in Clackamas.

The next Sunday, Chris went to look for his new friend's church. It turned out that there were four churches within a mile of each other on that road, and he couldn't remember the name or address of the one he needed. He chose one and went in. He looked around for the youth pastor, but he couldn't see him anywhere, so he sat in the back, listening and remembering. As sorrow and guilt poured over him, he begged God for forgiveness.

"Give me your whole heart, and I will lead you," God reassured him.

"I will," Chris replied as he prayed silently. At the end of the service, he found Pastor Dave so he could talk to him about what had happened and celebrate God's incredible forgiveness.

Realizing he had made a mess of his relationships with women, he began meeting with Dave to pray for a wife.

"I don't trust myself to make this decision," he told Dave. "But I know God can bring the right woman right here when He wants to."

Two months later, on January 19, 1985, he was at work when he got a call from a couple he had met at church, inviting him to come for dinner when he got off. And so, his prayers were answered.

The Sunday after our "arranged marriage" decision, Chris and I are sitting together in a back pew. Chris goes off to talk to someone, and Dan, the friend who originally wanted to introduce us, comes up to me.

"Well, I see you've met Chris," he says happily.

"Yes, I have," I smile back.

"He's the man I wanted to introduce you to last month," he explains.

"Oh, really?"

"So, is anything going on?" he asks with a sly smile.

"Yes, actually, there is. We're engaged!"

"What! You're kidding me! I *knew* this was going to happen. I can't believe it. I wanted to be the one to introduce you," he complains, and he walks away angry. I stand there, smiling. I seem to be smiling a lot more than usual lately.

"Are you ready?" the wedding coordinator asks me.

"I don't know. Maybe? I guess I have to be!"

I'm standing in the lobby area of our small community church, listening to my roommate, Marilyn, playing the piano. It's the prewedding piece she and I talked about her doing last week. Mum and Teesha have helped me put on the dress Mother made and have done my hair and veil. A fragrant bouquet of specially chosen flowers is in my shaking hands, and Teesha is standing with me in her long burgundy gown. Chris, his best man, Marcus, and Pastor Bill Mae are somewhere up in the front. My mother and Chris's mother, Juanita, have already lit the tiers of candles and sat down in the front pews. The day we will become husband and wife is here at last, August 3, 1985.

Marilyn finishes playing, there's a short pause, and the church organist begins her well-practiced rendition of the wedding march. I can hear the guests stand in eager anticipation. *Deep breath.* Our wedding coordinator motions for Teesha to begin her walk down the garlanded aisle, and now it's my turn. Reminding myself to smile so I won't look so nervous, I walk forward and stop at the end of the aisle, facing the front of the church. There is Chris, smiling broadly in his gray tux and burgundy cummerbund, unquestioningly the most handsome man in the room. He steps down and walks toward me. I'm relieved to no longer be alone as we link arms and walk slowly up the aisle together. I have no dad to do this important walk with me, but we like this idea of Chris coming to get me, as it is a picture of Christ coming for His bride one day. Loving family and friends nod and smile as we make our way past them, and I remind myself to take it all in, remember these details, stay focused. So many friends have told me they don't remember most of their wedding day, because they were so nervous. I want to remember it all. I'm only doing this once. We sing our favorite hymn, "Great Is Thy Faithfulness," and Pastor Bill shares a message from Isaiah 7 entitled "Send Me," knowing we are planning to go on the mission field. We nervously read the vows we each carefully wrote for the other, rings are exchanged, and Marcus sings "Our Love in Christ" while we take communion. Bill prays a sweet blessing over us and then announces, "So, by the power vested in me by the state of Oregon and God Almighty, I pronounce you husband and wife. You may kiss your bride." The nervousness of the morning melts away as we embrace for the first time as a married couple. We turn to face our loved ones as Bill adds, "Ladies and gentlemen, Mr. and Mrs. Chris Delaney." Clapping and cheering follow us down the aisle. *I'm a wife!*

We greet each guest on their way through the lobby. Chris cries as he hugs Solomon and Alice. We are so glad they could come. We spend a few minutes having photos taken, then we head downstairs for the reception. Like so much of our wedding, this feast is a gift of kindness from our church family, as everyone has brought food for a huge potluck. One lady has made the spectacular three-tier wedding cake that we soon get to cut. A florist friend has supplied all the flower arrangements, and the couple who are professional photographers are doing an amazing job on our photos. We receive an abundance of gifts and money toward our honeymoon. We feel so blessed and cared for. Before we know it, rice is being thrown on us as we run to Chris's now-decorated truck. *Thank You, Lord, for preparing us for each other and for bringing us together.*

———

Our honeymoon trip begins with two days at our favorite place—the Oregon coast. Then we head south for three days at Crater Lake and an overnight stay at Lake Shasta. We enjoy the redwood forest and the Oregon coast as we take a leisurely return trip up Highway 101. We talk and pray a lot about our plans for the future and decide we want to have our first baby in the U.S. before going overseas.

Two months later, I'm in the middle of my fall semester at Multnomah School of the Bible when I find out I'm pregnant. We're so excited! I graduate a week before our baby is due, but I end up having three weeks to get ready for this new role of motherhood, as she arrives two weeks late.

Mikeah Lynn joins us on June 3, 1986, by emergency C-section, a healthy miracle of God's grace. As I look into her perfect little face,

I'm reminded of Psalm 139 where David says of God, "You created my inmost being; you knit me together in my mother's womb . . . my frame was not hidden from you when I was made in the secret place."[19] *We love you, little girl, and pray God's richest blessings on you. May you come to know Him at an early age and serve Him all the days of your life. May He be preparing a husband for you even now, and may many be blessed through your service in His family and kingdom.*

Six months after the arrival of our daughter, we are preparing to head to Philadelphia for the five-month candidate course at our mission's headquarters. Our youth group wants to help with the travel expenses, so they organize an all-church spaghetti dinner. After the delicious meal one Sunday evening, they hand us a pile of checks and cash. The next morning, I deposit this much-appreciated gift into our bank account and go to a travel agent across the street to make arrangements for our flight to Philadelphia. The cost for the tickets comes to $563, the *exact* amount I have just deposited! We are shocked and blessed by God's faithful provision, and the youth group cannot believe He has used them to bless us in such a precise way. It is a wonderful lesson for us all that God knows what we need long before we do, and He delights in blessing His children. *Thank You, Lord, for taking care of us. I am discovering new kinds of love as a wife and a mother, new fears for those I care about more deeply than anyone else I've ever known, and a new level of trust in You for every part of our lives.*

Juanita with her children.
Top row: Frisco (Chris),
Juanita, and Marina.
Bottom row: Zanita,
James, and Paul, 1958.

---

19   Psalm 119:13, 15 (NIV).

Paul with Chris, 1953.

Frisco (Chris) Delaney,
two months old.
Born April 30, 1952.

Zanita (four), Marina (six), Frisco (Chris) (seven), James (three), and Paul (five), 1959.

Tommy, Juanita, and Jack, 1962.

Chris standing second from the left.
Bellflower LL baseball, 1963.

Chris (far right) on the Monrovia
High football team, 1970.

Frisco (Chris) Delaney.
Air Force recruit, October 1971.

Chris and Keith, 1987.

Chris and Celeste at the church Valentine's dinner, February 1985. This is their first photo together.

Chris graduates from Biola College with a Bachelor of Arts in Biblical Studies, 1978.

Marina, Chris, James, Tom, Paul, and Zanita at Tom and Bridget's wedding in June 1985.

Celeste and Chris. Wedding invitation photo, May 1985.

Letitia, Celeste, Chris, and Marcus.

Mr. and Mrs.
Chris Delaney.
Married
August 3, 1985.

Back row: Solomon and James.
Middle row: Stevie, Alice, Celeste, Chris, and Juanita.
Front row: Jessica, Zanita's daughter.

Celeste graduates from Multnomah
School of the Bible with a graduate
certificate in biblical studies, May 1986.

Mikeah Lynn Delaney.
Born June 3, 1986.

Alice and Solomon with two-month-old Mikeah, 1986.

chapter twenty-nine

A Slow Boat to China

As we move into our little apartment at our mission's headquarters in Philadelphia,[20] it's January 1987, and God chooses to show me His heart in another way. The crib beside our bed has no linens in it. The lady who is helping us settle in leads me down to the basement of the main building, where donated clothes, toys, furniture, and household items are available for missionaries to use.

I find a section that has some children's linens in it and discover a cute Winnie the Pooh fitted crib sheet. In a bag of items across the room, I pull out a bumper pad that has the same pattern on it. A few minutes later, my search takes me to another room where I find the matching crib comforter on a shelf! At that moment, I realize that having matching linens on my sweet baby's crib matters to me. I hadn't even thought about trying to find matching linens, I just needed something for her bed. But God knew it would matter to me and has provided something I like, not just something to make do. *Thank You, Lord, for knowing my heart and fulfilling a desire that I wasn't even aware of. You are such a good Father.*

About one hundred missionaries live here besides the new candidates who come for a five-month orientation course twice a year and others who are passing through for various reasons. We attend

---

20 The name of our mission is not included to protect those still working in closed countries.

classes each morning to learn about the mission, cross-cultural living and ministry, support raising and finances, language learning, taking care of ourselves and our family while living overseas, and functioning in a team setting. We each have jobs to do in the afternoon. I help with cleaning, and Chris is part of a team doing building projects and maintenance.

Once a week, we go downtown with Open Air Campaigners to do street evangelism. This feels like a full-circle moment when I remember my mother telling me about the Open Air Campaigners who baptized me on board the ship thirty years ago! Who would have guessed I would one day be working with the same organization?

As the five months pass, we continue to pray about where God wants us to serve. This is a faith mission; they do not assign candidates to an area of need. They ask us to pray and seek God's will as the leadership also prays to confirm that call. During one of the morning prayer sessions, a group of people are up in the front, as they are leaving for China soon. They share their plans and ask for specific prayer. It sounds exciting. Afterward, we talk to one of the couples who will soon be going.

"You know, you could come too," the wife assures us.

"We could?" We hadn't considered this closed country. Later, Chris and I talk and pray about this new information and both quickly know that this is where we are supposed to be going. We study the country's history, religion, and culture to write a fifty-page paper for our class. The assignment is difficult but essential for preparing us for the new country where we will soon be serving. In order to get into China, we need to resign from our mission and register as students who are there to learn Mandarin. We will live on a university campus and study with students from all over the world. Friends from our mission will be living in other parts of the country and will be either registered as students or working as teachers. *Lord, we are so grateful for Your leadership in making this decision. We know this will be a challenging place to live, but we trust You to prepare us and to take care of all the details of how we will share Your light there.*

Little Mikeah has been in a baby nursery with three other candidate children each morning while we study. She is learning to talk and is toddling around by herself at only nine months old. Having been on the mission field as a single woman, I can tell it is going to be a lot more challenging to deal with the difficulties of life in a third-world country with a baby and husband to take care of. I'm scared. It's one thing to suffer illness and harsh conditions yourself; it's another thing to watch your child go through something like that. *Lord, You're going to have to teach me a whole new set of skills for this assignment.*

We arrive in Hong Kong on January 15, 1988, after seventeen hours and three flights to get us across the Pacific Ocean. We are here for orientation before we eventually head to mainland China. Hong Kong is a crowded, very modern city with a mixture of Chinese customs and many other cultures. It is currently part of the British commonwealth, but everyone knows that it will go back to Chinese control soon. This has caused many people here to seek citizenship in Australia, New Zealand, and Canada so they can leave if that control is too tight. Six million people call it home, and most live in tall high-rise buildings that hold up to a thousand small apartments in each.

We stay at a team house on the outskirts of the city with fifteen other team members. As we do orientation classes, several people share about how difficult it is for English speakers to learn Mandarin. They also talk a lot about the frequent water and power outages in the area where we will be living. While it is great to meet our team and to have help adjusting to the new culture, I can't help but wonder how this is going to work with our eighteen-month-old still in cloth diapers.

A few weeks later, I'm standing on the bow of the rusting old Danish cruise ship that now serves the route between Hong Kong and Xiamen in mainland China. I'm feeling tired and discouraged. Chris takes Mikeah down to find something to eat, and I look out over the bleak rolling China Sea before me. Suddenly, a large pod of bottlenose dolphins bursts into the wake on either side of the ship, their sleek bodies flying in and out of the turbulence as they race and dive beside us. I watch in awe, knowing this is a gift from my heavenly Father—a little surprise to remind me that He is with me. *Thank You, Lord. I haven't seen dolphins out in the ocean like this before. It's such a special reminder that You have everything under control.* Chris and Mikeah get back in time to see our swimming friends for a few minutes before they disappear into the depths.

It is not a great night's sleep aboard the rattling old ship, so we are glad when the dawn finally breaks, cold and clear. Standing on deck, we take photos of the picturesque harbor of Xiamen, surrounded by large freighters and old Chinese wooden junks with their characteristic sails. Ancient and modern buildings stand side by side between the rocky hills and sandy beaches. It's easy to see why this city is popular with both Chinese and foreign tourists. After twenty hours on board the decaying ship, we are happy to disembark, but it takes several hours to clear customs. Stern looking young men in green uniforms wave us through checkpoints, look through our papers and luggage, and ask us questions. We're relieved when we are finally allowed to clamber into a rented van and speed through the crowded streets to our university home. *We're in China!*[21]

We're standing beside our stack of trunks in the bike-filled lobby area when we find out we've been assigned a room on the fifth floor.

---

21 Photos are limited to our family only, and no names are shared to protect the privacy of friends in China.

Fortunately, help quickly arrives in the form of several able-bodied fellow students who haul our possessions up the five flights of stairs to our new home away from home. It has painted concrete walls, a tile floor, two twin beds with mosquito nets, two small tables and chairs, and a metal door that leads out to a narrow balcony. The space definitely needs cleaning, but we know we have to deal with the cockroaches first. Per the instructions of more experienced residents, we draw lines with borax chalk around the edges of the room to poison any new arrivals, then we crunch the ones we find hiding under the beds.

The next day, we find our way to the market to buy what we need to make our small space comfortable. We add a little bed and mosquito netting for Mikeah, curtains to cover the windows and balcony door, straw mats for the hard floor, and a bookshelf. We also find a small table, an extra chair, and a highchair to set up an eating area. The twin beds push together to make a roomy king-size bed, and we arrange the desks to make a study nook.

Within a few days, we begin the routine of morning language classes, where pronunciation drills, grammar, listening skills, and written characters flood our brains. Mandarin, the official language of China, is one of six hundred dialects here, but there is only one written language. Because there is no alphabet, the graphic characters must be individually memorized, and eight thousand of them need to be learned for basic literacy. We spend most of our afternoons and evenings reading, writing, and reciting Mandarin. After four months, we know about five hundred characters and can converse in very simple sentences. Mikeah spends her mornings in the campus childcare center, where about a hundred children play and listen to stories. There is one other American girl, who is a little older than she is, and they become best friends. The children are divided into rooms by age level, with one teacher per twenty children. Each room has one long table surrounded by little chairs. There are no books, toys, or craft materials, no pictures on the walls, and no outside play area. Daily activities include singing songs and doing group dances together. Potties line the back wall of each classroom, as the Chinese children are potty-trained by eighteen months at the latest. There are no diapers in China, so the caregivers are a bit uncomfortable dealing with these two American girls who are still wearing them. Mikeah likes the singing and dancing, but her favorite part is eating the noodles they have at snack time.

Figuring out meals for our family can be stressful, as all ten families on our floor share one makeshift kitchen/shower room. A refrigerator and a counter topped with two camp stoves line the left side of the room. On the far right corner is a large sink where we wash our dishes. The drain to this sink empties into an open channel that is built into the floor along the right wall. Two shower stalls also empty into this channel, and the water runs down a slight slope to the outlet pipe. This trench makes a convenient highway for the large rats who regularly climb the pipe in search of leftover food from the sink. There's nothing quite like the shock and disgust of seeing a cat-sized rodent scurrying past your bare feet while you're showering or bathing your baby.

If we don't want to cook, there is a campus cafeteria that serves very basic Chinese food at good prices, and there are also many restaurants along the beach. Xiamen is part of a "free economic zone," which means the local people can own small businesses and have more than one child if they are willing to pay for all the medical expenses and schooling for that child. In most parts of the country, the government controls when you have the one child you are allowed to have by assigning the number of births permitted in a given area each year. Couples must get permission to have a child, and if they get pregnant during an unassigned time, they are required to have an abortion. Many of the women I meet have had several abortions. We talk about how Americans are protesting for the right to have abortions. Here the women would like to protest for the right to *not* have them. Of course, they can't do that; there is no freedom of speech in this country.

All day and well into the evening, a middle-aged man in a worn uniform sits at a small wooden desk at the top of the stairs leading to our floor. In a large ledger, he documents what time we come and go, and he checks the identification of any Chinese person who visits our floor, noting their name and who they came to see. Needless to say, if we want to talk to Chinese friends, we meet them elsewhere to ensure their privacy.

At Easter, Chris is invited to speak at a small international church gathering of mostly Filipino believers who are studying here. What a joy it is to sing songs of faith with them and enjoy a wonderful meal together after Chris shares the victorious resurrection story. One very gifted young student from Norway comes to this gathering, seeking to know more about our story. He doesn't know much about Christianity but asks us a lot of thought-provoking questions during the meal.

A few days after the service, we are told the power will be off for two days. Because of the extreme heat, many people plan to sleep on the flat roof, but our new friend from Norway chooses to sleep on his balcony instead. Sometime during the night, he rolls off the table he has made into a bed, falls seventy-five feet to the ground, and is seriously injured. Friends take him to the hospital nearby, but the hospital is not admitting new patients due to the power outage. The next morning, he is found dead in his room. We hold on to hope that while he lay dying during the small hours of the morning, he remembered Chris's talk and chose Jesus. It is a sad reminder that we never know when our time here on earth will be over, but we can know where we will be spending eternity, and we can help others to make that decision too.

———————

They say that culture shock usually hits around three months after arriving in a new country, and this is definitely true for us. The honeymoon period where "all this is so new and different and exciting" has worn off, and the daily difficulties of life begin to weigh heavily on us. One morning during his quiet time, Chris is discussing this with the Lord and confesses that he just can't do this anymore.

"I don't have the love I need for these people. I have no joy or peace, and I don't feel like I can be kind or patient. I just can't do this."

You never could, he hears the still, small voice from the Lord say. *I am the One who gives you all those things. This is my work, remember? I never expected you to do it in your own strength.*

It hits us both how easy it is to accept an assignment from God and then act as if He has left us alone to handle it! We struggle with living in one room, sharing a kitchen and showers with so many others, and coping with cockroaches, mosquitos, and rats in our living space. We battle the mold that grows on our walls, books, and clothes because it's so humid and hot here. We have to constantly haul buckets of water up five flights of stairs just so we can bathe, flush the toilet, or do laundry when the water is off. It isn't easy to deal with finding worms or bird feathers in our food, let alone the regular bouts of stomach illnesses that result from these conditions. We labor daily to learn the language and understand the culture. Sacrificing life's comforts to help others hear the good news is hard but *so* worth it in light of eternity. We pray together to keep our eyes on Him, and we keep going.

Just when we are beginning to get used to all this, our team asks us to move to another part of the country to help begin a new language program. Changsha is a large city that is further north and inland from where we are living. It was the home of Chairman Mao Zedong, who led the Cultural Revolution from 1966–1976. His goal was to preserve Chinese communism by purging remnants of capitalism and traditional culture from Chinese society.[22] There are five universities in Changsha that are very close together, and our

---

22 Alessandro Russo, *Cultural Revolution and Revolutionary Culture* (Durham. Duke University Press, 2020).

small class will be comprised of the first foreigners to ever study in the area. We wrap things up in Xiamen with a second birthday party for Mikeah, a farewell picnic with our friends on the beach, and a sightseeing trip to see the Buddhist temple and gardens nearby. *Lord, it's hard to be heading into the unknown yet again. Please help us keep our eyes on You, no matter what comes along.*

By the end of July, we are back in Hong Kong for a seven-week break, and while we're there, we get to announce that we are expecting a baby brother or sister for Mikeah! We are ecstatic. I get an early prenatal checkup at a local clinic and plan to have the baby here in March of next year. We attend our team conference in August so we can hear what's happening with the others who are working all over China and so we can plan for the next year. We finally get to read our mail, which is always delivered to the Hong Kong base. Mail sent into China has the potential to be checked and censored and may not get to us at all. We write letters home, happily telling everyone about our pregnancy, and we shop for the supplies we'll need in our new home in Changsha.

Just before dawn a month later, I wake up with spotting and cramps. I had some of this when I was pregnant with Mikeah, so at first, I'm not too worried. As it continues throughout the week, I get more anxious and go alone to the maternity clinic to find out what's happening. The nurse at the clinic can't find a heartbeat, so they transport me by ambulance to a local hospital for an ultrasound. It reveals that our precious baby died around the ten-week mark, and they recommend a D&C. Shock and sadness overwhelm me as I sit in the cold hospital room alone. *This just isn't fair. I know people who are having their third or fourth illegitimate child, and they are doing fine. I'm here serving You in this difficult place, and You allow our dearly wanted baby to die. Why? This doesn't make sense.*

Chris comes to get me but doesn't know what to say or do, and I'm too distraught to talk about it. He goes with me to the hospital the next morning. Since he didn't see the ultrasound the day before, he insists that they do another one to be sure the baby isn't alive. They kindly agree to do it, but the result is the same. They wheel me into surgery. After a lonely, frightening two days in the hospital, where only the nurses speak English and I share a ward with fifteen other female patients, I just want to be alone for a while. I'm glad to be out of the hospital, but sharing this team house with so many people makes it hard to have any privacy. Even though many are trying to be kind and understanding, I need space to sort this out with the Lord.

But there is little time to grieve, as we are leaving for Changsha in a week. It's an overnight train ride, and we will have lots of luggage to haul up and down long stairways in the train stations, as well as a busy two-year-old to keep track of amidst the hurrying crowds. I know this is all in the Lord's hands, and even though I don't understand it or like it, I'm choosing to trust Him. *Lord, I need Your strength to begin again in another new place. Please use me to bring light to lonely hearts, even though I feel empty and numb myself.*

Celeste doing afternoon chores with Mikeah during candidate training in Philadelphia, 1987.

Chris helping with a renovation project at our mission's headquarters, 1987.

Celeste (far right) teaching with Open Air Campaigners in Philadelphia, 1987.

Chris, Celeste, and Mikeah arriving
in Hong Kong, January 1988.

New sights, sounds, and smells to get
used to in the Chinese markets.

Chris, busy with daily writing
and reading practice.

Mikeah, twenty months old.

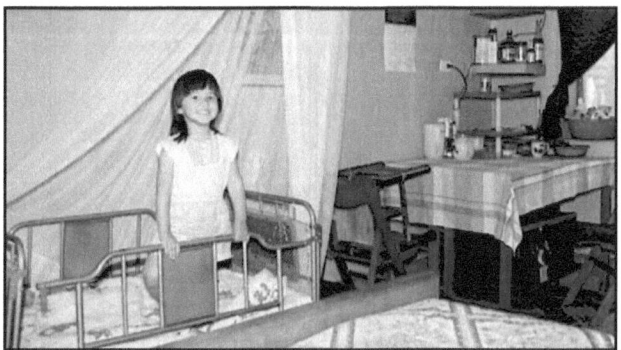

Mikeah loves her new bed in our dorm
room in Xiamen, China, 1988.

Chris, Celeste, and Mikeah
visiting a park in Xiamen.

Mikeah's second birthday party, June 1988.

Chris shares at the Filipino gathering at Easter in Xiamen, China, 1988.

chapter thirty

I Will Restore What Has Been Taken

Exhausted after a twenty-six-hour train journey, we join the checkpoint line, knowing we have a lot of Bibles hidden amongst our clothes and we could easily be deported or imprisoned if they are discovered. We pray silently as we move forward. When we finally reach the first officer, he stamps our passports and waves us on. We slowly walk along, wondering what will happen next. To our surprise, a path opens up in the crowd, and none of the guards are looking at us. Within a few minutes, we are standing outside, realizing God has made a way and we're heading for our new university! The building that the school officials have chosen for us is usually used for visiting dignitaries, so each room has nice carpet, wallpaper, and its own bathroom with a bathtub, sink, and western toilet. However, we are disappointed to find that the promised arrangements of hot water in our bathrooms, wardrobes for our clothes, and a kitchen/laundry area have not been completed yet. There is a dining room downstairs where we eat while we wait the two weeks it takes for them to add a camp stove, sink, counter, and washing machine to a small room on our floor. Wardrobes eventually arrive, and the hot water heaters they provide work when there is water and electricity available at the same time. All in all, though, it is quite comfortable after we again rearrange the twin beds into a king-size bed and buy a little bed for Mikeah.

Our fourth-story room looks out on the open field of the local primary school, where we watch all six hundred children gather twice a day for twenty minutes of synchronized exercises that are guided by a loudspeaker that counts down and shouts encouraging propaganda messages. It's a pretty walk through the campus grounds and local vegetable gardens to the market where we can buy meat, fresh produce, and any other groceries we need. It's not as modern as Xiamen is, but we are excited to be the first foreigners to attend this school, and we look forward to meeting some of the many students who come here from all over the country to study English.

We attend an official opening of the new language program that was created to teach foreigners Mandarin, and classes begin with all seven of us in attendance. There is no nursery for Mikeah, so Chris and I take turns going to class at first—most of this is review for us, so it's not hard to keep up with the others who are just starting to learn the language. Our writing teacher also happens to be the communist leader for this area, and he asks us to write a diary about where we go and who we meet with each day. Needless to say, we are careful about what we write and certainly don't include everything.

Changsha is a very old city. People have lived here for more than three thousand years, and the current population is around 2.6 million. It is the capital of Hunan province, which, although it is located on some of the richest land in China, is one of the poorest and most underdeveloped provinces. Hunan is also the birthplace of the much-loved leader of the cultural revolution, Mao Zedong, and many people here still wear the traditional navy-blue uniform that everyone was required to wear when he was in power. This clothing rule was supposed to produce a feeling of equality and reduce the class distinction created by fashion.

Labor is all done by hand here, as there aren't many machines to help. We watch construction workers making concrete support beams in wooden forms on the ground in our front yard. When they are set, eight men carry each one to the new building site down the road. One afternoon, we watch a huge boiler being transported on rollers inch by inch to the new building. Life is hard here. We are told there is no unemployment—a lot of underemployment, but everyone has something to do. We don't see any homeless people, and begging is not allowed.

Many of the young people who are here to study English find us so they can practice speaking this strange new language. We are never quite sure who to trust, as we know we're not supposed to share our faith here. So one night when we hear a knock on our door, Chris answers cautiously.

"Yes? Can I help you?" he says through the closed door.

"Yes. I want to meet with you. I want to know about Jesus. Someone told me you could help," comes the man's reply.

We look at each other, not sure what to do. Is he actually a spy from the government, checking to see how we respond to this request? What should we say? We could easily be thrown out of the country if this goes south.

We offer up a quick silent prayer, and Chris takes the man downstairs to talk with him. It turns out he is a teacher from another province who has sincere questions. They meet several times, and a few months later, he returns to his home with Bibles we have smuggled in and a new heart to share the truth with others.

God hasn't forgotten my shattered heart. I'm slowly dealing with the grief and loss of our sweet baby when one of our teachers suggests that we each enter something in a writing competition the school is having for students. I have no clue what to write about, but as I pray about it, I feel led to try to express my deepest feelings of sorrow in a short poem. I write it in English, and our teacher translates it for me. It is placed on a bulletin board with all the others. I don't win any prizes, but that was never my goal. There is now something written down that says this little person once lived and mattered deeply to us. It's a small mark on the world, but it's tangible, and it helps my heart to settle and move forward. I know many women here have lost children to abortions they didn't want. I hope that some will see this and realize their child lives. *Lord, I pray You will somehow use this tragedy for good.*

You never know how God is going to work, especially in a place where sharing your faith is risky and often secretive. Out of the blue, Chris is asked by the dean of students to speak at an evening meeting. He's not given a topic to speak on, so he chooses, "Holidays in America." About forty students are seated in the room, with the usual communist party supervisors standing at the back. Chris shares the meaning of the Fourth of July and Thanksgiving, then he talks about Christmas and Easter, including an explanation of their original meanings and why we celebrate them today. During the question and answer time at the end, a man stands up. "So, do you believe in God?" he asks.

"Yes, I do," Chris replies.

"Why?"

Chris goes on to explain his faith, even writing the Four Spiritual Laws on the board to explain salvation. That night as we talk about what happened, we are excited by the way things unfolded, but we worry there will be repercussions after sharing such a clear message of faith. Instead of getting in trouble, however, we're shocked when he is asked to share again a few weeks later!

In his second talk, Chris explains "What Americans Believe About God." Three students follow him out of the hall and cautiously tell him that they, too, want to believe in God. Here is another opportunity to share very directly. The dean meets with Chris a few days later and asks if he will give that same talk again. The morning after the second version of that talk, a large group of students surround him while he's walking to school, again asking him if he believes in God.

"Yes, I do," he answers.

"There's no such thing as God," challenges one of the students.

"How do you know that? Tell me something; if there was a terrible car accident down the road that you didn't see, but someone who was there came and told you what he saw, would you believe him?" Chris asks him.

"I guess so," the young man replies.

"Well, that's the same for me. The Bible was written many years ago by people who were there and saw what happened. I have no reason to not believe what they are saying."

I wish I was as good as Chris is about speaking up in these situations.

A few days later, he brings a young woman to me who wants to know about God. It is a delight to read Scripture together and explain God's plan. We have a Bible that has both English and Mandarin, so I read the English and she reads the Mandarin as we talk together each week. Before long, she prays to receive Jesus. The next time we meet, she is beaming as she explains that reading the Bible I gave her makes her "feel clean." God is changing her life from the inside out. What a privilege and a joy it is to baptize her in our bathtub a few weeks later. *This* is why we came. These times with her become the highlight of my week.

Meanwhile, Chris has led several young men to the Lord and decides he would like to form a discipleship group with them. As he suggests it to each of them individually, they refuse to join such a meeting. They are very nervous about sharing their faith with strangers because it's hard to know who to trust here. Suddenly, the freedom we have at home to meet whenever we want to seems like a huge privilege we take for granted. Not that there aren't gatherings here. The Three-Self Church is the official government church for protestants in China. The government controls where and when they can meet and what will be taught, especially to children and young people. Many are afraid to attend, as you have to register and everyone is closely watched. Services can be raided by the police at any time, and leaders are often jailed.

So the underground church is a growing movement—small secret meetings in homes where believers can worship and read the Word together. Bibles are highly valued here, since they are banned, and even though all of us bring as many as we can each time we come into the country, it's never enough. They are often taken apart. and the individual chapters are carefully passed around the group.

As the winter weather sets in, we have blankets of sparkling snow outside but no heat in our rooms. We brought a small heater with us from Hong Kong, but there is often no electricity to run it, so we dress in multiple layers when we're at home studying, including our jackets and a heavy bed quilt. Sometimes it's so cold we can see our breath inside the room.

In early February, we make the long train trip back to Hong Kong to gather supplies, write a newsletter, and answer mail. A trip to the pharmacy confirms what we have suspected—I'm pregnant again! Although we are delighted, we feel much more cautious this time, and we wait to share our news.

Back in Changsha, we resume classes and look forward to the warmer spring weather. But there are changes brewing. In early April, the students from the five universities around us abandon classes and begin daily marches into the city. They are protesting the imprisonment of a government leader who had been promoting greater freedom for the people.

The local government authorities tell us, in no uncertain terms, that we are not to join in these protests or take any photos. We must stay in our room as much as possible. They want all foreigners to leave the country, but the students have closed the airport and the railway stations. We are stuck in our dormitory room, trying to find out the latest news by listening to the unsanctioned BBC and Voice of America broadcasts on the radio. A few students visit us, but they are closely watched, so we discourage these visits, as we don't want to get them or ourselves in trouble.

We hear about the huge gathering at Tiananmen Square in Beijing and watch some of the protests on TV. As the movement grows and spreads to every city in the country, we all wonder what will happen next. We no longer have any classes, and hundreds of students march past our window in long noisy demonstrations every day. Their actions reflect the general feeling of dissatisfaction among the people here. How the government responds as the world watches will be important for China's development and its standing in the international community. We pack up all our belongings so we are ready to leave whenever that becomes possible.

June 3, 1989, is Mikeah's third birthday, and we have a small party with friends to celebrate. That night, the tanks roll into Beijing. Over a thousand people are killed as the military opens fire on the crowds of gathered students. Many others are beaten and arrested. The government has quietly infiltrated the protesters to discover who the leaders are. Once those leaders are removed, the movement soon falls apart.

By the beginning of July, it is mostly over, and we are relieved to fly to Hong Kong on our way back to the U.S. for a break. We're not sure if we will return to mainland China or go to Taiwan after this, but we know we need time to sort out some things and have a rest. Dealing with the stress of moving, having a miscarriage, and surviving the protests and the lockdown has brought out issues in our marriage. We need to be in counseling, and in the midst of all this chaos, we have another baby to prepare for. We talk through all this with our team leaders in Hong Kong, and they agree that we should take a furlough. *Lord, this has been a difficult time, but what a privilege it has been to see people come to know You in such a closed place. We have met believers who face daily persecution and uncertainty, but they still remain faithful. We have watched You open doors we never imagined could be opened, and we have seen You take care of us through confusing situations. Thank You for bringing us here. Please take care of our Chinese friends. We will be praying for them.*

I'm six months pregnant and haven't seen a doctor yet when we arrive in Portland, Oregon, in late July. We enjoy catching up with Paul and Annie as we stay in their comfortable home. Three-year-old Mikeah doesn't remember America and is amazed at how clean the bathrooms are after our experiences with the filthy public toilets in China. Our church generously helps us to buy a used station wagon, and we're soon heading south to catch up with Chris's family in Los Angeles. The last stop is my mother's home in Oklahoma City, where we will be living for the foreseeable future. As we settle in, Chris gets a job mowing grass for the city, and I begin going to a free prenatal clinic, as we have no medical insurance. This means long waits and a different doctor every time. As my due date comes and goes, they start to get concerned since I had to have a C-section the first time. I'm hoping to avoid surgery this time around, but that does present its own set of risks. I have my first ultrasound and a pelvic x-ray to make sure the baby can be born without a C-section. The doctor agrees to try it and insists I come into the hospital as soon as I'm in labor.

I wake up from a nap on a Saturday afternoon, eight days past my due date, with the familiar feeling of early contractions. Mum takes charge of Mikeah, and Chris and I head to the hospital. In this large maternity department, there are twelve labor rooms and four delivery rooms, and they're all full when we arrive in the early evening. I wander the halls in an effort to get things moving along, but around 8 p.m., they decide to send me home. They need the space, and I'm just not progressing fast enough. Back at Mum's house, Mikeah is disappointed there's no baby. Everyone goes to bed except me. I spend the night alone, breathing through the contractions and doing laps around the living room and kitchen.

By 4:30 a.m., I can't focus enough to keep breathing correctly, so I wake up Chris.

"I think we need to get back to the hospital," I explain.

When we arrive, the admitting doctor seems skeptical but checks me anyway.

"Ah, yes. You're at nine centimeters. I guess we'll keep you," he jokes.

Joseph Paul is born an hour later on October 15, 1989, delivered by a doctor who didn't seem to know beforehand that my last delivery was a C-section.

"You should never have been sent home," he tells me. "You could have bled out on your kitchen floor." I thank the Lord for taking care of me and our healthy baby boy. It is such an amazing miracle to look into his little face and know God grew this new human being inside me for the last nine months. What a gift! *Please bless this precious baby boy, Lord, with a mind and heart to know You from a young age. Teach him Your ways, and lead him like You led the Josephs in the Bible. Prepare a bride for him, and may he be a man after Your own heart. We love him so much already and are delighted to welcome him into our family.*

Three weeks later, we're driving north to Philadelphia, where we stay for two months at our mission's headquarters. I spend a week in the hospital over Thanksgiving because of an infection in my leg related to being very anemic after Joseph was born. We marvel as God takes care of the $10,000 bill for us through a hospital funding plan for low-income patients. It is suggested by leadership that we go to Taiwan next, but we don't have the financial support for such an expensive country. "God's work, done in God's way, will never lack God's supply" is a reassuring quote from Hudson Taylor, a pioneering missionary to China, so we continue to pray and seek His guidance for the next step. In the meantime, we are adjusting to being a family of four, and Chris and I begin reading through *The Marriage Builder* by Larry Crabb together. We submit the needs of our marriage to our heavenly Father. *Lord, You know we each love You. Show us how to love each other, accept our differences, and support each other's walk with You.*

No decision has been made about where we might serve next, but we pack up and head west in early January 1990. While we wait for clear guidance from God, we let our prayer partners know we are still seeking God's will for the future. We're also planning to find a good counselor to help us sort through our marriage issues. The weather is unseasonably warm as we drive all the way across the country and only deal with one snow-covered mountain pass. Back in Oregon, we stay with Pastor Steve and his wife, Barbara, while we look for an apartment to rent. *Another new beginning.*

Chris is back working at Fred Meyer. They have been so good about always finding him a job as we have come and gone over the last five years. Of course, he is one of their best salesmen, so I understand the incentive to rehire him. We rent a two-bedroom apartment in Gresham and settle into a daily routine. We find a counselor who can help us sort through what is going on between us, and we do some initial sessions together before seeing him separately.

In a one-on-one session, the counselor asks me to choose from a list of adjectives the ones that best describe me. I circle all that seem to apply. There is one empty space where I can add anything I feel is missing from the list. I add "unlovable." He asks if I have any history of physical or sexual abuse, and I admit I do. As I cannot bring myself to talk about it, he asks me to write it down and read it to him in the next session.

And that's what I do. I describe with minimal detail the incident that happened during our summer camping trip when I was nine years old and how both my stepfathers were physically and verbally abusive. He reads it, and we talk about the impact this has had on me. He tells me I should share it with Chris. It feels so hard to do, but that night, I ask him to read what I have written. He doesn't say much and doesn't seem to know how to respond. I'm happy to not talk about it too much, but I did hope for a more sympathetic response. I'm hoping that, in time, the counseling will help him to see my need for support. We move on.

Talking about my past has at least taken away the isolation created by a secret and has opened the door for further healing. I'm grateful for the counseling. I'm talking and being heard by someone for the first time in my life. I realize how much difficulty I have expressing my needs or even identifying them. I don't like to ask for help and cannot deal with conflict. Often, I push difficult feelings aside, remain quiet, and keep moving. When I do venture to say something, Chris doesn't know how to deal with my feelings of sadness or worry. Instead of listening and helping me to talk it through, he just asks if I've prayed about it. He offers no support or comfort or reassurance. He needs me to be strong and take care of everything, like I have always done. The problem is, my feelings and needs don't disappear, and I find myself becoming resentful and bitter.

Compounding the problem is the dilemma of being married in a missionary setting. Chris's attitude on the field is that "we came here to serve God, and that is my first priority." On the rare occasion where I get up my courage and finally ask him for help, it feels like I'm taking him away from the pressing task of leading people to God. Which is more important, helping with the dishes or saving souls from an eternity separated from God? I feel guilty even asking for help, so most of the time, I don't. Instead, I try to hold it all together, but the hostility between us is growing. The anxiety, sadness, and loneliness I feel is coming out in anger and animosity toward my husband. It's clear that something needs to change.

After I share this with our counselor, he talks to us both about our family always being the priority, because our first ministry is to those closest to us. Our witness as a loving family is huge in any community, and raising our children to know God is job number one. *Lord, help us to find balance in our lives. We love our children and want them to know You, love You, and serve You. Give me courage to speak up for my needs, and please help Chris to listen. Replace our anger and frustration with love and patience. Take away the feeling of "please just get me out of this," and give us the courage and strength we need to build a happy marriage together. I know we both have deep wounds from the past, but I also know You are the God who heals and can make all things new.*

———————

Mikeah turns four and wants to go to preschool. Meanwhile, Joseph teaches himself to walk at eight-and-a-half months old and is into everything. They love playing together. Most mornings, I find Mikeah in his crib, playing house or singing songs with him. During the summer, they both enjoy the apartment complex pool, and Mikeah becomes quite a confident swimmer. In August, we discover our family is about to be complete, as we're expecting another baby! We have always wanted to have three children of our own and leave room to adopt or foster children if God leads us to that possibility. I'm so happy to be back with the doctor who delivered Mikeah and to get to "meet" our addition, as he now does routine early ultrasounds. Looking at the wiggling twelve-week-old on screen, I fall in love immediately and just know she's a girl. At the same time, we realize we are not going back overseas for now. The funding has not come in that would allow us to live in Taiwan, and God has not led us to consider any other country. We have children to take care of and lots of opportunities for ministry right here.

Our sweet Erin Marie arrives on April 9, 1991, by induction. My doctor was concerned because my first two babies were late and each had the cord wrapped around their neck multiple times, so he induced me on my due date. After a long day in labor, she finally arrives at 4:35 p.m. She looks a lot like Mikeah, and I am in the same room I was in five years ago, with the same doctor and some of the same nurses who helped to deliver her older sister. It's so nice to have a newborn in the house again. Mikeah and Joseph can't get enough of holding her and want to give her things to play with constantly. *Thank You, Lord, for this beautiful baby girl we all love so much. Please bless her with coming to know You at a young age and with a strong heart to follow You all the days of her life. May she be an instrument of Your peace everywhere she goes. Please be preparing a husband for her who knows You and will help her raise a family to serve You well. Our family feels complete. Thank You.*

A month after Erin is born, we move into our first home. It's a simple three-bedroom, one-bathroom ranch on half an acre of land. There are fruit trees and lilacs and lots of room for the children to run and play in the fenced yard. We plant a big vegetable garden, and the older two often play in the kiddie pool while I hang diapers on the clothesline. One evening, a neighbor knocks on our door to introduce himself and ask if we want a dog. His daughter left her American Eskimo puppy with him, but his dog doesn't get along with it.

"Bring him over," Chris suggests, and Kodi becomes our first pet. Six months later, I go back to work as an on-call occupational therapist one morning a week. Chris watches the children for the five hours I'm gone then heads to the evening shift at the store. This arrangement keeps my license current and helps with the budget as well.

Chris is an assistant manager now, but they are constantly asking him to take a management position. When the offer to lead the store in Bend comes up, he feels we have to show some interest or the bosses will stop offering to promote him. We drive over to Bend, visit the store, and look around the area. We're not impressed by the dry, brown landscape and don't really want to move here. However, as we drive back across the mountain pass, God changes our attitudes, and Chris accepts the position. We rent out the home we've owned for only a year and pack up everything. It's hard to start again in another new place, but God provides a home for us to rent with a beautiful mountain view. Eight months later, we buy a manufactured home out in the woods. We find a loving, supportive church, make lots of new friends, and help to form a wonderful homeschooling group that meets regularly to do field trips and learn together.

While I'm getting three-year-old Erin ready for bed one evening, I'm telling her that Barney says various things as we play with her Barney toy.

"Mom, Barney can't talk. He's just a toy," she assures me.

"I know that," I reply. "I was just pretending."

A few minutes later, I leave her in the bathroom to brush her teeth with the already prepared toothbrush. When I return to complete the task, I find the toothbrush still sitting on the counter, with the toothpaste still on it.

"Did you brush your teeth?" I ask her.

"Yep," she replies as she continues to play with the water in the sink. It's obvious this isn't true, so I give her the lying lecture. She looks up at me and says, "How come when you do it, it's pretending, and when I do it, it's lying?"

Oh dear. If this is three, what will thirteen be like? This little girl is way too smart!

Chris is teaching a discipleship group with some men at work, and I am leading a mom's Bible study and support group. I'm also working one day a week at the local hospital, and we have a home group meeting in our house each week as well. Life is busy, but we haven't forgotten about missions. It has been nearly six years since we left China. We have considered several possibilities, but God hasn't opened any doors yet. We're aware that we're not getting any younger. I will be thirty-nine this year, and Chris is already forty-three. We both feel passionately about global missions, and as we see the increasing evil in the world, we sense it is time to get back on the field. We contact our mission in Philadelphia, and they set up a reorientation time starting in September 1996. We put our house on the market, and when it sells four months later, we move into a rental home. We sell and give away belongings and wait to see what He has next. We pray together as a family for guidance and strength.

Homeschooling continues, and the children are busy with swimming, gymnastics, soccer, piano, and Sunday school. Leaving here is going to be a big sacrifice for each one of us. We all have friends we love, activities we are a part of, and belongings we don't want to part with. We continue to talk about it and pray together.

We buy our first computer so we'll be able to write our newsletters and get online no matter where we end up. So much has changed since the days when we had to write letters from Hong Kong, even though it wasn't that long ago. Now we can send our letters by email without having to deal with the unreliable postal services. It feels like such a luxury! We're not sure how long we will be away, but we're planning on being gone for at least two years. *Lord, we're heading back to our mission's headquarters with no idea where You will take us. We've boxed up our lives, cried through the goodbyes, and packed our passports. We're ready to go wherever You lead. This is a new challenge for all of us, especially our children. Please help us all to trust You and Your plan for us.*

University guest house. Changsha, China, 1989. Our room is on the top floor, the second from left.

Mikeah, Celeste, and Chris.
Christmas 1988. Changsha, China.

The market where we shop for food and supplies.

A small meat stall in the market. Meat hangs in the open air and is sold by the jin (pound).

Mikeah with adopted "grandparents," Di and Terry, fellow students from Australia.

Chris and Mikeah playing outside in the snow. Changsha, 1988.

A public taxi built on a modified motorcycle.

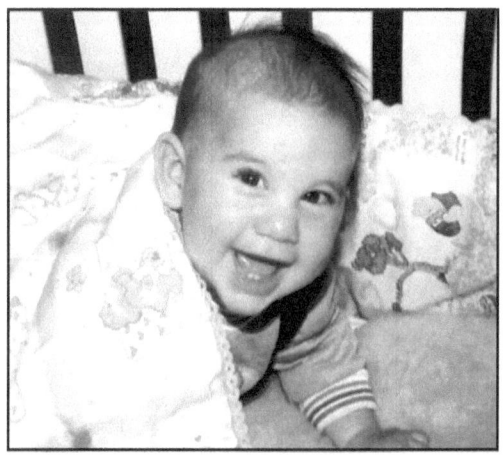

Joseph Paul Delaney, five months old. Born October 15, 1989.

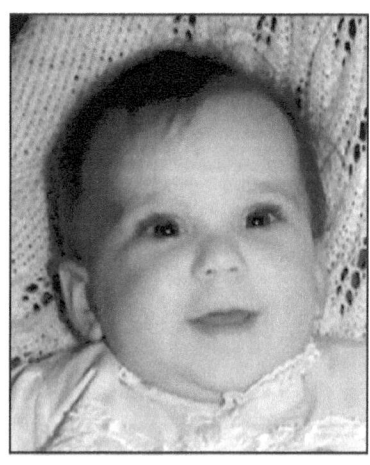

Erin Marie Delaney, two months old. Born April 9, 1991.

A trip to Disneyland, 1993.
Joseph (four), Erin (two), and Mikeah (seven).

Celeste and Chris,
Erin (eight months), Joseph
(two), and Mikeah (five),
December 1991.

Grandma Eunice comes to visit us in Bend, 1994.
Mikeah (eight), Joseph (five), and Erin (three).

Visiting with
godparents, Paul and
Annie Lesko, 1991.
Joseph (two),
Mikeah (five), and
Erin (eight months).

chapter thirty-one

¿Cómo Oirán Sin un Predicador?
How Will They Hear
Without a Preacher?

Before we know it, the five of us are packed into our minivan and pulling a U-Haul for twelve days and three thousand miles across the country. Along the way, we enjoy visits with friends in Montana and Chicago, and we make sure to squeeze in a stop at Mt. Rushmore as well. As incredible as the famous landmark is, the kids are more excited when the motel near there turns out to have a huge waterslide. It is a welcome break after hours in the van.

On September 4, 1996, we're all relieved to finally make it to Philadelphia for our third visit. We quickly settle into a three-bedroom apartment. Chris is working in the maintenance department, while I am helping in the office and homeschooling our children. They are making new friends here and enjoying the freedom the missionary children have to play in the thirty-five acres of gardens and woods. We fit in a trip to New York City to visit Ellis Island, the Statue of Liberty, and the World Trade Center. And all the while, we are praying about where to go next. Mexico and Venezuela are at the top of the list. We talk, pray, and spend time listening to the wise counsel of staff, waiting to hear from the Lord.

I love being at the headquarters. There are so many godly people here who share their stories of God's work in them and through them, all around the world. We feel supported as we seek God's direction for the next step. Eventually, the answer comes as we meet some new team members heading south—Mexico will be our next home. It feels so right with Chris's grandparents being from there. I hope that as he learns to speak Spanish again, he will also find the positive aspects of the Mexican culture he has inherited.

Our first stop will be a year in Edinburg, Texas, to study Spanish at RGBI (Rio Grande Bible Institute). They will provide us with a small furnished apartment to rent, but we will need to take our own household items, like dishes, pots, pans, and linens. We don't have any, so I head down to the basement supply rooms where I first found the matching crib linens nearly ten years ago. I find some things we need, but there are no dishes. When I explain our need to the woman in charge of this area, she asks me what kind of dishes I would like.

"Plain white seems the most practical," I reply.

"We'll pray about it," she tells me.

A few days later, she calls.

"Your dishes have arrived!"

Two huge boxes of white dishes have just been donated! It's another reminder that He knows our needs long before we do. *Thank You, Lord.*

A month later, eighteen of us are studying together here at RGBI, where missionaries learn Spanish and Spanish-speaking people from Mexico and South America study the Bible. Our children attend a small Christian school that uses the same curriculum we have been using for homeschooling, but it still takes them some time to adjust. As it was when we were learning Mandarin in China, I do well in class but struggle with shyness when trying to speak to others in Spanish; Chris struggles in class but is very good at using what he knows. He is part of a ministry team that visits a prison across the border in Reynosa, Mexico, once a week. There, he gets to lead several men to the Lord and disciple them as he practices his language skills.

As part of the immersion into the language and culture, we are required to attend a Spanish-speaking church. This is challenging. We have Bibles that have both English and Spanish, so we can at least follow along once we know which passage we're reading, and the hymns are familiar tunes as we try to learn the new Spanish words. But it's so hard for me to try to talk to people, and it's no better in the classroom. Reading aloud in Spanish every morning, I discover that the problem from my childhood is still lurking in the recesses of my brain, and I struggle to read out loud fluidly, even though I understand what I'm reading. Embarrassed and humbled, I plod on.

Our finances have been really tight this whole year. Three days before our final exams, we get word from headquarters that we won't be able to go to Mexico unless our financial support increases by at least $200 a month and we get enough money on top of that to buy furniture when we arrive. We send a note to our prayer partners and begin to pray earnestly. During the next two weeks, we receive $2,000 in the mail from various people, a promise of $1,000 for furniture, and letters from people saying they are planning to support us! This increases our support by $400 a month and provides for our initial moving expenses. God's work, done God's way, really will have God's provision! Unlike our experience a few years ago, when the money did not come in for going to Taiwan, this time the generous provision confirms that God is leading us to Mexico.

It is no small feat to cross the border into Mexico with a trailer full of household items. We are required to stop and empty the entire thing so the uniformed officers can decide how much we need to pay in "import taxes." After it's reloaded and the bill is paid, we're on our way to the town of Matehuala. This small town is about halfway between the U.S. border and Cuernavaca and has an American Bible school that provides a little cabin for us to stay in overnight. Late the next day, after nearly ten hours of driving, we finally arrive in Cuernavaca. For the next four weeks, we housesit for team members who are on furlough while we look for somewhere to call home.

Cuernavaca is at about five-thousand-feet elevation and an hour and a half southwest of Mexico City. It is known as "The City of Eternal Spring" because of its abundant water supply and many flowers, especially the spectacular bougainvillea that seem to grace every wall. It is a popular destination for locals and tourists, as it's on the route between Mexico City and Acapulco.

We find a small two-story cinderblock house to rent in a gated community on the outskirts of the city. It has three small bedrooms, one and a half bathrooms, and an open kitchen and living room area. The white walls are made of concrete blocks, and the floors are white tile. There's a large water tank on the flat roof that functions as a reservoir when the water is off, which it often is. Behind the house is a small fenced-in concrete slab where the washing machine and clothesline reside. We buy furniture from the local market and set up house. There's a community pool and play area that our children enjoy, and we are soon getting to know our neighbors.

Chris immediately finds all kinds of opportunities to share his faith with people. We have been in our little home in Cuernavaca for only a month when he leads the landlord and his wife to the Lord and begins a weekly Bible study with them. He often spends long hours sitting at the entrance of our gated community, sharing Scripture with the guards there or going to visit one of the families we have become friends with nearby.

Teresa lives right next door to us. She was living in Mexico City when the last big earthquake hit, and the fright caused her to have ongoing debilitating rheumatoid arthritis. She moved here because there are fewer earthquakes, and she feels safer. She doesn't speak much English, but we never seem to have difficulty communicating with her. After Chris leads her to the Lord, she is the first person we baptize in the community swimming pool. She begins coming to church with us and invites several of her family members to come too.

Sara lives around the corner and has become my language tutor. She is a new Christian, so we combine my Spanish lessons with her discipleship. I also learn a lot from her about what is going on in our neighborhood and how Mexican women are expected to put up with their husbands going to strip clubs and having affairs. Some of her friends tell her that she's being unreasonable when she complains about her husband wanting to do those things, and they tell her she won't be married for long with that attitude. She sticks to her guns and remains happily married.

We form a weekly neighborhood Bible study with Teresa, Sara and her husband, Victor, and four other friends from our community. It is wonderful to share gospel truths and watch them learn and grow in their relationships with God. At the same time, they teach us so much about the Mexican culture and traditions. For example, when you go to someone's home and they offer you a drink, it's polite to refuse at least twice before agreeing to have something. I realize I have unwittingly been rude to many guests, as I've taken them at their word and not offered them anything more than once! Apparently, the neighbors who visit regularly have learned to say "yes" straight away if they really do want something at our house.

The children and I are happy to return to homeschooling and settle back into a daily routine. We have found a good church to attend, and we join in several ministries, including Sunday school, AWANA, and Bible studies. We're grateful for the previous experience of immersion into a Spanish-speaking church back in Texas, but I still find it hard to fit in with only very basic language skills. Everyone here is patient and kind, but it is taking me time to adjust. Shopping in open markets where haggling over the prices is expected terrifies me even more than the constant flow of scorpions, tarantulas, cockroaches, black widow spiders, and rats who continually try to take up residence in our home. There's often no water or power, and driving requires more than the typical "defensive" skills, as road signs are more of a suggestion than a requirement for many. *Lord, this is a lot to get used to. There's much I don't like, but I'm so grateful to have a comfortable home, new friends, and a great church family here. Thank You.*

Two years roll along in a steady rhythm of ministry and family times. There's not much on TV here, so our evenings usually consist of reading books together, like the biography of Eric Liddell and *The Wheel on the School.* We often celebrate birthdays at one of the popular local water parks and take several trips to the beautiful beaches.

The most exciting adventure is swimming with dolphins when Mum comes to visit. These amazing animals are much bigger than they seem from a distance and are so smart and gentle. We take turns being pulled around by them and are amazed at how carefully they move around us as we swim beside them in their deep pool. It's an unforgettable day.

We love celebrating holidays here and learning new traditions. Christmas starts on December 16 each year with "Las Posadas" (The Inns). For ten days, families walk around their neighborhoods, knocking on doors and asking, "Is there any room at the inn?" They are usually given a small gift or candy, but they may also be invited in for a party. The Christmas meal is eaten at midnight on Christmas Eve and often includes pozole (soup with shredded meat and hominy) and ponche (a warm spiced punch made with fruit). There are large piñatas with candy and toys for the children and others for the adults that include cigarettes. Some people give gifts on Christmas morning, while others wait until January 6, King's Day, which honors the wise men who brought gifts to Jesus as a small child. Sara and Victor introduced us to these festivities last year during our first Christmas here, but they have moved, so this year we celebrate with team members and neighbors instead.

Our growing team of twenty-three adults and seventeen children meets weekly, as most of us live in or around Cuernavaca. We are from ten different countries, which can make team meetings interesting as we deal with group decisions about issues like finances, insurance, schooling options, and whether we should expand into other cities or not. Being from so many different cultures, there's a wide range of opinions, and it takes patience and humility to find a consensus and move forward. That has to be the work of the Holy Spirit. Whatever else we each bring to the situation, we all have the same Spirit of God who unites us as we seek His plans. Even with the challenges, we are a happy team. We often have potlucks and game nights together and share birthday, Thanksgiving, and Christmas celebrations.

Mikeah arranges activities for the children to do during the weekly team meetings and organizes a mime group for performances at church and with short-term teams. All three of our children serve in the worship band for our church and are involved in Sunday school and youth group events. They all learn to perform puppet shows and make balloon animals in order to help with VBS and street evangelism programs.

Chris and I help organize and care for visiting short-term teams who come to work with churches in our area. I plan which church they will work with, the ministry schedule, accommodations, meals, transportation, and a day-off activity, and Chris supervises each team. They come to do a variety of ministries, including children's events, building projects, medical clinics, and street evangelism. Each outreach gives a local church an opportunity to learn new skills and to reach out to people in their community they may not otherwise meet. Many people here are nervous about protestant churches. When they see caring people meeting needs in their town, it helps to open doors of communication and possibilities for future ministry. The visiting team members also learn about God's love across cultures as they face all kinds of challenges and realize they can make a difference for God's kingdom, both here and at home.

These visitors are not the only ones God is teaching. As I'm walking down the road with the kids one day, a woman suddenly calls out to us in English. She had heard us speaking and was excited to meet other Americans besides herself living in Cuernavaca. She invites us in for a visit, and we enjoy the novelty of meeting someone new here who speaks our native language. When we leave, she sends us home with Calvin and Hobbes books for the kids to borrow and magazines for me to look at. At first, I enjoy looking through them, but I soon find myself wishing that I had the American homes and yards that I see in the photos. I can feel the discontent growing, and I don't like that it's pulling me away from the joys of service here. I give the magazines back and feel much happier once they're gone.

Not all the lessons are that easy. After our whole family spends a long day helping out at a medical clinic put on by a team of visiting medical students, we return home to find that our house is one of several in our neighborhood that has been broken into. Our computer and a guitar have been stolen. It's a huge loss, and the feeling of violation and vulnerability is awful. We ask our landlord to add bars to all the doors and windows, which he is happy to do. A month later, someone breaks into our van, which is parked on a street downtown while we're visiting a local church. The thief steals Chris's tools and Erin's Bible that he probably mistook for a purse, as it had a cloth cover. These items are added to the list of things that we will need to replace when we're on furlough next month.

When one of my friends on our team asks me if I experienced abuse as a child, I tell her I did. She asks if I will speak to a group of women she is counseling who have all been abused, but I'm not sure I'm ready for that. When I mention it to Chris, he asks what abuse I'm talking about. I re-explain my childhood experiences, and he says, "Oh that. That was nothing!" His dismissal of the pain I went through and still carry is so hurtful I just stand there in disbelief, unable to even comment. *Lord, I need help with this hurt and anger. I don't know what to say or do to help Chris understand how deeply what he says and does affects me.*

Family vacation
at Ixtapa,
December 1998.

Chris baptizes Teresa in our
community pool, 2001.

Chris fishing for tuna near Ixtapa, 1998.   Our little house in Cuernavaca, 1998–2001.

Erin, Mikeah, Eunice, and Joseph with the dolphins, 1999.

Grandma Eunice visits, 1999.

Family photo, Chris and Celeste, Erin (seven), Mikeah (twelve), and Joseph (nine), November 1998.

chapter thirty-two

The End of Life as We Know It

In March of 1999, two and a half years after leaving Oregon, we embark on a three-month furlough through Texas, California, Oregon, and Washington. We travel eleven thousand miles, stay in thirty-three different places, present a video about our lives in Mexico more than thirty times, and speak in many churches and small groups. It is an opportunity to explain the work in Mexico to current and new supporters, and we are so happy to see friends and family. We enjoy many wonderful meals and birthday celebrations. Our kind hosts provide comfortable beds and take us on adventures to local farms, mountain snow, museums, and even Disneyland. They shower us with gifts, including lots of Beanie Babies for the kids.

As we head south again in June, we visit family in LA, see the glorious Grand Canyon, and stop at RGBI for the night. The days in the van are long, with ten or more hours of driving. Every evening, we make sure the hotel we stay in has a pool so our tired children can relax and play. We get back to Cuernavaca in time to work with several more short-term teams over the summer and to start preparing for the dreaded Y2K. We've been warned that the world may end if computer systems cannot switch to the year 2000. Predictions range from a minor inconvenience to a major world crisis. There is particular concern in less developed countries like Mexico, where the power and water supply systems are not very advanced. The government here decides to close all offices, banks, schools, and businesses before midnight on December 31. Everyone has stocked up on food, water, and gas, anticipating months of shortages and closures.

On New Year's Eve, we each hold our breath and pray. Midnight rolls around. There is no loud bang, no sirens, no screams—nothing happens. Our computer seems to be working fine. We watch the news and talk to friends. Although there have been a few minor problems with local businesses, the major crisis that some anticipated hasn't happened, and life has gone on as normal. *Thank You, Lord.* Now to get rid of the huge sacks of rice and beans we bought. Thankfully, we're able to bless the poor in our community by donating the extra food to them.

Several times a year, Chris travels with "Amigos Sin Fronteras" (Friends Without Borders) to remote villages in places like the mountains of Oaxaca. These trips are long and grueling. Sometimes, team members have to stand for hours on the back of a pickup as they travel for days on dangerous mountain roads. Many of the places they manage to reach haven't seen medical help in years, if at all. They sleep on concrete floors and eat whatever the villagers provide.

People hear about these clinics through hand-carried brochures that are distributed in their remote villages, and they walk for days along mountain trails to come. Once they arrive, they spend hours waiting in line to see a doctor or dentist. During that time, Chris shares Bible stories with them, as well as his personal experiences with God. He makes balloon animals for the children and plays games with the teens. He also helps with handing out food and clothes that the team has brought for those in need. The Mexican doctors and dentists treat patients, provide medications, and do minor surgeries in very simple but professional conditions. All the work is done with interpreters present, as most of the villagers speak only indigenous languages like Nahuatl instead of Spanish. It has taken years of repeated outreach to gain the trust of these reclusive villagers, but now the teams are welcomed whenever they can set up a medical clinic in the area.

Meanwhile, I'm busy with homeschooling and the responsibilities of family life, church ministries, and team tasks. I attend a women's Bible study at our church and enjoy the fellowship with the ladies there. I also help out with AWANA each week and various potluck meals that we have. Besides the planning for short-term teams, I'm also responsible for setting up some of our yearly team conferences and for writing our personal newsletter as well as one for the team. I love what we are doing here, but I'm exhausted. When I talk to Chris about helping me more, he reminds me that he came here to reach the lost. I thought we had dealt with this during the counseling we had four years ago, but I find myself stuck in the same dilemma of balancing our family needs against the eternal needs of lost souls. I still struggle to stand up for myself, maybe because part of me thinks he might be right and I'm just not handling this well enough. The combination of exhaustion, anger, loneliness, and guilt breeds a deep resentment in me. This leads to me being very critical of Chris in front of others. Some well-meaning friends try to help by challenging me to be kinder to my poor husband. It's obvious to them that what I'm doing is detrimental to my marriage and family, and while they are right, they don't understand what is causing it, and I can't seem to vocalize my side of the story to them. Their good intentions only leave me feeling like more of a failure. I stay quiet, and the cycle continues. *Lord, please give me answers and patience and the strength to keep going. Help me to find a way to voice my needs.*

———————

As 2001 begins, the team leadership finally addresses the obvious marriage issues we are having and suggests that we return to our headquarters for counseling. Chris also has some medical issues that need to be addressed, so we plan a three-month trip to Philadelphia.

Our goals are to get some rest, work on our marriage problems, have Chris seen by a doctor, and hear from the Lord about our next step. With Mikeah in high school now, we are considering returning to the U.S. so the children have time to adjust to life there before going off to college. It's a hard decision, as we also see the needs in Mexico and would miss being part of such important work. We drive north in early March 2001 and settle into an apartment at the headquarters. We all get medical and dental checkups, and Chris has an outpatient surgery to correct an umbilical hernia.

We meet weekly with Tom, the mission's counselor. We explain our issues and go over our upbringings. We do reading assignments on specific problems, like anger, and he leads us through one-on-one healing prayer sessions that help uncover the lies we believe about ourselves, allowing God to heal those deep wounds. I find comfort in Isaiah 53:5 that tells us that Jesus died not just for the sins we have committed but also for the sins committed against us so that we can receive healing and extend forgiveness to others. We feel strengthened and encouraged as we each find new freedom and hope for our marriage. *Thank You, Lord. You truly are the God who sees us.*

As part of our counseling, we ask for help to make the decision about the next step for our family. Chris wants to work on a master's degree in counseling, and Tom agrees that giving the children time in the U.S. before they go off to college is a good idea. So in early September, we begin the journey back to Mexico, unsure how long it will take to wrap things up there and head back to Oregon. We love working with the team in Cuernavaca and have made so many precious friends in our church and on the team. But I know I can't continue carrying the load of our family without help. Chris is not happy about leaving. He likes the missionary life, but he agrees to put that on hold for the children's needs. I appreciate his willingness to finally put family first and to go to Western Seminary to study counseling. I'm not sure what's next, but I'm trusting God and so glad we had this time to get wise counsel.

Early on the morning of September 11, 2001, we are standing in a small office on the Mexican side of the border, waiting to get a permit for our trailer as we head back to Cuernavaca. There's a small black and white TV behind the officers doing the paperwork and a long line of travelers, eager to get on the road.

"Is that real or a movie?" one man asks as we all watch a plane crash into a skyscraper.

"It's real," another man replies. "That's footage of a plane that crashed into one of the Twin Towers in New York City about an hour ago."

"Deliberately? Or was it an accident?" I ask him.

"Well, they weren't sure at first, but then a second plane crashed into the other tower about fifteen minutes later, so now they know it was deliberate. There's something about the Pentagon being hit as well," he explains.

We all stand there in disbelief as the coverage moves to a live shot of both of the Twin Towers engulfed in smoke. Who could do such a thing? What's next? A cry of shock goes around the room as we witness the horrifying collapse of the south tower. *Can this really be happening? Lord, what is going on?*

We finally get the papers we need and are on our way. We are one of the last cars to cross the border before it closes. We spend two days driving south through Mexico with no real news about what is happening. Once back in Cuernavaca, the "9/11 attack" is all anyone is talking about. Government buildings, tourist destinations, schools, and banks are closed here, as Mexico wonders if they are next. We talk and cry and pray with friends, choosing to trust God but wondering what else will happen.

I feel as if the world has suddenly changed and there's no going back to "normal." We have lost our innocence and our sense of security. My heart breaks for our children, who are facing a different world than what we grew up in. It takes time to find out who instigated the deadliest terrorist attack in U.S. history and for the leaders of the nations to determine how the world is going to respond. It's hard to get news down here, and we wonder what life will be like back in the U.S.

We decide to leave Mexico before the end of the year. We are busy packing, selling, and giving away belongings as we pass the baton for various ministries at church and on the team. We're happy to see that our home group and the men's group have each done well while we were gone and to know they will be in capable hands after we leave. We have a wonderful team conference at the end of October and are excited to see plans moving ahead for the purchase of a camp property. God is good. We will miss these people *so* much, but we are grateful for all God has done in us and through us here. I'm sure He will use what we have learned in some future plan He has for each of us.

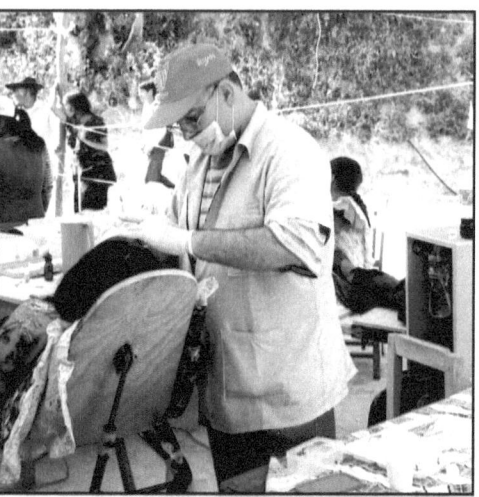

Joel and Chris spending eight hours tied onto the back of a truck on their way to Oaxaca with Amigos Sin Fronteras, 1998.

Antonio Moreno, who helped to form Amigos Sin Fronteras, with a dental patient in Oaxaca, 1998.

Mexico team conference, 2000.

Chris and a friend playing chess during a church potluck, 2001.

Our children serving on the worship team at our church, Rey de Reyes.
Omar, Joseph, Erin, Madai, Pastor Louis, and Mikeah, 2001.

Visiting family in L.A. on the way home.

Amanda, Kathy, Jennifer, and Tom.

Baby Dylan, one month old.

Paul, Tom, and Chris.

Grandpa Jack.

Cousins! Back row: Jennifer, Mikeah, Jeremiah, Amanda, and Joseph.
Middle row: Gregory, Don, Aaron, and Jessica. Front row: Erin and Jordan.

chapter thirty-three

I Will Make All Things New

"I met a girl at Sunday school today who is from Alaska," Erin tells me as she comes in the door.

"Oh really? I met a lady who's from Alaska at my Bible study group yesterday. They must be related."

Indeed, they are, and soon the members of the Smith family are our best friends here in Oregon. Gerry and Janel moved down here from Alaska in August with their two children, Kathleen and Jackson. Gerry is going to Western Seminary, where Chris is starting classes, and he also works at the church we joined soon after getting here. They homeschool their children and are adjusting to life in Oregon like we are. We quickly develop a tradition of getting together with them on Thursday evenings to have dinner and watch *Survivor*.

We buy a house in Gresham with the inheritance money that Mum gave us as a down payment. Chris is back working for Fred Meyer and is finding opportunities for outreach ministry. We miss our Mexico team and friends but are grateful to be able to represent our mission at a few West Coast missions conferences and to welcome several traveling missionaries into our home.

In June, we are all excited to celebrate with Teesha as she graduates from the University of Washington with a PhD in Anthropology. Teesha is now living on Vashon Island, and Mum organizes a weekend stay at a bed and breakfast there for all the family, including the New

Zealand crew. Jamie and Jane fly over with their two daughters, Sam and Sarah, but Trudy tells us she's too afraid to fly. I'm sad she can't come, but we have a great time honoring Teesha's accomplishment and enjoying time together as a family.

———

I was so exhausted when we returned to Oregon from Mexico that I resolved not to be involved in any ministry for a year. However, within a few months, I was asked to lead the small Bible study I had been attending at our new church, and I happily did so. By the beginning of 2003, I'm feeling better, so when I'm asked to lead the "Care for the Lost" branch of our women's ministry, I agree. I enjoy leading teams that organize outreach events, including a summer fiesta and a women's tea that allow us to minister to people in our community. I also take classes at Western Seminary that are part of the "Pastoral Care to Women" program. To be honest, in the past I have rarely attended women's events, as they often struck me as being lightweight and silly. I'm beginning to see that differently as I learn more about the needs of women and how we can help them grow in their relationships with God. I'm also feeling more comfortable in personal relationships and learning how to speak out more. *Thank You, Lord, for this new beginning and all that I'm learning through these classes and the example of the women at our church. I have much to learn.*

———

Waking up with sandpaper in my throat and every muscle refusing to move was not in my plan for today. I'm in the middle of doing jury duty in between homeschooling, running our household, and keeping up with ministry. I don't have time to be sick. A week later, it's worse, and I'm so tired I can hardly keep moving through each day. I reluctantly visit our doctor. I have been home only a couple of hours when they call with the results of the blood tests. I have mononucleosis!

"Take it easy for a couple of weeks, and you'll be fine," the nurse tells me.

Three weeks later, I'm sitting in an examination room again, still not "fine." The virus has spread to my thyroid, causing all kinds of nasty complications. Several months of medications and visits to specialists don't really yield much, but I slowly recover enough to limp along. Our church family supportively provides wonderful meals and help when needed, but I'm really sick and tired of feeling sick and tired.

Mikeah finishes her senior year of the high school curriculum we've been using, passes the SATs, and makes plans to attend George Fox University to study elementary education in the fall. Joseph and Erin are asking about attending a local high school instead of homeschooling. As I'm dealing with this long-standing exhaustion, it seems like a good idea in order to simplify my life as well as to provide the opportunity for them to adjust to classroom life before college. By the end of the summer, Joseph is registered as a sophomore and Erin as a freshman at Gresham High School. It's very strange not to be homeschooling after doing it for fourteen years. *Lord, please bless my children on these new adventures and show me what You have next for me.*

Mum turns seventy this year, so Teesha and I fly her up from California and arrange a whole week of pampering and fun. We visit Mikeah at George Fox on our way to the coast, then continue on to Lincoln City, where we stay at a beach house, fly kites, visit antique shops, watch glass blowing, and relax. Back in Gresham, there's a trip to the spa, afternoon tea with Janel and her mother, and a nighttime riverboat cruise, where Mum even gets to skipper the boat for a while. She is talking about moving up here sometime soon to be nearer to all of us as she ages. I think that's a good idea.

Mum traveled back to New Zealand a few years ago and reestablished relationships with Jamie and Trudy. She also confirmed what she had suspected for a long time, that her "sister" Daphne was actually her mother. There are still many unanswered questions about how Daphne got pregnant at fourteen years old and who Mum's father is, but she has written her story down and seems to have found some peace with her difficult past. I continue to pray for her to truly know God and be healed of all those past hurts. I'd love to be able to read the Bible with her and watch her face light up as she discovers some new truth about His love for us.

2005 is a busy year, as I work part-time as an office assistant for my friend Lynne, teach a women's Bible study, organize events for women's ministry, and take care of Mum, who moved up here last October. She is staying with us until she can move into an apartment of her own at an independent living community near us. She takes care of a lady in her nineties on the other side of Portland, so she stays there overnight during the week and commutes back here on the weekends. She seems happy to be living here, but she doesn't like the bleakness of the winters without leaves on the trees.

Chris continues to work at Fred Meyer in the jewelry department and is constantly frustrated by the emphasis the world puts on money above all else. He has taken some interesting classes this year but took this fall semester off so we can work on our marriage issues again. One evening, we finally come to the point of wanting to give up. Tired, angry, and unhappy, we ask each other why we are staying together. There's no fun, no joy in our relationship. We're like roommates, going through the motions but not even friends. We sleep in separate rooms that night, contemplating our lack of a good answer. In the small hours of the morning, he comes to me to say he doesn't want a divorce, and I know I don't want one either. I am grateful beyond words that he wants to keep trying. We begin working through a marriage CD series and have tickets for the "Weekend to Remember" marriage retreat in November. Last August, we celebrated our twentieth wedding anniversary, but we know we're a long way from happy. *Lord, thank You for Your grace, which has kept us together. Please help us to understand each other better, even though we are so different. Help us to find a connection that pulls us back together.*

The children are doing well. Mikeah successfully completes her first year in college, and Joseph is selected as a high school sophomore to do a special summer research program at Portland State University. Erin takes up photography and has one of her photos published in the high school paper. We always plan some family fun into each year, and this year, we go to see *The Lion King*, take a vacation at a friend's house on the Columbia River, go to the kite festival in Lincoln City, and spend a long weekend at the beach. Chris baptizes Mikeah's roommate, Katie, in the Sandy River, and it is such a joy to cheer her along as she follows God's plan for her life. Three missionary families come through and stay with us, and there's a whole gang here for Thanksgiving. Life is busy. Maybe too busy?

I start the new year with a plan to renew my occupational therapy license but get ambushed by another round of extreme fatigue, shortness of breath, weakness, and tachycardia. As these symptoms continue to come and go throughout the year. I cut back my schedule and my doctor sends me to one specialist after another, trying to find the cause. No one has answers, and I often feel frustrated by being "sidelined" from life, as I'm too weak to participate in activities I love to do. God meets me through times in Scripture and prayer to reassure me that He is using this to build my trust in Him and to lead me into something new. I write out this verse to keep reminding myself that God's ways are not mine: "Rejoice always, pray constantly, give thanks in all circumstances, for this is the will of God in Christ Jesus for you" (1 Thessalonians 5:16–18). Who I am is more important to Him than what I do. *Lord, You know I like to be doing, not sitting. Thank You for reassuring me that You love me even if I can't do anything. You are more concerned about my heart than how I am serving You. Help me to rest in this reassurance of Your love.*

Weeks drag into months as I visit one doctor after another, each telling me that they don't know the cause of my symptoms. As one cardiologist puts it, "Look, I don't know what is causing your heart to be racing, but I do know there is nothing wrong with your heart." Nearly two years after all this started, I find my way to a medical doctor who is also a naturopath. He determines that my vitamin D level is extremely low and asks if I've taken antibiotics in the past. Of course I have, so he starts me on a good probiotic and high doses of vitamin D, as these are essential for a strong immune system. It turns out, I have chronic fatigue syndrome, which can be triggered by having a virus like mononucleosis. We also talk about how much stress is contributing to my poor immune response. I resolve to be more aware of taking breaks and not overloading my schedule. The final piece to the puzzle is the poor sleep I get because of Chris's loud snoring and restless sleeping. We buy a split king bed, and I start using ear plugs. What a difference restorative sleep makes! Within a few months of starting all these changes, I'm back to my old self and able to rejoin life again. *Thank You, Lord, for these answers to prayer.*

Teesha graduates with a PhD in Anthropology from the University of Washington,
June 15, 2002. Back row: Jane, Jamie, Celeste, Chris, Mikeah, and Joseph.
Front row: Sam, Sarah, Teesha, Eunice, and Erin.

Eunice, Celeste, and Teesha at the beach, 2004.

Delaney/Smith clans, 2008. Back row: Gerry and Chris.
Middle row: Joseph, Celeste, and Jackson.
Front row: Janel, Kathleen, Mikeah, and Erin.

Erin (fourteen), Joseph (sixteen), and Mikeah (nineteen),
Celeste and Chris, 2007.

chapter thirty-four

Letting the Next Generation Fly

The nest is empty, though the young birds still revisit it often. Joseph graduated from high school and moved to George Fox University in 2007, and Erin did the same in 2008. We joyfully welcome their return for holidays and summer breaks, their energy and exuberance filling the house that is so often quiet now. When the children were small, I never thought about what it would be like when they weren't at home all the time, when we wouldn't all be together to celebrate every birthday, and when getting together for some time at the coast would be difficult to orchestrate. It seemed like we had so much time and that was how life would always be.

Chris and I are learning that the balance has changed as they have become adults. We are listening more and not giving as much advice. We have to ask, "How can we be praying for you?" because we don't see them every day to know what is going on in their lives. We enjoy learning from the insights they share from Scripture as God leads them into new maturity with Him, and we're figuring out how to trust God with them when we can't be right there to help. Even though each of them prayed to receive Christ as a child and got baptized when they were old enough to understand that choice, we are under no delusion that that is enough. We know they will each need to make a personal decision to follow Jesus as adults, and we pray for them daily that they will each seek His will for their own journey.

The new year begins with my finally signing up to do an online reentry course for occupational therapy to renew my license after twelve years away. By May, God leads me to the only pediatric clinic in the area that has an opening. Suddenly, I'm learning about autism, ADHD, PTSD, sensory processing, and traumatized children to be able to help them and their families learn the skills they need for daily life with these issues. It's scary and amazing and rewarding all at the same time, and I love it. Chris is still working full-time and taking one class at a time to get through his master's degree. For someone who never got higher than a C in school, this requires incredible perseverance and focus. By doing one class at a time, he's getting A's and B's in most subjects.

In the spring of 2010, there's a new bridal shop opening near us that will sell donated dresses to raise money for an organization that helps victims of sex trafficking. I'm looking for something nice to wear for our twenty-fifth anniversary celebration, and I ask Mikeah if she wants to go with me. At the grand opening two days later, we walk out of the store with a wedding dress for Mikeah and nothing for me! She doesn't even have a boyfriend, but the brand-new dress she found was too gorgeous on her to pass up for only $200. We'll trust God for the right man to come along. In the meantime, I find a simple gown at another store that makes me feel like a princess when Chris and I renew our vows in August.

One hundred friends and family gather around us to celebrate. Like our wedding, many help to make this special day happen by doing my hair and makeup, decorating the church, arranging flowers, cooking a fabulous meal, making the cake, and taking photos. All three of our children and Chris's brother James stand with us as our friend and pastor, Gerry, officiates the ceremony. *Lord, even though our marriage is not perfect, we continue to trust You to grow us together and use us in Your kingdom as we celebrate Your incredible grace in our lives.*

In lieu of gifts, our guests generously help us pay for a spectacular Alaskan cruise the following month. Our good friends Jerry and Candy join us for an unforgettable adventure. We can hardly take enough photos of the incredible sights we see as we glide along the pristine coastline, visiting Juneau, Glacier Bay, Sitka, and Ketchikan. We take a helicopter ride up to the Taku Glacier, where we walk cautiously on the ice-covered rocks and peer down into a deep crevasse. Each town has its own special charm as we visit historical parks and shop for souvenirs. We enjoy endless sumptuous meals onboard and are delighted by the decorative towel creatures that greet us in our cabin each evening as we return tired and happy.

Our children are finding their own directions. Mikeah graduated with her bachelor's degree in elementary education. After spending several months with Teach for America in Baltimore, she found a unique teaching position in the cancer ward of a pediatric hospital here in Portland, Oregon. She has always loved hospitals, and this job seems to be a perfect fit. Joseph has added an engineering degree to his schedule. He will stay an extra year in Newberg, but he will graduate with degrees in both philosophy and mechanical engineering. Erin switches from being an art major to pursuing a nursing degree, as she is planning to be a missionary in the future. *We thank You, Lord, for guiding each one of them. Please give them wisdom as they make important decisions and continue to draw them each closer to You.*

I'm just getting home from work one evening in early February when Mikeah calls. She has met someone and seems excited and nervous. I ask her to tell me about him, and she launches into a long explanation about how they met at a weekend getaway for ministry leaders from their church. Some of them went cross-country skiing, and when her foot got stuck down a hole, it was Michael who came back to rescue her.

"He's the same age as me, and he's smart and kind and funny. He loves the Lord and works as a barista while he's finishing school. He's from Vancouver, Canada, and loves the outdoors," she tells me.

When I ask if we will meet him soon, she's not sure. I can sense that she's feeling overwhelmed. This is obviously serious. The enormity of the future decision she may have to make is already weighing heavily on her heart.

I assure her that there is no rush. "I know this is exciting, but it can also be overwhelming. You don't have to do this alone. We are here to pray with you and help. We look forward to meeting him whenever you're both ready."

She thanks me, and we laugh about the fact that she already has a wedding dress if she needs it.

We all meet Michael within the next month. By the end of May, he asks Chris for permission to marry our oldest daughter. Erin helps him pick out the engagement ring (Mikeah had already told her which one she wanted), and he proposes at the beach on Mikeah's birthday in June. The wedding is planned for August 28, 2011, so there's a lot to do in the next two months. Mikeah will be gone for sixteen days in Uganda on a missions trip she committed to doing last year. Before she leaves, she takes her dress in to be altered and we add an edging to the long veil. God knew she would need this dress just a year after we bought it! *Thank You again, Lord, for meeting a need before we even knew we had one.*

Chris and I were asked earlier this year to take a team to Bolivia, and our trip is also scheduled for the short months before the wedding. After weeks filled with preparation meetings, vaccinations, fund raising, team building, and Spanish review, we're off. Four flights and twenty-three hours later, our team of ten arrives in Santa Cruz, Bolivia, where missionaries Ron and Jeanie Burgin work with Campus Crusade. They have been training Christian university students to do outreach on various campuses around the city. During the mornings, we join them as they start conversations with other students, or we offer a time to practice their English with us. By the end of our trip, the campus workers have long lists of contacts who have shown interest in knowing more about God.

In the afternoons, we help start two new satellite churches in poor rural communities. We lead Vacation Bible School activities for the children from each area, help to build a meeting structure for one of the villages, and show *The Jesus Movie* at night for the adults. It's wonderful to see God reaching people in these communities, but it's also so encouraging to see Him work in the hearts of our team members, many of whom have never been outside of the U.S. before. We are all challenged to trust Him in new ways and to be more purposeful about sharing Him in our own communities at home.

As the wedding day dawns clear and cool at 5Rock Ranch in the Yamhill countryside, friends and family pitch in to put up decorations, set out chairs, and prepare the tables for an outdoor ceremony. Gerry officiates after completing the Hood to Coast run just hours before. Michael sings the song he wrote for the proposal, and Mikeah reads the entry from her diary where she prayed for her husband two years before they met. After singing, prayer, and the recitation of the vows they wrote together, their first acts as a newly married couple are to take communion together and then to wash each other's feet in the river flowing beside us.

At the reception, hamburgers, mountains of bacon, and ice cream sundaes fill the outdoor tables. Flowers, dancing, toasts, and a wet getaway through the sprinklers make it a day to remember. *Welcome to the family, Michael. We wish you both many happy years together and a deep shared walk with Jesus.*

Through all this activity, I am feeling well. I'm working three days a week at the pediatric clinic. They are long, stressful days, but it is very rewarding to see the children making progress, and I'm grateful to be able to help many of the parents learn new skills as well. I'm also co-leading a women's Bible study each week and am responsible for organizing a couple of church events during the year. *Keeping my eyes on You, Jesus.*

Chris is currently doing an internship at the Portland Rescue Mission while still managing the jewelry department of our local Fred Meyer. I have come to realize that I must accept the things I cannot change in him. I try to be less critical and trust God with the rest. Although it's easy for me to be negative, I also know that Chris is a man who prays faithfully for his family, often at 3 a.m. His prayers have kept our family under God's love and protection for many years, and I really appreciate that. *Thank You, Lord, for a godly husband who keeps serving You as a priority.*

In April of 2012, Joseph graduates with bachelor's degrees in philosophy and mechanical engineering. He quickly gets a job with an engineering consulting firm and starts working in cost management at the new Intel facility. He buys a new car and moves into an apartment with a friend from school.

Erin spends three weeks in Kenya on a medical missions trip with some of her fellow nursing students before heading into her final year in college.

Mikeah continues to work as a hospital teacher while Michael works as a mortgage loan originator and studies for his degree in psychology. His hope is to work as a marriage and family therapist in the future.

Chris's sister Marina and I have been talking about doing a dual birthday party in Los Angeles for Chris and his mother as he turns sixty and she turns eighty. Marina outdoes herself with all the planning and arrangements for the big day in May. Our happy group of siblings, cousins, and aunties takes over one corner of a Mexican restaurant with laughter, stories, food, drinks, gifts, cakes, and elaborate picture boards. The highlight for me is getting a photo of Chris's mother, Juanita, with all six of her grown children for the first time in the twenty-seven years that I've known them. It's so rare to have everyone in one place these days. With my own children scattered, I know a mother's heart sings when she has all her babies under one roof, even if it's only for a short time.

The housing market is struggling to recover from the recent recession, but we know it's time to move. We have lived in this house for over ten years, the longest we've ever lived in one place, but we don't need such a big house for just the two of us. We would like a ranch home with a small yard as we prepare for retirement years in the future. We have an offer on our house within four months, but the house we want to buy is a short sale that takes over nine months to process. It is well worth the wait, and in March 2013, after it is painted and the new carpet is installed, we move in. It's the first home we've owned that's just for the two of us. Well, maybe.

"Ummm, Mom? How would you and Dad feel about us moving in with you for a little while to save some money before we head east?" Mikeah asks.

"I think we can do that," I reply.

A month later, Mikeah graduates with her master's in special education, and she and Michael move in. They are preparing to move to North Carolina to be part of a church plant in the Tri-City area. Three months later, the moving truck is loaded, and they are driving their car across the country to begin a new life. It's hard to see them leave, but we know they are in God's hands. *Lord, please take care of them as they travel and settle down on the other side of the country. Help them to continue to serve You and bless others.*

The day after they leave, Erin arrives back from her summer in Lodi, California, where she helped out on a friend's ranch, sat the NCLEX (the exam nursing graduates must pass to become licensed as a registered nurse), and looked for a local job. It took leaving Oregon for her to recognize how attached she was to it. She's back now and living with us while she looks for a job in the Portland area. Her graduation back in April was the last ceremony we will attend in the George Fox University gym. We proudly watched her walk to get her nursing degree and wished her years of happiness and success. Now we're praying with her that she finds the perfect nursing job nearby.

Our annual Thanksgiving revelry with the Smith family takes place in our new home. With Mikeah and Michael across the country and Kathleen in Cameroon with the Peace Corp, we're a smaller group than usual, and we miss their lively presence. But we still have lots of great food, followed by games of Bingo, Turkey Foot, and Dutch Blitz. As Erin notes, "New house, new dishes, same old friends!" *Just the way we like it.*

As I glance through my emails one evening after work, I am not expecting to see a message from Gerry Breshears, a professor at Western Seminary where Chris is studying. Gerry is also on the elder board of our church and often preaches there. He wants to know if I can fill in for the main speaker at a women's conference next weekend, as she can't make it! I've never spoken at a conference and certainly don't have four talks prepared, so I have to say no. But God puts it on my heart to be ready in the future for an opportunity like this one. After all, Peter says to "always be prepared to make a defense to any one who calls you to account for the hope that is in you."[23]

A year later, I'm in charge of planning our women's weekend retreat at the coast, and I am the emcee. Our guest speaker for the weekend is my friend Lynne, and she shares a story of her trip to Kenya to see her daughter and son-in-law who are missionaries there. At the end of their time together, they decided to go whitewater rafting. As their guide was handing out life jackets, he explained the rules.

"When you fall into the river—and it is when, not if—stay in the river. You might be tempted to swim to the side, but that's where the crocodiles live, and they will eat you!"

Lynne uses this story to illustrate our need to trust God in all situations. When we face difficulties and long battles, we just want it to end. It's tempting to try to find another way or to beg God to get us out. If we stay in the flow of what He has allowed into our life, we will find that it is not happening *to* us but *for* us. We may be facing the consequences of our own mistakes to show us not to go down that path again. We may be in a trial that will bring us to the end of ourselves so we can learn to truly trust Him and His plan. We often will not see His purpose immediately, but if we "stay in the river," we will avoid the one who waits on the edges of our lives, seeking whom

---

23   1 Peter 3:15.

he may devour. This will take patience, wisdom, and perseverance, all of which God is ready to supply through His Holy Spirit within us.

As I listen to her speak, I feel the truth of what she says resonate in my soul. There have been many times in my life when I didn't like the circumstances that surrounded me—long periods of illness and the grief over the loss of our baby come to mind. But today her words speak directly to my marriage issues, as there have been so many times I have wanted a way out. God has always convinced me to keep trying and has given me support and encouragement along the way. I have been struggling recently and praying about why Chris's anger incapacitates me. He sometimes stops talking to me for days at a time. I often don't know why he is angry, and I am too afraid to ask, as it may make him angrier. So the silence goes on as he comes and goes from the house without more than the briefest of words.

A month ago, during one such long silence, I finally got up the courage to ask.

"What's wrong? You seem to be angry. Have I done something to upset you?" I asked.

"No. What are you talking about?" he replied.

"You haven't talked to me for over a week! You've been coming and going and barely saying a word. I don't know what you're thinking or feeling," I explained.

"Oh. I'm not upset with you. I'm just so angry about how the Jews are being treated in Russia."

What! He isn't angry with me at all? He was just preoccupied and had no clue that his behavior was destroying me and our relationship.

"When you don't talk to me like that, I feel really hurt and unlovable and so sad that I don't want to live anymore," I tried to explain.

"Oh. You shouldn't feel that way. It has nothing to do with you."

This pattern has been going on for years. Even though I have tried to explain how I feel when he doesn't talk to me, he doesn't understand why his behavior affects me. I wish I could just accept that he's absentminded and not feel so hurt when he's silent. It feels soul-destroying at the deepest level to have the person I entrusted my heart to all those years ago trample it underfoot because he's preoccupied with more "important" matters.

I have recognized for years that my marriage leads me into anger and bitterness, but now I start to wonder if the cause is deeper than I previously thought. I think back to the counseling we did at our mission's headquarters. Our counselor told us that when an emotion seems way more extreme than the situation warrants, we should look for the lie we are believing. It is probably something from way back, but it is still influencing our reactions.

I take some time during a conference break to pray about the root cause of the anger I feel when Chris ignores me. And God leads me back to the all-too-familiar lie, "I'm unlovable." He gently reminds me of times in my life when He has faithfully provided for me and protected me and loved me, like the father I never had. And for the first time, I actually feel loved.

I realize I will probably be confronted with the same hurt, lies, and anger again, but at least I understand what's happening now. I'll "stay in the river" and trust God's guidance. I realize that this does not excuse Chris's behavior, but it frees me to not be so hurt by it. *Thank You, Lord, for continuing to love me and heal those wounded places, one at a time. You are a good Father.*

Mikeah graduates with a Bachelor of Science in Elementary Education, April 2008.

Our twenty-fifth wedding anniversary, August 2010.
Erin, Chris, Celeste, Joseph, and Mikeah.

Chris and Celeste at Glacier Bay
during a cruise to Alaska, 2010.

A helicopter ride to the Taku
Glacier in Juneau, 2010.

Joseph, Mikeah, and Erin at the Oregon coast, 2006.

Family gathering at James and Rhonda's home, 2011.
Back row: Jake, Nicole, Ryan, Jared, Michael, Joseph, Chris, James, and Don.
Front row: Rhonda with Braelyn, Juanita, Mikeah, Celeste, and Marina.

Mr. and Mrs. Sleigh. Married August 28, 2011.

Michael and Mikeah's wedding at 5Rock Ranch in Yamhill, Oregon, August 2011.
Celeste, Chris, Erin, Michael, Mikeah, Eunice, Joseph, and Teesha.

Erin graduates with a Bachelor of
Science in Nursing, April 2013.

Joseph graduates with bachelor's
degrees in philosophy and mechanical
engineering, April 2012.

Marina, Paul, Zanita, Chris, Juanita, Tom, and James.
Birthday celebration in Los Angeles, 2012.

chapter thirty-five

Celebrating the Milestones

In April 2014, Chris graduates from Western Seminary with his Master of Arts in Counseling degree after twelve years of extremely hard work and dedication. He retires from Fred Meyer and spends most of the year looking for a counseling job. After a short stint with DHS, he decides to take a sales job at Zales, just two minutes from our home, while he continues to look for that right counseling job. He has also started taking two friends with him to do street outreach in an impoverished area near us. He loves being able to share the gospel, hand out tracts, ask people about their stories, and share the care bags that others at church make for him to take along. He is so good at sharing what he is learning with others, and his naturally friendly demeanor draws people to him. Now that he has more space in his schedule, he begins attending a men's Bible study at church and enjoys sometimes getting to teach there.

Mum turns eighty this year, and I organize a big celebration that includes my brother, Jamie, and his wife, Jane, coming to visit from New Zealand. I had hoped that Trudy would come so we could have had all four of Mum's children together with her for the first time in forty-two years, but Trudy is still fearful of flying and won't come. We Skype with her during the visit so we can include her in the family photo.

Mum makes a final trip to New Zealand in 2015 and is happy to spend time with both Jamie and Trudy as well as their families. She goes on the annual camping trip with Neil and Audrey and has the time of her life fishing and hanging out at the beach. I'm so happy she and Audrey have remained such good friends since they met all those years ago in Te Atatu. But the long plane trip back is exhausting, and it takes her several months to recover from it. Sadly, she knows she won't ever be able to go back again.

Macular degeneration is taking more and more of her eyesight every year. I often take her to doctor's appointments to help her remember what questions she wants to ask and to help recall the answers later. We include her in all birthday and holiday celebrations, and Teesha makes the three-hour drive down here from Seattle to go on adventures with us too. Mum is less mobile and not always steady on her feet. She begins to have difficulty with meal preparation and can't keep up with her garden. I suggest she move in with us, but she refuses. She doesn't want to be a burden on any of her children. I remember the difficult years when her mother was so demanding of help, and I understand why she doesn't want to be remembered that way.

She decides to move into an independent care facility where meals are provided. There, she makes a beautiful garden on her balcony and keeps busy despite her deteriorating eyesight. A year and a half later, she is having difficulty keeping up with her medications and has had a couple of falls. It is time to move into assisted living, so we find her a nice place near our home. She enjoys the comfort and help there and makes new friends. Always the one to have ideas on how to improve any place she lives, she works with the staff to start a writing club and enjoys writing poems that are published in the monthly newsletter. She makes suggestions for outings, social groups, and exercise-group activities and attends them all. On her birthday weekend each year, we travel up to Vashon Island to visit with Teesha and enjoy the peace and beauty of her sweet cabin on the water.

"Miss Celeste, are you tired?" one of my patients asks during our time together.

"Yes, I guess I am, Miguel."[24]

It seems like a simple and common interaction, but this moment is huge for this child who was nonverbal when I first started seeing him a few years ago. Not only has he noticed my yawn and interpreted it correctly, but he has also asked an appropriate question! For a child on the autism spectrum, this is an amazing step and one we celebrate when I return him to his father later that afternoon.

I am learning so much while working with these incredible children. I attend workshops to learn the information and skills needed for this job, and other therapists are also a constant source of ideas and help. The children with autism fascinate me the most, maybe because I'm not great with social skills either and understand their loneliness. They so desperately want to have friends and feel included, but they are often living on the edges of social interactions, not knowing how to get into the action. Teaching them social skills is so important, as depression, mental illness, and suicide rates are high in this lonely group. Having a friend or a spouse can be the difference between life and death.

As I learn about sensory processing issues, I begin to understand my own sensitivities to loud noises; crowded, busy places; and certain smells. Several children come in with dyslexia, and since I have been studying this disorder, I'm often the therapist they are sent to. And somewhere along the way it finally dawns on me—I have dyslexia. The backwards writing as a child and the difficulty I always had with reading aloud in class suddenly makes sense. It wasn't recognized as a learning disability when I was a child. Now, the problem I never wanted to talk about is the very thing God is using to help me reach these frustrated and often discouraged children. Lena is eight years old and struggling to learn to read. She's a very bright, energetic girl who is creative and funny, but reading just isn't coming easy for her.

---

24 Names of children have been changed to protect their privacy.

At first, she's embarrassed when I ask her about it, but when I talk about having the same problem and overcoming it and that I can help her do the same, she begins to cry. Her concerned mother asks what she is feeling. "Happy," she replies with a brief smile, and soon we're all crying. In that moment, God heals a deep part in me that has always felt like an awkward failure. I would never see Lena as "less than" because of this issue that is not her fault, so why have I let it make me feel that way all these years? Through God's grace, both of us find encouragement and a new freedom.

The summer of 2015 finds Chris on a plane, heading to the Philippines with a short-term team from our church. They have a great time on the Island of Negros, working with several churches and seeing 1,140 people come to the Lord as they present the gospel in local schools, churches, and homes. The follow-up with these new kingdom members begins before the team leaves, with a huge celebration dinner and a church service that fills the community with joyful singing. The team comes home with an abundance of exciting stories and plans to return next year.

At the same time, I'm flying east to North Carolina, where our first granddaughter, Naomi Hope, arrives July 12. I soak up ten days of sweet baby snuggles while I help the nervous, sleep-deprived new parents, Mikeah and Michael, adjust. It just isn't enough, and we're soon crying at the airport as we reassure each other that we still have Skype to keep in touch. Children are a blessing from the Lord, but grandchildren are a double blessing. *Lord, please bless little Naomi with strength and joy all the days of her life. May she come to know You at a young age, and may all her ways be pleasant and filled with hope as her name suggests.*

Erin has been attending a college group at church for over a year when an attractive man shows up one night. Unfortunately, he's very reserved, and it only takes a quick glance toward his left hand to see that he's married.

"There's no good-looking single men in this group," she laments to her friend. "Trent is attractive, but he's married."

It isn't until later that an offhand remark reveals that he is, in fact, single. Apparently, he just doesn't know which hand to wear a purity ring on. Not one to wait around, Erin makes a plan that night. Oleg, a friend and a leader in the group, jumps on board and happily agrees to be the go-between. He and his wife, Crystal, invite Trent and Erin over for dinner to give them a low-pressure first date.

When we meet him, we discover that Chris knows his dad from working at Fred Meyer together years ago. It isn't long before Chris and I have another awkward meal with a nervous young man. We gladly give him our blessing to marry our sweet Erin. On July 2, 2016, she marries Trent Jennings in a sunny outdoor ceremony at a beautiful church near our home. One-year-old Naomi is the flower girl, and Oleg officiates the wedding. Friends provide desserts for the indoor reception, and everyone enjoys eating, dancing, and laughing together. Romantic photos at the coast are taken a few weeks later, and years of happily ever after begin. They move into an apartment not far away. Trent begins a new career in banking, and Erin continues working as an educational assistant with photography on the side. Welcome to the family, Trent! *Lord, please grant them both much joy and laughter as they grow together, serve as one, and live out Your love in a world that needs it so much.*

———

While romance blossoms for the next generation, Chris and I take a much-anticipated trip to Israel with a group from our church. As the plane lands in Tel Aviv, and we see the first lights of the city in the nighttime darkness, I cry. *Jesus, I'm so excited to be visiting the place You called home while You were here on earth, to see some of the places You saw so long ago, and to walk in this Promised Land. Thank You for this amazing opportunity.*

We visit locations we've read about for years, and we walk where Jesus walked. We step into history at archaeological digs, peer into several empty tombs, and stand on the Mount of Olives, where Jesus will one day stand when He returns—unforgettable! My favorite place is the Sea of Galilee, because even though it is several feet lower than it was two thousand years ago, it is still very much the same. I can imagine the Son of God looking at these same hills, watching the sun rise and set, heading out on the same water in a wooden boat, and calming one of the storms that develop so quickly here. In the old city of Jerusalem, Chris starts up a conversation with two rabbis, and as I listen, it's as if the ancient and modern meet. It's sad to see that there are still people here who talk about God and even serve Him but don't know Him personally. *Lord, we pray for the peace of Israel. Protect Your children who live here. Bring truth to hearts that don't know and open eyes that haven't seen who You are.*

Although we have lost many relatives and friends over our years together, losing Auntie Alice in 2016 and Uncle Solomon a year later brings the heaviest and saddest of farewells for us so far. It's hard to describe the blessings these two poured out on Chris as second parents to him throughout his childhood. They led him to a relationship with God and taught him the Scriptures. Later, they welcomed me and all our children into their family, supported us on the mission field, and always opened their home to us when we were in Los Angeles. It's hard to believe that "Sugar" and "Super" don't still live in that little east Los Angeles home. It feels like they must still be there, Solomon busy barbecuing lemon chicken while the rest of the family gathers under the shady porch, telling stories and laughing together. We will miss them *so* much. Heaven just got more wonderful to us, knowing they are there and we will be with them again someday. *Lord, help us to make the most of every day. We really don't know how long we have or if we'll get another opportunity to share You with others. Thank You for these two amazing people who loved well and left a legacy of serving You every day.*

In the fall of 2016, Mum asks me what I would like for my sixtieth birthday, and I suggest skydiving. She's a little hesitant but agrees. Late one Saturday afternoon in October, I meet the young man I will jump with as we don harnesses and talk strategies. We get some photos with the family members who have come to support me, walk across the tarmac, and climb aboard the Cessna with three other tandem teams and four individual flyers.

It's a clear, sunny afternoon, and the view from thirteen thousand feet is amazing! We're the second ones out of the plane. Freefalling at a hundred and twenty miles an hour is noisy and not very comfortable, but looking around at the 360-degree view takes my mind off that. After a minute, John pulls the parachute cord, we jolt upright, and we're quietly suspended above the earth. As we slowly float down, we can see the Pacific Ocean to our left, Mt. Rainier up ahead, and the Cascades with Mt. Hood to our right. It is indescribably beautiful—I could stay up here all day! We take photos and talk about the joy of sharing this view with the circling birds far below us. I don't feel nervous or hesitant. I've always loved heights. After about six minutes, we approach the airport and make a perfect landing. Wow! This was definitely the best birthday present ever. I'd love to do it again anytime.

Chris graduates from Western Seminary
with a master's degree in counseling,
April 2014.

Eunice and Celeste at Rockaway Beach, 2014.

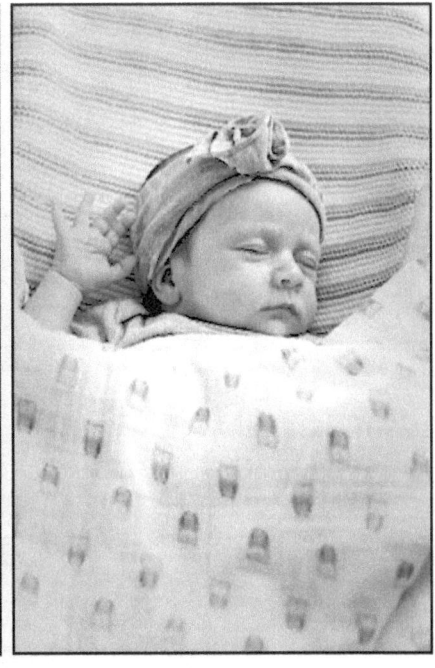

Eunice and the fish she caught while visiting
with Audrey in New Zealand, 2015.

Naomi Hope Sleigh.
Born July 12, 2015.

Erin took this beautiful photo of Celeste, Eunice, and Teesha in 2015.

Solomon and Alice Orona, June 2015.

Trent and Erin's wedding at Harvest Church in Troutdale, Oregon, 2016.
Chris, Celeste, Erin, Trent, Joseph, Mikeah, Naomi, and Michael.

Mr. and Mrs. Jennings.
Married July 2, 2016.

Chris and Celeste looking
at Jerusalem from the
Mount of Olives during
a tour of Israel, 2016.

A boat trip on the
Sea of Galilee.

Celeste tandem skydiving, 2016.

Celeste C. Delaney, 2018.

chapter thirty-six

Numbering Our Days

Each day, we all walk that fine line between here and eternity. We watch a new baby start their journey as we see others move on to the next life. In between these bookends of life, we get to help others through their struggles and offer the gift of knowing why we're all here. Moses contemplated how short life is at the end of his forty years of long desert wanderings and prayed, "Teach us to number our days."[25]

In the summer of 2017, Chris and I head in opposite directions on separate short-term teams. He is in Lebanon, working with Syrian refugees who are housed in makeshift shelters on the outskirts of Beirut. There are more than a million displaced people, and many of them share stories of losing loved ones in the long war that is destroying their country and so many lives. They talk about daily facing the reality that this could be the moment they die for their faith—nothing is certain or stable or comfortable. Their courage inspires the visiting team as they work in medical clinics, children's programs, and supply distribution. The generosity of the Christians in Lebanon is astounding considering the fact that they are helping the very people who were occupying and harshly ruling their country not long ago.

---

25   Psalm 90:12 (NIV).

Meanwhile, I'm in eastern Oregon. Washington Family Ranch is owned by Young Life and is nestled in the hills near the town of Antelope. The property is best known for being the former home of Rajneeshpuram, a cult commune in the 1980s. Today, it is a well-run Christian camp where events are held year-round. I'm here with a team of women from our church to take care of energetic toddlers so their teenage mothers can have a week of fun, discipleship, and affirmation. Many of these young women make decisions to receive the Lord and raise their children to know God. We're all exhausted by the time we make the two-hour trip back home, but our hearts are full as we talk about a job well done.

———————

On the front end of life, we have two additions to our family in 2018. Edward Joshua Sleigh joins Michael, Mikeah, and Naomi in North Carolina on February 17, and I get to spend a month with them as they adjust to family life with two children. As the first boy born into his father's line, this smiley baby is named "Edward" by tradition, like his father and grandfather before him, but he will be known as Joshua, which means "deliverer." *Lord, thank You. We are blessed by this sweet new baby, and we pray he will know You and serve You all the days of his life. May he be used by You to help deliver many people from their sins and into eternal life with You.*

And joy of joys, Trent and Erin welcome their first baby, Eleanor (Nora) Adeline Jennings, into the world on December 1. She's such a loveable, wee bundle, whose name means "light of God." I'm glad they live close so Erin can hang out once a week while we try new recipes and marvel at Nora's every move. *Lord, our hearts are full as we welcome another granddaughter into our family. Please bless her with a heart for You, and make her a light that shines brightly so that many will see Your truth and love everywhere she goes.*

———————

It has turned out to be quite a year for me too. In March, the children's book I have been working on for several years finally becomes a reality. I wrote *ABC Ready for School* to help children learn social skills and prepare for kindergarten. I daily see many children at work who are not ready for this big transition, so I initially wrote a checklist for their parents, which eventually became this book. It's exciting to see families enjoying it and children gaining the skills they will need to be confident learners.

I also have two speaking opportunities. The first is at the Oregon Occupational Therapy Association's annual conference, where I do a workshop on "Teaching Social Skills to Children." In October, I attend a women's conference and have fun leading a breakout group about "Living a Life Worth Remembering."

How did God take such a shy, awkward child and train her to speak in front of large groups of people? I don't really know—slowly and gently, as He always does. He delights in using even unlikely people from difficult backgrounds because then the glory is all His. At the same time, I'm reminded of something Charles Spurgeon said: "Like the moon, we borrow our light."[26] The moon is just a chunk of rock; it has no light at all. We see it in the night sky because it reflects the light from our sun. We are the same. Without God, we are "darkness itself," Spurgeon says. Everything we have is from Him. There is no place for pride in anything we have done or any work of grace He has done in us. We are simply reflecting His light so the world can see His glory. This is His kingdom, won by His power, for His glory.

As 2019 begins, we know we are walking into the valley of the shadow of death with Chris's sister Zanita, who has been fighting

---

26 Charles L. Spurgeon, "Evening, June 29," *Morning and Evening Daily Devotions with Charles Spurgeon (Annotated)*, https://www.ccel.org/ccel/spurgeon/morneve.d0629pm.html.

pancreatic cancer for several years. He visits her in California in February and can tell it won't be long. Always the life of the party—funny, sweet, brave, and outgoing—she is profoundly missed by the whole family when she leaves for heaven in March. The memorial service for her highlights her love for the beach, and many family members share funny stories and precious memories of this deeply loved sister, daughter, mother, and friend.

Jeff and JoAnne Bantz are the couple who introduced us thirty-four years ago on that stormy night in January, and we have remained friends with them over the years. We visited them last October, having no idea it would be our last chance to be with Jeff on this side of eternity. He had been fighting bladder cancer for three years and thought he had beaten it, but it returned, and this time he lost the fight. He leaves his grieving wife, two sons, daughters-in-law, and grandchildren in March. He gave them a meaningful legacy and a strong foundation of faith to live by.

When Chris moved up to Portland in 1978 with his best friend Keith, they rented an apartment in a duplex and met their neighbor Martha, who was a single mom. They became good friends as they shared meals and life in close proximity. Eventually, Chris led her to the Lord, and a year later, Keith married her. They have been more like family than friends to us over the years, and we were grieved to find out last year that she was battling uterine cancer. Our last visit with them is on August 28, and she is in the arms of Jesus by September 4. She exemplified a servant's heart, always making sure everyone around her was doing well. More than anything, she was always eager to see others come to know the Savior she loved. We are so glad her suffering is over, but our hearts will take time to mend.

Lord, this has been a year of hard goodbyes. Please take care of these loved ones who we will always miss. We grieve as those who have hope, knowing You are the resurrection and the life.

Mum has been having a lot of muscle aches, stomach problems, and fatigue for quite a while, but she is eighty-four, so she always says it is just "old age" and carries on. She's enjoying life in the new assisted living place near me and stays actively involved there. We also take regular outings to museums and places she wants to explore.

After a checkup reveals some blood issues, her doctor insists that she see an oncologist. I go with her for the bone biopsy in March, and we return in April for the results. The doctor looks somber as he walks into the room and comes straight to the point.

"Well, the bone marrow biopsy revealed that you have acute leukemia," he says slowly.

He begins to talk about possible chemotherapy and what that would involve as we're still trying to accept this new reality.

"I don't want to do anything," Mum tells him.

"In your situation, I think that is wise. You would be spending several hours here in the clinic for five days a week if you did chemotherapy. It wouldn't be much of a life."

"If I don't do anything, how much time do I have?" Mum asks.

"I would say four to six weeks," he replies.

We sit there in shocked silence, each trying to process what he just said. *Did he say WEEKS?* He talks about getting hospice set up right away and assures us that dying from leukemia won't be a painful process. He's fighting tears as he leaves the room, and we move down the hallway, through the lobby, and into the hospital waiting area, still silent. As we navigate the parking garage, a fast-moving car suddenly comes around the corner, and I instinctively put my hand onto Mum's arm to stop her from stepping in front of it.

"I don't think that matters now. I'm dying anyway. It won't matter if I get hit by a car," she says with a smile in her voice.

On the drive back home, we start to discuss this news we suddenly have to accept. She talks about seeing people in heaven and mentions wanting to see Alison, who she still believes is her twin sister.

I think about her life, with so much sadness and so many unanswered questions. She lived through a painful childhood where she always felt unwanted and inadequate. She overcame rickets and was exposed to TB and polio before she was even a teenager. She survived three unhappy marriages and the constant struggle to make ends meet. But somewhere along the way, she found her voice and moved from accepting the role of a victim to taking control of her future. She challenged herself to learn new skills and get over her fear of animals and people in authority. As she wrote her life story in her sixties, she took responsibility for her mistakes and mourned her losses. She realized that no matter what life threw at her, she kept going and made the best of each situation.

It takes a while for it to really sink in. I am concerned about getting hospice in place and making arrangements for a wheelchair and a hospital bed, but my thoughts are mostly on her need for salvation. Over the years, I've shared the gospel with her and prayed she would see the truth of how much God loves her. I'd love for her to be set free from the guilt, anger, and bitterness that block the peace and forgiveness she needs. I want to know she will be waiting for me beside Jesus when I get to heaven. I ask everyone I can to be praying for her in the coming weeks.

Teesha comes down to stay with me so she can be close to Mum and help out when I have to be at work. As we talk about what's going on and our concerns, I notice her priority is to make sure Mum feels loved and happy through the days to come; she doesn't want to deal with the hospice schedule and the acquisition of needed equipment. I'm happy to do those things, but I'm aware that I'm not good at the emotional support piece. I'm so glad we have each other during this difficult time; we need our different skills to do this well.

It is a stressful six weeks as we manage Mum's care, trying to balance her quality of life with her safety and medical needs. I'm grateful I have Teesha here to act as a sounding board when I need to talk things through. She is able to work remotely, so she is often sitting beside Mum's bed with her computer on her lap when I come in from work.

Easter is Mum's last time with our family. We share a traditional lamb dinner and take some family photos—four generations together for the last time. I watch her interacting with others, especially talking to Nora, and I can't wrap my head around her not being with us much longer.

We never talk to her about how much time has passed since the diagnosis day when she was told she had four to six weeks, but Mum will often say something about it, so we know she's keeping track. We take her for walks in the wheelchair, arrange visits with many people who want to see her, and keep track of the hospice nurses, who are so caring and helpful. When we were children, Mum always listened to records of Jim Reeves singing gospel songs, so I buy her the CD of one of the records, and we enjoy listening to them all over again. Many are about going to heaven. *Lord, speak to her heart.* When the six-week mark arrives, she is sitting up in her chair, visiting with Gerry and Janel. In the evening, she decides to go to dinner, although at this point she is only drinking a little water and sometimes eating a bit of ice cream. After she returns, the hospice nurse arrives to give her a bath, so Teesha and I leave, knowing the nurse will get her into bed and settled for the night.

I head to work the next morning, and Teesha goes to the assisted living facility. Mum is still asleep when she arrives, and Teesha soon realizes she's not waking up. Suddenly, we're in the coma stage. The next day, the hospice nurse tells us the end is close, so we stay with her all day, helping to turn her and talking to her as she rests, her breathing deep and steady. I read Scripture aloud and pray for her, asking God for some sign that she knows Him. Nothing comes. We go home for a quick meal that evening and return around 9:30 p.m. to sit with her. We sing "PōKareKare Ana"[27] together for her—she always loved to hear that Māori song we learned as children. We

---

27 "Pōkarekare Ana," Wikipedia Foundation, last updated June 8, 2025, https://en.wikipedia.org/wiki/Pōkarekare_Ana.

thank her for being our mum and reassure her that we will take care of each other. We say our goodbyes and leave around 11 p.m.

The hospice nurse calls me just after midnight—she has gone. We go over to wait for the funeral home people to arrive. We say goodbye then quietly stand beside death, still not believing it. Several of the staff come to talk to us and say goodbye to her too. Through the tears, we are moved by their kindness and are grateful to hear how she has touched their lives. Numbly, we make our way back home. It doesn't seem real. *Bye, Mum. Thank you for all you taught us over the years. I really hope you met Jesus while you were in the coma and that now you are free from all the hurt and sadness that filled your life.*

Back in her room the next morning, everything looks the same, but she's not there. It's still not real, but there are tasks to keep us busy. After we visit the funeral home to make arrangements, we return to divide her remaining belongings between her children and the garage sale pile. Things that meant so much to her yesterday now have no value to her at all. It's a reminder to hold possessions lightly.

Mum attended a Unitarian church a few years ago, and she had been planning a memorial service there since her first week on hospice. She had definite ideas about what she wanted, and we try to honor as many of them as possible. A memorial board and favorite objects from her life are set in the entryway, and a beautiful violin recital leads us in as a reminder of her years playing the violin her father made for her. Caring friends give various readings and share her story. Teesha and I speak our thoughts and thanks, and a friend sings meaningful songs that Mum has picked for each of us. A potluck luncheon and fellowship time follows. Before we know it, we are making our way home, acutely aware that a whole life cannot be summed up so briefly. We are grateful for the many words of kindness from those who shared about Mum's impact on their lives. So many people cared about her.

A deep sadness surrounds me in the following weeks as I lament not really getting to say goodbye to Mum. Neither of us could say what really needed to be said, even when we had times alone together.

I wanted to hear some kind of "blessing" from her, something that said she cared about me. So many of her words to me were impatient and unkind, especially toward the end of her life. A few months later, as I'm sorting through a drawer, I find an old card from her saying how much she appreciated my kindness and how proud she was of me. She said she felt very loved and blessed when she spent time with our family. It was the blessing I needed to hear. *Thank You, Lord, for these simple words of affirmation. I'm trusting You with whether she knew You or not. Thank You for all she taught us and the many ways You blessed our lives through her.*

At the beginning of this year, before any of these losses, I had asked the Lord about what I should be doing. This year is an important anniversary for me—fifty years since I gave my life to Him in that church so far away in New Zealand. I want to do something significant to acknowledge the decision that has taken my life down such a different road than I might have gone. Joseph asked me what I would do if I could do anything to celebrate.

"I would love to go back to that church where it all started and have some time to sit there and thank Him for saving me, but I don't have the money to do that," I told him.

Three months later, we found out Mum wouldn't be with us much longer, and we talked about the plan we'd had for a long time to take her ashes to New Zealand. She told us not to bother, but then I heard her talking to a hospice nurse about being in the U.S. for over forty years. The nurse had suggested to her that this must be home now.

"Oh, no. New Zealand will always be home for me," she had replied.

And I knew then that we had to take her ashes back there. She had, after all, put money aside for this very reason.

The arrangements have been made. Teesha and I will take her home, and we will finally have all four siblings together for the first time in forty-seven years. And I will be able to visit the church I had described to Joseph in January and celebrate fifty years of walking with Jesus. God has made a way—His timing is so amazing. The sadness of this journey will be mixed with gratitude for knowing Him all this time. This is also the fifty-year anniversary of Donna and me meeting in intermediate school, so I tell her we must plan an adventure together to celebrate.

Our Boeing 777 banks slightly to the right as we make our descent toward Auckland International Airport. We've spent the last thirteen hours traveling across the ocean, cramped into a plane with four hundred fellow passengers. Teesha and I strain to see some sight of land through the window across the aisle from our middle-section seats. I'll be glad to stand up and move around when we land.

I have Mum's ashes in my carry-on bag and all the required documents to get them into the country. I wait nervously, hoping it won't be too complicated. But I needn't have worried. The uniformed customs official doesn't even ask to see any documents or the container of ashes! As my bags go through the next x-ray machine, the woman in charge yells out, "Whose blue bag is this?"

"Mine," I yell back from fifteen feet away.

"There seems to be a large box of some kind. What's in that?"

"My mother's ashes," I reply awkwardly.

A dozen shocked people turn toward me then quickly look away as the x-ray technician nods, avoids eye contact, and sends my bags through. *Welcome back to New Zealand, Mum!*

———

Two days later, Jamie, Trudy, Teesha, and I are on a small boat, speeding across the Waitemata Harbor, enjoying spectacular views of the Auckland skyline and the surrounding islands. I haven't been on this water since before Teesha and I left in 1978. I can't help thinking about Mum and Wendy as teenagers, rowing around in a bay off this harbor so many years ago. The morning is cool and cloudy, but the sun greets us as we pass by Rangitoto Island on our way to Motutapu Island, where we anchor in a picturesque little bay. Our boat captain waits while we take turns spreading Mum's ashes onto the water, followed by some flowers to mark the spot. We talk about Mum, open gifts from Trudy, take photos, and watch the current take the flowers out into the main channel. It's a bit awkward—we haven't all been together since we were children, and so many years stand between then and now. But we have marked Mum's passing, returned her to the water she loved, and honored the life she gave each one of us.

Back on dry land, we make our way to a fish and chips shop in Mission Bay, where the rest of Jamie's family waits to join us for lunch. We spend a couple of hours talking and catching up, and we take more photos of the four of us, because who knows when we'll all be together again? Jamie takes Teesha to her friend's house and then drops Trudy and me off at Trudy's home. *Thank You, Lord, for this day I will never forget. Thank You for the bridges that were mended and the celebration of Mum's life. I'm glad we came.*

Trudy makes me feel comfortable and welcome in the little house she shares with her son Jordon, his girlfriend, Zoe, and their son, Drake. I have the fun of giving her some treasures from Mum's home, and I share the details of Mum's last days. We drive around some of the places we lived as children, reminiscing and retelling family stories. I pray with her daughter Clare, who is in the hospital, and we have her younger daughter, Hayley, and her family over for a visit. On Sunday morning, Trudy and I go to the Anglican church that Trudy has been attending, and I get to meet a lot of her friends there. After dinner, we go to the evening service at the Church of

Christ in Mt. Albert, just as we did fifty years ago this month. This is what I've been waiting for.

It's like stepping back in time as we make our way from the parking lot into the sanctuary. The red cushioned pews and high wooden platform at the front are still the same. We sit on the far right side near the front row where I sat fifty years ago—a nervous twelve-year-old, praying with a stranger and finding Jesus's forgiveness and presence for the first time. We talk briefly with some of the older ladies sitting near us, and I wonder if one of them was the one I sat with right here on that day. *Lord, I can't believe I'm here. You made this happen. It means so much to me to be able to remember what You did that day fifty years ago in the very place it happened. The place seems unchanged after all these years, but I know You have made many changes in me. I am blessed beyond words to be Your daughter. Thank You.*

Trudy drops me off at Donna's home, and we say goodbye. I'm so grateful for her hospitality and for her help in making it possible to visit the church that means so much to me. The next day, Teesha and I join Jamie and his partner, Robyn, at a waterfront cafe for coffee and lamingtons. We take the scenic route home as we try to soak in all the sights and smells of this beautiful city. It is so special to have time with our brother, laughing and teasing as only family with the same ridiculous sense of humor can. We spend some time at their home, where he opens gifts from Mum before we enjoy lunch together.

That evening, deep in the bush near the Scenic Drive in Titirangi, we make our way down a very steep driveway to visit Mum's friend Audrey in the home of her daughter Sharon and son-in-law Dave. I brought my family photo album from last year to share some pictures of our lives in the U.S. with her. She tells us over and over again how much she loved our mother. She reminisces about the first time she saw Mum walking down the street in Te Atatu and thought to herself, "I need to get to know that woman." Tears fill her eyes as she says, "We were more like sisters than friends. I miss her so much." It is an emotional time, but we have a wonderful dinner and such a meaningful visit. I'm glad we brought some closure for Mum's best friend. Mum would have wanted us to come here. She couldn't bring herself to say goodbye to Audrey during their final phone call a few months ago, so I hope this makes up for that.

Back at Donna's home, we fall into the easy comradery of friends who have known each other for fifty years. After visiting with her brother one afternoon, we stop by Mum's old home on Waiatarua Road and walk down the street to the bridge and watery inlet where she spent so many happy hours rowing around with Wendy. I take pictures of the old house that she hated to leave when she was a teenager. The orchard has been replaced by another house now, but the long driveway and Meadowbank Primary School are still there, just as she described. I can imagine her as a young child, finally out of those braces, wandering up the hill, looking at all the gardens and homes along the way. I can see Ethel in the garden, Pop making Mum's braces and the violin she played for years, Gena up to her old tricks, Daphne's wedding, and little Lorraine and her dad, Leo, sick with TB here. So much of Mum's life and heart were in this special place. *Thank You for letting me see it all and for being able to bring Mum's ashes back here. This is the right place.*

The next day, Donna and I set off on our daring three-day adventure. We drive through lush, green farmland to Cambridge and visit the stables where one of her horses is in training for this season's racing. Next, we take a leisurely walk through Tolkien's enchanting village of Hobbiton, expecting to see Frodo, Pippin, Merry, and Samwise

Gamgee at any minute. We arrive in the geothermal wonderland of Rotorua by evening and settle in for the night.

Early the next morning, we step back in time as we wander the old pathways of a town buried by the eruption of Mt. Tarawera in 1886. After a light lunch, we make our way to the escapade Donna has been hoping to avoid—zip-lining! Bravely, we don the gear, sign the required waivers, and join our assigned group five stories above the old growth forest. Over the next hour, we fly along zip lines, walk across swaying bridges, hang off ledges, and learn about this tour group's goal of returning native species to the bush. Back on the ground, we recover with a soak in hot mineral pools and eat dinner in the nearby street market.

On day three, we visit bubbling mud pools and spectacular geysers at Orakei Korako on our way to Lake Taupo. We part ways for a few days as Donna heads home and I settle into a rented bungalow with five occupational therapy friends from college. We enjoy two glorious days of sharing stories, wandering around the lake, and making delicious meals together.

Thank You, Lord, for Donna and the fifty years of friendship we have enjoyed. I'm so grateful for her willingness to make this odyssey happen. And for Jill, Jenni, Sue, Alice, and Rachel, who took time away from their regular lives to hang out. Whenever we're together, we pick up right where we left off, as if no years have passed at all. How true it is that "a friend loves at all times, and a sister is born for adversity."[28] Thank You for this amazing time together and for all the new memories we will always share. You are so good to me.

―――――――――

Two days later, Donna takes me to the airport, and Jamie comes to say goodbye. Teesha has gone over to Tasmania to visit a friend, so

―――――――――

28 Based on Proverbs 17:17.

I'm on this leg of the journey alone. It's hard to leave, not knowing when, or if, I'll ever get back here. *It's all in Your hands, Lord.*

Back in the U.S., I realize our family has racked up some traveling miles this year. Besides my journey Down Under, Chris went to the Philippines again, and Joseph took his first short-term missions trip with a team going to Cuba. They shared in homes and visited three churches, getting to see what God is doing inside this country that we rarely have access to. Joseph enjoyed the happy, outgoing culture of a people who have little material wealth but so much joy in the Lord. *Thank You, Lord. You are always working in our lives and challenging us to trust You in new situations. What will 2020 have for us?*

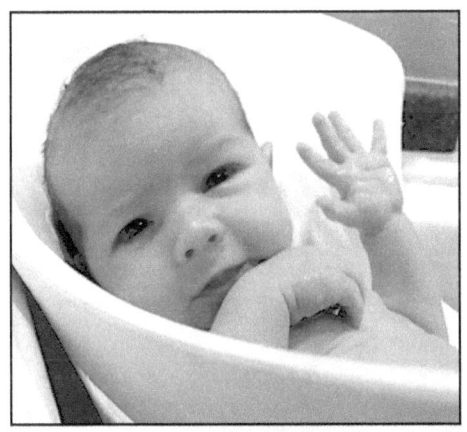

Edward Joshua Sleigh.
Born February 17, 2018.

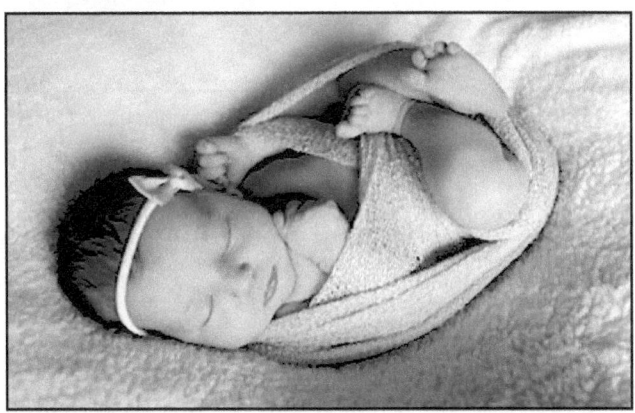

Eleanor Adeline Jennings. Born December 1, 2018.

Zanita with her daughter, Jessica, enjoying a California beach, 2018.

Chris and Celeste visiting JoAnne and Jeff, 2018.

Martha, Ryan, Keith, and Nadine, 1987.

Chris visiting a family during his trip
to the Philippines, 2019.

Chris and Celeste after
completing the Lilac Run 5K
in Gresham, Oregon, 2019.

Audrey, Eunice's best friend for
more than fifty-nine years, 2019.

Chris making balloon animals for Filipino children, 2019.

Easter together, April 2019.
Back row: Joseph, Chris, Trent, and Erin.
Front row: Celeste, Eunice with Nora, and Teesha.

Joseph standing in front
of the "B" in the CUBA
sign in Santiago.

Joseph with the team heading to Cuba, 2019.

Jamie (Jim), Celeste, Teesha, and Trudy, together again
for the first time in forty-seven years.
Waitemata Harbor in Auckland, New Zealand, 2019.

Sarah with Caleb, Sammi, Jane, Jim, Teesha, Robyn, Celeste, and Trudy.
Family gathering at the fish and chips shop in Mission Bay, 2019.

Celeste and Donna visit Hobbiton in Matamata, New Zealand, 2019.

Celeste and Donna zip-lining in
Rotorua, New Zealand, 2019.

Visiting with Trudy and family, 2019.
Back row: Jordon with Drake, Celeste,
Hayley, and Jordee with Harmony.
Front row: Zoe, Cassie, and Caleb.

chapter thirty-seven

Who Would Have Thought?

I n January, as I read the verse, "No eye has seen, nor ear heard, nor
the heart of man conceived, what God has prepared for those who
love Him,"[29] I'm thinking about the splendors of heaven that await
us. I contemplate the events God put into place last year in order
for me to visit New Zealand, and I'm wondering what I should be
planning on doing this year. I have long wanted to write my story,
and I strongly feel that God is saying it's time to start, not with mine
but with my mother's story first. I pull out the notes she wrote long
ago and start trying to piece them together into a readable account.

I'm not a narrative writer. I usually just write the facts as clearly
as possible. It is a learning process, and sometimes, I get stuck in
the sadness of my mother's story and don't want to go on. The Lord
encourages me with the reminder, *This is what I redeemed you from.
Keep writing.* With work, Bible study, and home commitments, I don't
have much time to really work on it, so it's frustratingly slow going.

When we first start hearing about some new virus in Wuhan,
China, it doesn't seem like a big deal. We go through this every few
years: bird flu, SARS, H1N1, and Zika. They come; they go. How
bad can it be? The reports say it's a type of coronavirus, like most of
the others, but Wuhan is struggling to deal with it. We lived near

---

29 1 Corinthians 2:9.

there when we were in China. We know how poor their medical system is, and we're sure we could easily deal with it if it came here.

We're busy with preparations for Chris to lead another team to the Philippines, and Joseph is planning to go to Uganda this year. Mikeah is expecting a baby in June, so I'll be over in North Carolina for at least a couple of weeks for that. We're not going to let the threat of some distant virus slow us down.

As we flip over the calendar on March 1, the news reports are getting more urgent. The first official U.S. case of what is now being called COVID-19 is a man in Washington State who had recently returned from Wuhan. Others quickly follow, and travel between China and the U.S. is closed. But now it's all over the world, and visitors are bringing it into our country. Panic begins to set in as the nation's leaders realize we are not prepared to deal with this. We don't have enough tests or hospital beds or ventilators. Italy is the first country outside of China to fall under the overwhelming tide of illness, and we all watch in horror as our news anchors assure us that we could be next.

At work, some parents become reluctant to bring their children into the clinic, as the schools are closing and authorities are urging everyone to stay at home. The governor talks about closing down the state and what that will mean. The CDC (Centers for Disease Control) warns that everyone over sixty years old should stay at home, as this disease is hitting the elderly most severely. I talk to my doctor, and he agrees that, as I'm sixty-three and have a history of chronic fatigue, I should be careful. On March 20, I'm laid off at work, and I apply for unemployment that day. They tell us the shutdown will only be for two weeks. It might be nice to have a break.

Two weeks of shutdown becomes one month, then two months. The information we're receiving keeps changing as the distant virus becomes a worldwide pandemic.

"No, cloth masks do not help contain this virus. Don't wear medical-grade masks. They are needed for the hospital staff fighting on the front lines," eventually turns into, "Wear a cloth or medical-grade mask at all times, in all public spaces, indoors and outdoors, even in your home if you share a space with elderly relatives."

"Social distancing" becomes a mantra for all of us as we "stay six feet apart." We can't leave our homes, except to get supplies. All nonessential businesses, including restaurants, are closed. The schools are all closed, and children are learning to do their work online. Life comes to a screeching halt as we all "shelter in place" and wonder how long this will be our new "normal."

Suddenly, there's no toilet paper, hand sanitizer, or flu medicine available in any store. I find myself getting up at 5 a.m. to shop during "senior hour" so I might get what we need while it's still on the shelves. It reminds me of shopping trips I took in Russia and China, where empty shelves are normal. The panic and rationing feel like stories my mother told of WWII. Attending church from our sofa is a novelty at first, but we soon miss having real contact with friends and family. The short-term trips for Chris and Joseph are canceled. We're wondering what God is trying to teach us through all this. It's scary to see how quickly the government can take over your life and individual rights take second place to whatever they decide is "good for the community." It's even scarier to see neighbors turn against each other, fear driving people to treat others as threats.

Life slows down to a sloth's pace, but now I have time to write. Recording my mother's story flows into my own, and God continues to work in my heart to heal pain and replace lies. I can see how he has been teaching me to know Him throughout my life, and no lesson has been wasted, as each has prepared me for the next challenge I would face. I feel a new, deep sense of peace and an exquisite awareness of His love for me. I can see His hand leading and providing through this strange COVID existence. "In thy book were written, every one of them, the days that were formed for me, when as yet there was none of them."[30] These peculiar days are part of His plan for us all. *Thank You, Lord, for Your faithful presence with me over so many years, and for using challenging situations to show me I can always trust You. Help us all to keep trusting You through these uncertain days, where sickness and death loom large. When we're not sure what to believe from the world news, You are still the way, the truth, and the life.*[31]

June arrives with us still in lockdown, but I'm going to North Carolina anyway. Mikeah is having a lot of painful Braxton Hicks contractions that are much worse than with her other two children, and she needs help earlier than we expected. So I don my mask, wander through the quiet ghost town that used to be the Portland airport, and follow the social distancing rules on two planes to get there. She's exhausted and relieved to have help with the children. Naomi is almost five and is constantly busy with various crafts and activities. Joshua is two and is in the middle of potty training. Baby is due June 13 but, thankfully, comes early on June 9—a sweet little girl her parents name Saraia Anne. The older two and I keep busy at home while Michael stays with mom and the new arrival at the hospital for three days. COVID restrictions don't allow for him to leave or for us to visit, so it's very exciting when they finally get home. Naomi is so ready to hold her new little sister, while Joshua stands back, watching her from afar, assessing this new addition to his life. *Lord, please bless sweet Saraia with a saving faith from a young age. Her name means "Princess." May she come to know that she is a daughter of the King of Kings, and may she represent Your royal family with grace, dignity, and kindness all the days of her life.*

---

30   Psalm 139:16.
31   John 14:6.

Chris has moved to the apparel section of Fred Meyer, as the jewelry department has closed because of COVID restrictions. He is happy to be working with his old friend Kevin, who is our son-in-law Trent's dad, and enjoys the slower pace. Sadly, over the last year, he has also discovered the world of internet misinformation. He has trouble discerning what is true versus what is there to create anger, fear, and hopelessness. He spends hours on his computer, watching video after video of conspiracy theories and sending the videos to others. Despite attempts by me and members of our family to reason with him, he succumbs to deeper and deeper anxiety as he worries about what he is supposed to do to protect his family. He wonders what will happen next as these men take over our country, forcing us into socialism and one-world government. I can see that there may be pieces of truth in what he's reading, but much of it seems designed to cause anger and polarization. The fact that these people are profiting from the exploitation of his fears is infuriating to us but disregarded by him.

We talk about what God is doing by revealing evil and showing how the church can be light in times of darkness. We review what we know will happen at the end of this world from Scripture, that God is always in control, and that He will use this time to refine us all. Ultimately, nothing is outside of His plan, and He will be glorified through all this craziness. We need to keep our focus on Him, not our circumstances.

But continuing to consume a heavy diet of negative news, Chris spirals into cynicism and depression. He is very upset when people start lining up for the COVID vaccine that he has been told will kill everyone who gets it. He hears about the "big reset," a supposed plan to kill millions of people and control the rest with implanted microchips. His fear turns to anger, which spills into our relationship. He is moody and withdrawn much of the time, and he's very angry at me for not agreeing with everything he is listening to. He wants to move to a bunker somewhere, store food, and plan for the end of the world. I have no sense that what he's saying is an accurate reflection of reality, and I keep trying to trust God and to help Chris do the same. *Lord, I have no idea what to do with this. I've tried to talk about You. I've prayed with Chris and for him, over and over. Only You can shine truth into his heart and mind. Only You can lead us out of this darkness.*

Riots take over downtown Portland. What started as a protest over the death of George Floyd quickly becomes a way for people to vent the anger and hostility that's been building during this election year. Once-in-a-century winds tear through our area, pushing forest fires to consume whole towns and over a million acres of trees. The middle of the country deals with record cold and snow, and the southeast has five hurricanes heading across the Atlantic to prepare for. Murder hornets from Asia are discovered not far from Oregon, threatening our bee population and our ability to sleep at night. The NEOWISE comet comes through, and when they announce a "Christmas Star" will be here in December, we all agree, "Why not?" So many other apocalyptic events have happened in 2020—an unusual reminder of God's faithfulness and hope would be a welcome end to this craziness!

August is making way for September when it becomes clear that the clinic I have worked in for eleven years is not going to rehire me as they originally promised. On one level, I'm disappointed to be treated that way, but I'm also grateful not to have to return to such a stressful environment. I hear of an opening at a smaller pediatric clinic nearby, and within a few days, I'm working two days a week and learning hippotherapy as well.[32] *Thank You, Lord, for this wonderful provision. You never cease to amaze me. We are so glad this horrible year is almost over. Surely 2021 will be better.*

---

32 Hippotherapy is used as part of occupational, physical, and speech therapy, as horseback riding challenges gross motor coordination and balance skills while providing helpful sensory input.

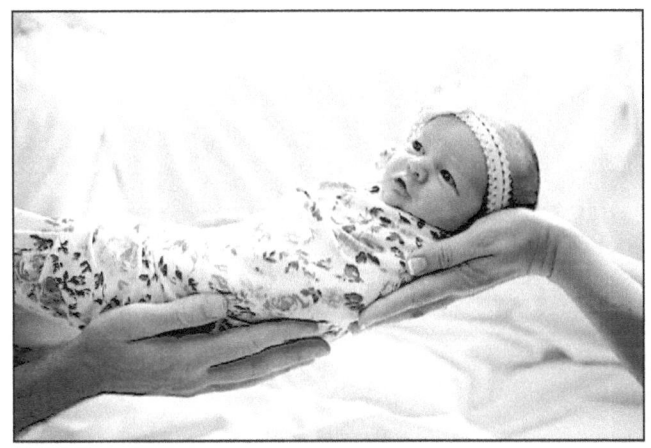

Saraia Anne Sleigh.
Born June 9, 2020.

A new family of five, 2020.
Mikeah holding newborn Saraia and Michael holding Joshua (two) and Naomi (five).

chapter thirty-eight

New Mercies Every Morning

The pandemic drags on into 2021, with the big push to vaccinate the whole world as quickly as possible being the main priority. Conflicts deepen as people can't agree about whether the vaccines are safe and if we should open restaurants, schools, and churches yet. Are masks really needed? Is social distancing working? A fiercely fought, contentious election refuses to end as the argument continues about who was elected. Riots and fighting at every level of society create a growing sense of fear and uncertainty. The splits grow wider in families and friendships and political opinions across the whole country. It's hard to know what is true anymore. Lawlessness increases, and decency and kindness seem to have flown. But life goes on, and we continue to seek God through it all.

I'm enjoying working at the clinic and getting to know the children and the horses there. Chris retires from Fred Meyer and begins working in the custodial department at Multnomah University. Joseph is still working there as he takes classes and waits for another trip to Uganda to get organized. All short-term trips overseas have been canceled again this year. We shovel mountains of heavy, wet snow to make a path to the front door during one of the biggest blizzards in recent memory. Nora visits often to play, drink hot chocolate, and sit with Grandpa in the comfy "Grandpa chair."

"Nana Banana," Nora says as we play together at her home.

"Who's calling me a banana?" I reply with feigned indignation.

Nora looks around at me with a cheeky grin on her sweet two-year-old face and, quick as a whip, picks up her favorite toy flamingo.

"Kiki, don't call Nana a banana," she says to her, and we burst into laughter together. This becomes an often-repeated dialogue as I spend a week taking care of her while Erin and Trent are at the hospital, bringing her baby brother into the world. We have fun dancing to Swan Lake, reading, doing crafts, taking walks, and playing with a dinosaur who likes pink shoes.

On May 7, 2021, Rhett Timothy arrives by emergency C-section due to a serious complication during labor. They transfer both mom and baby to a Portland hospital, where she recovers from surgery, and he spends six days in the NICU while we wait and pray. We are all relieved when they both recover well, and Nora is delighted to be a big sister when they finally get home. *Lord, we are so grateful for your protective hand over Rhett and Erin. We are delighted to have this gorgeous baby boy join our family. Please bless him with strength to follow You from an early age and all the days of his life. May he learn to offer wise counsel as his name implies, and may many come to know You through his words and through the example of his life.*

We are all excited when we find out that Mikeah's family is moving back to Oregon from North Carolina. We pray for them as they tackle the huge task of sorting, packing, selling, and shipping their belongings while they try to sell one house and buy another one three thousand miles away! In June, Mikeah flies to Oregon with the three children, and Michael makes the long trek across the country with a friend in a heavily laden rental truck. They quickly fix up their new house, find a new church, and become regulars at the local pump track. I love having them only two and a half hours away.

Chris is still really struggling with anger, frustration, and depression as he tries to make sense of all he's listening to on the internet and watching around the world. He's angry at me and everyone else, and there's nothing that brings him joy anymore. He drags himself along, and I keep trying to encourage him to keep trusting that God is still in control. He begins meeting regularly with our friend Joby to talk about life, but he wants to change churches and doesn't attend the weekly prayer meeting with me anymore.

Out of the blue one Saturday morning, he suggests we get a breakfast sandwich and some coffee and drive over to the Columbia River Gorge. We take our Bibles and devotionals so we can read, pray, eat, and talk while we enjoy the spectacular view. This becomes our weekly routine every Saturday morning, a few minutes away from the concerns of life, a chance to focus and be together. I start hoping that we can find our way back to each other. *Thank You, Lord, for this sweet time together. Please draw us closer to each other and to You.*

"I think God is asking me to go downtown every day for forty days," Chris announces to me in mid-August.

I'm happy he wants to do something that will help to keep his focus on the Lord and will mean less time on the internet. He has been going into Portland once a week to visit people on the streets for years, but going every day will be a challenge.

He plans to begin next week and lets Butch and Mary Lou know he will need extra care packages to hand out. They have been providing these so faithfully for years whenever he needs them. He always sends them an email when he gets back to tell them what happened and who to be praying for. I ask him to send those to me now too. I read them each day and pray for the people he has seen. I have never gone with him on these trips, so I'm amazed to learn how God uses him in so many lives as he talks to people living in tents, passengers waiting to catch the MAX train, workers cleaning the streets, security guards, businessmen, and tourists.

He often asks a leading question to get the conversation started, like, "How do you feel about what's happening in our city?" or "If you could ask Jesus for anything, what would you ask for?" I can see in his early notes that he is angry and wants God to judge this city and its people. But after about thirty days of daily conversations with people, hearing their stories, praying with them, and sharing his own life failures and successes, he begins to remember the compassion of God. It changes Chris's heart and reminds him that God forgives.

He is also learning that helping the homeless is complicated. Some want to get housing and jobs, others don't. Mental illness is a huge factor for many, and poor life choices often lead to situations that are difficult to get out of on your own.

He is excited to meet other people who are helping too. Roger,[33] whose homeless brother died on a park bench in Portland while his family knew nothing of his desperate situation, has come here to work with those who live on the streets and help them find their families. There are also several people who were homeless until they got help and have now come back to help others get off the streets as well. During these short forty days downtown, Chris helps Julie find her way to a rehabilitation center, and soon she is able to get her own apartment. He leads Simon to the Lord, who in turn reaches out to his own family. Tommy and Felix and Billy and Ricardo and Martin and Colin and so many others—he touches their lives with the love and the grace of God.

I'm reminded that everyone has a story, and everyone needs God in that story. Chris shares parts of his own life and any Scriptures that God brings to mind. If we know God personally, we have a story too, and sharing it honors God and gives Him a way to build faith in the lives of others.[34] *Lord, help me to be braver about sharing my story and praying with others. Thank You for speaking to so many needy people through Chris and for working in his heart during this time too.*

---

33 Names have been changed to protect privacy.

34 I'm sorry I don't have space to share all of Chris's notes here, as they really do tell the story of so many needs. They are available in a separate booklet, *Forty Days in Downtown Portland,* that I would be happy to send to anyone who is interested in reading about this time. Contact: stayintheriver25@gmail.com.

Rhett Timothy Jennings.
Born May 7, 2021.

Erin and Trent with Nora (four) and Rhett (one and a half), Christmas 2022.

chapter thirty-nine

Weeks of Sickness

In mid-October, two days after Chris's final downtown visit, Joseph tests positive for COVID-19. He is still living with us, so we all go into quarantine. Five days later, Chris gets his first symptoms of it, and three days after that, I have it as well. We're not really concerned and feel glad to finally get it over and done with after twenty-two months of this pandemic.

Joseph recovers quite quickly, although he loses his sense of taste and smell for months. Chris and I are more seriously ill, with raging headaches, coughs, fevers, body aches, and extreme fatigue, all typical for the Delta variant that is dominating the end of 2021. Since Mikeah lives two and a half hours away, she helps by contacting everyone she can to pray for us and keeping them updated. Erin and Trent need to avoid getting it, as their condo is on the market and they are actively looking for a house to buy. They drop off food for us, pray, and keep in touch. Our church family begins a meal train, and a constant supply of carefully prepared dinners, generous gift cards, and restaurant deliveries grace our doorstep for several weeks. Joseph keeps track of all of them and shops for us when he gains enough strength to go out.

Friends send over medicines and an oximeter to keep track of our oxygen levels. By day five, I'm concerned because Chris's oxygen levels are very low. He is lethargic and doesn't even have enough strength to be concerned. I call the nurse helpline to explain his symptoms, and she wants me to take him to the nearest emergency room. He is very reluctant to go and begs me to make sure they don't admit him. I have no idea what they are going to do, but I try to reassure him that he needs oxygen, and they can send him home with that.

At the ER, they let me stay long enough to get him through the sign-in process, but then they whisk him away to sit at the far end of the waiting room with the other COVID-positive patients, and I have to leave. It's awful to be home, wondering how he is doing and not being able to help him negotiate the hospital system that is so familiar to me. He has never been an inpatient in a hospital. I pray and wait.

It's several hours before he gets back to an examination room. They start him on oxygen, but he refuses most of the medications they want to try. They call me, and I try to reassure him that they know what they are doing and to encourage him to relax. He is beyond anxious. In the middle of the night, he is transferred to another hospital and admitted. We keep in touch by phone, but I am too sick to visit. Joseph goes to see him and is a big encouragement to his dad. Two days later, a doctor reassures me that Chris is going to do well since he has no underlying conditions. They are sending him home with oxygen, steroids, and cough medicine. We are all relieved.

We settle into a daily routine of medications, vitamins, small meals, and rest. I am now having difficulty breathing and am moving very slowly, and Chris doesn't seem to be improving at all, even with the oxygen. On the morning of November 8, he asks Joseph to take him back to the hospital. He doesn't want to go, but he is really struggling to breathe, and it frightens him enough to overcome his immense fear of the hospital. They admit him immediately. I'm relieved that he's somewhere they can take care of him. I just don't have the energy or mental capacity to keep up with his care anymore. They increase his oxygen and add antibiotics to the steroids because he still has a significant fever. Joseph and Gerry take turns visiting him in the progressive care unit. Chris admits to them that he hasn't taken COVID seriously enough and realizes now that he has had a bad attitude toward people who disagree with his point of view on vaccines, treatments, and the politics of the situation. He apologizes and asks for forgiveness from everyone he talks to.

Joseph takes me to an appointment with our family doctor. X-rays show I have bilateral COVID pneumonia, like Chris, so the doctor puts me on oxygen, antibiotics, and steroids. I go home with instructions to go to an ER if my oxygen levels fall below ninety. He calls me daily to check in.

I have never felt this sick and weak and helpless. I often feel dizzy, cough constantly, and can only stay up for a few minutes at a time. Joseph brings me light meals and the medications I need. I'm trying to keep in touch with Chris. After he drops his phone and it stops working, we switch to Zoom calls with the kids whenever we can get the nurses to set it up. He's extremely anxious and in a lot of pain, but he's still able to communicate. One evening, a doctor calls me to talk about how things are going.

"People this sick don't make it," he explains to me bluntly. "We need permission to ventilate him if that becomes necessary."

I'm stunned. Mikeah is on the line with us.

"I'm not sure he would want that," I say, knowing that he believes ventilation kills people. Besides that, we agreed we didn't want any extraordinary life saving measures when we set up our living wills a few years ago.

"We have to do *something*," Mikeah interjects. "We can't just let him die, struggling to breathe."

"I totally agree," I manage to say between both of us sobbing. The next morning, the doctor calls to tell us that Chris is now in the ICU and on the ventilator. His oxygen levels are finally where they should be.

Mikeah drives across from Redmond to see him. She sits with him, calling family and friends so they can "talk" to him, even though he can't respond, as he is heavily sedated and comatose. She decorates his room with pictures and cards from family and puts up a note she has written, explaining who he is and how he loves to share Jesus with everyone he meets. She wants the staff to know that this often-uncooperative patient is a man who cares about others. I'm so grateful she can be there and ask her to send me photos so I can see where he is and how he looks.

It's miraculous when, two days later, they take him off the ventilator because he's breathing well enough with just supplemental oxygen to keep his levels up.

"This doesn't usually happen," they tell us. "If this keeps up, he'll be back home in a week or two."

The news quickly goes around our prayer warriors, and we're all relieved and grateful that the worst is over.

Erin suggests that we send a CD player for Chris, so Joseph takes one to the hospital with a collection of their dad's favorite music along with more cards, photos, and notes from everyone. During an evening Zoom call, Chris seems encouraged as he talks about watching Christian television and realizing God is teaching him a lot through this suffering. He goes on and on but doesn't once ask how I am feeling or how any of the kids are doing. I know he's sick and he's probably just happy to have someone to talk to, but I'm disappointed.

The next night as I'm preparing for our Zoom call time, I suddenly feel very angry at Chris. The hurt and frustration I've carried for years rises to the surface, and I just don't have the strength to hide it anymore. I'm tired of feeling unseen and like I don't matter. I'm angry that I have allowed Chris's anger to control so much of my life, keeping me silent when I should have spoken up. I'm angry that we failed to take better care of our marriage and each other. *Lord, what do I do with all this anger? Help me. I don't know how to change this, how to process it all, how to move on. I need You to help me sort this out.* I miss a couple of the calls.

A few days later, Mikeah makes the long journey around Mt. Hood again to be with her dad. They share stories, and he tells her about some of his experiences when he worked as a hospital chaplain and how he would anoint people with oil when he prayed for them. A few minutes later, a chaplain comes into the ICU room and introduces herself.

"You got oil?" Chris asks. "I'd like us to pray and for you to anoint me with oil."

"Are you Protestant?" she asks.

"Yes."

"I can come back tomorrow," she offers.

"No, my daughter is here now, and I need to do it today, please."

She looks a little flustered. The precautions needed to get into an ICU room with a COVID patient are extensive—gown, mask, shield, gloves—it all takes time. She would have to take it all off, wash up, go across the hospital to where the oil is stored, come back, and put it all on again. But she nods in agreement and returns an hour later. She and Mikeah pray over Chris and apply the precious oil. He talks briefly on the phone with a few people but doesn't have the strength to talk for long before settling down for the night.

The nightly calls are getting harder and harder as Chris struggles to breathe and talk. He's so anxious despite all the medications they are giving him to help him stay calm. As I pray often for him, my anger is slowly replaced with the deepest sadness as I realize how much I care for him despite the years of struggle. I cry every time we get off a call. I hate seeing him struggling like this and not being there to help. I have taken care of this man for thirty-six years, and now that he really needs me to be there, I'm too sick to go. *Lord, how much longer must he suffer?*

Early on the morning of November 22, Chris is up in a chair when the nurse sets up the Zoom time for us all. He is alert and talkative as he shares how God has been teaching him about suffering. He remembers the life of Richard Wurmbrand, who spent thirteen years in prison in Romania because of his faith, and the testimony of Joni Eareckson Tada, who has lived all her adult life as a quadriplegic. He talks about Jonah and the mercy of God to allow suffering in our lives so we can learn to trust only in Him. Later, I try to get a phone call through to him, but the nurses are always too busy to make it happen. After I've gone to bed, Mikeah gets through, and as they chat about life, he encourages her to write her stories down so she can share them with others. They pray together before saying goodnight.

The next morning, we are told that Chris is back on the ventilator. His lungs are getting worse instead of better, and his heart is struggling to pump blood into them because they are so inflamed. He still has an unexplained fever and blood clots, and now his kidneys are failing as well. Dialysis may be needed. We talk about options and probable outcomes and long-term effects of all these procedures with his doctors. I realize he had been having symptoms of kidney issues for several months before all this. Sleep apnea has also been a problem for as long as I've known him, and now they are saying that's an underlying condition too. *Lord, please be close to Chris during this comatose time. Speak to him while none of us can. Reassure him of Your presence and love.*

Daily updates with the doctors do not bring good news, and a decision is needed. I talk with all our children, and we weigh Chris's desire to not be kept alive on machines against our wanting him to stay. Mikeah and Erin sense, as I do, that it would be a mercy to let him go. Joseph is not so sure. He wants to know how his dad would feel about it. I show him the living will Chris signed a few years ago. I pray for God to reveal His will to Joseph. That night, he has a very vivid dream in which his dad comes into his room, smiling and happy. "They tell me I have only one more day to live," he says to Joseph. Seeing Joseph's reaction, he adds, "Don't be sad. I'm happy." Joseph has his answer. On Friday, November 26, Chris is in complete, permanent kidney failure, so we plan to take him off the ventilator the next day. *Lord, You could still turn this around between now and then. We are trusting You.*

I make my way through the morning of Saturday, November 27, feeling very fragile as, one by one, Erin, Joseph, Gerry, and Janel say goodbye to Chris. I am finally well enough to handle being up for a while, so Joseph takes me to the hospital around noon. Gowned and masked, I sit holding Chris's very swollen hand. I look around the ICU room at the ventilator forcing him to breathe at a steady tempo, the cards, photos, and notes on the wall behind the CD player, and the special quilt over him that was made by hospital volunteers.

"So this is where you have been for the last nineteen days. I'm so sorry I couldn't be here. I'm doing better, but this is such a hard fight. You've fought it well, but we are going to let you go to be with the Lord you have loved and served for so long. It feels like the merciful thing to do. I know you haven't been happy for a long time. You have struggled with the way the world has been going and wondered what you could do to protect your family. You've said you want to go, and God seems to have made a way. We love you and will all miss you, but we will be okay. I will write your story, and we will not forget."

Mikeah arrives around 3:30 p.m., and I let her have some time alone with her dad. After an hour, I return to the room, and we talk about this COVID journey and God's grace to us all. The nurse on duty has been coming and going quietly, gently answering our questions and telling us the plan. Friends turn up unexpectedly just before five o'clock as the nurses are preparing to take Chris off the ventilator, so they have only a few minutes to say goodbye. We wait outside in the hallway with them, talking about Chris's life as they turn off the machine that has been keeping him alive.

"It's time," the nurse says as she leads me back in. She closes the doorway curtains to give me some privacy. They can't tell us how long he will live while struggling to breathe on his own, but I know I'm staying until the end, however long it takes. I will *not* let him die alone here. I wish we could talk. I hope he can hear me.

"How did we get here? This is not how either of us thought our life together would end. How do I say goodbye to someone I've shared life with for thirty-six years? I'm sorry I wasn't a better wife. I was too critical and didn't encourage you enough. We weren't good at being married, but we raised three wonderful children together. They all love the Lord and are raising their children to do the same. Thank you for loving us and for sharing so many exciting adventures all around the world with me. The Lord has used us in so many lives, and so many people love you. Thank you for always praying for us in the middle of the night. I know those prayers were precious to God and kept our family safe. I love you."

The nurse softly puts her arm around me and asks what I need when she checks on us twenty minutes later.

"Can you ask Mikeah to come in, please?" Mikeah sits beside me as I stroke Chris's hand. His breathing is slower and shallower. She plays hymns on her phone, we pray, and we talk to Chris through our tears.

"It's okay to go and be with Jesus, honey. He's waiting right there. We love you and will miss you. Say hi to Solomon, Alice, and Zanita when you see them. We'll be there with you all before we know it."

"How Great Thou Art" is playing about forty minutes after the ventilator is turned off. Two tears roll down Chris's cheek. I wipe them away, wondering if he can hear us. His breathing slows to nothing as he takes his last breath here on earth and steps into heaven, finally free from the battle, soaring above it all, seeing that spectacular place we all long to see, engulfed in the love, mercy, and peace of our wonderful God. *And I'm a widow.*

Mikeah stays the night, Joseph is home, and Erin brings breakfast over the next morning. The four of us have a wonderfully unplanned time to talk about their dad, his life, his dreams, his fears, his passions, and what we should do for his memorial service. All three of them want to talk and think I should too. As we prepare over the next three weeks, the fog of grief descends. I know Chris is gone—I was there when it happened—but my brain keeps suggesting he would like to know about that old friend who just called or that he may have an opinion about the new rug. Once this is all over, he'll be back, and we can just go on with life. Processing this huge loss takes up so much bandwidth in my head, I can't deal with much else, but there's a seemingly endless amount of paperwork to get done. I'm taking it just one day at a time, one task at a time, and I'm so grateful for the constant support from friends and family.

I'm happy to be going through photos for the PowerPoint of Chris's life so the memory of how he looked in the hospital can be replaced by happier memories. A strange mixture of sadness and relief coexist. I'm so glad he's no longer suffering or anxious. He's safe now, and Jesus is taking care of him. I don't have to worry about him. But the house seems empty, our big bed feels empty, and there's so much space where he once lived in my heart and thoughts. *This is going to take time.* I'm so glad we had our trip to the beach with all the children and grandchildren in September. We had no idea it would be our last time all together and the last family photo with him in it. We treasure our memories of flying kites, playing in the sand, collecting shells, and running after the frisbee. *It's hard to believe this is all real.*

We finally make it to Chris's memorial on Saturday, December 18, 2021. So much planning and help combine to make this a wonderful day to remember Chris's life and share the gospel story he loved to tell. Two hundred people attend, and eight hundred people watch online as we tell his life story with memories, photos, and songs. We laugh and we cry; we hug and we share. Chris's life revolved around telling people about God. He could talk to anyone, anywhere, and turn the conversation to the Lord. He cared that people were going to spend eternity without God if they didn't make a decision for Him in this lifetime. It wasn't just a nice idea to him that all Christians should be sharing the gospel. Like Paul, Chris was compelled to share what he knew with everyone. As Paul wrote, "For if I preach the gospel, that gives me no grounds for boasting. For necessity is laid upon me. Woe to me if I do not preach the gospel!"[35] Chris felt that way too. One tract found by his uncle so long ago led to Chris's decision to give his life to God. That decision led to hundreds of souls waiting in heaven

---

35 1 Corinthians 9:16.

to greet him when he arrived. I wish I could have seen it. Small and large acts of faithfulness work together to change eternity.

Each of our children does an amazing job of sharing their memories and their hearts. So many people tell me how Chris's life has affected them, even a stranger who was hearing about it for the first time today. We give out tracts so others can continue the legacy of reaching out. The grandchildren have drawn pictures to pass along too. Family have come all the way from Eugene and Los Angeles to share in this celebration of life with us. We have a festive meal together after the service and hear more funny stories of Chris's childhood and college years. Everyone comes back to our place afterward. It is exactly what Chris loved most—noisy family gatherings with food, laughter, and fun. He is here in every memory and every heart present.

When he was in grade school, Chris's teacher asked the class, "What do you want to do with your life?"

Here was a question he could answer. Chris raised his hand and said, "I want to get married, live a good life, and go to be with Jesus when I die."

Well, honey, you did it! You completed your plan. Thank you for living a life faithful to God. Thank you for working hard to provide for your family and for loving us through all the ups and downs. Thank you for sharing dad jokes with us and for never letting us win at a game until we really could beat you. We love you and miss you, but we know that one day, we'll see you up there, and we'll walk on that beautiful shore together. In the meantime, we'll keep telling your stories, and your legacy will live on as a man of God.

———

In the early months of 2022, I am still dealing with the brain fog of COVID combined with the disorientation of grief. I tire quickly, and half my hair has fallen out, but I'm getting around. Joseph has been fixing up Chris's old truck so we can sell it, and that feels like a good way for him to work through his grief. I head back to work two days a week, as I'm not sure how things are going to work out financially. Eventually, the life insurance pays off the last of our mortgage for me, which is a huge help. The church pays some of the medical bills, and Social Security decides I can get Chris's benefit for this year. *Thank You, Lord, for continuing to take care of me.*

When our children and I talked the day after Chris went home to be with the Lord, we decided we didn't need to have a gravesite here in Oregon and would like to take his ashes back to Los Angeles instead. His sister Marina begins organizing a second memorial and a military burial ceremony for the weekend of April 30, which would have been his seventieth birthday. It is wonderful to be with his extended family, especially as so many could not make the long trip north for the first memorial. After the moving church service, Patriot Riders lead us through the rolling green hills of Riverside National Cemetery. Air Force personnel stand respectfully at attention, and the pastor shares briefly as the flag is held aloft. A gun salute shatters the quiet of this peaceful setting, and the expertly folded flag is handed to Chris's mother, Juanita, per my request, with those deeply moving words, "On behalf of the President of the United States, the United States Air Force, and a grateful nation, please accept this flag as a symbol of our appreciation for your loved one's honorable and faithful service." His ashes are buried in a field of the honored, right across the street from the March Air Force Base where he served so long ago. A boisterous family gathering follows at a restaurant Chris and Marina frequented many years ago. Many gather again at Tom and Kathy's later that evening and the next day. *Thank You, Lord, for this time here in this place and with these wonderful people whom Chris loved so much. This feels right. He would have loved it.*

Chris at our favorite beach,
Rockaway, 2015.

Chris on the left—one of the many
fishing trips he loved so much.

A marker placed for a man of God.

The solemn folding of the flag at the
military memorial for Chris, 2022.

Juanita receives the flag for her son.

Family gathering for the military service for Chris at the Riverside
National Cemetery, California, April 29, 2022.

Our last family photo with Chris, September 2021.
Michael holding Saraia, Mikeah and Joshua, Joseph, Celeste and
Naomi, Chris, Erin holding Nora, and Trent with Rhett.

chapter forty

Lessons Learned

I cry as I leave the DMV early one rainy morning a few months after Chris died, having just taken Chris's name off the vehicle titles. It feels as if we are erasing him from our lives—like he never lived. The Lord gently reminds me that I have all the notes Chris wrote when he was meeting with people in downtown Portland for forty days. I begin writing his story with those. God's impact in the world through Chris continues as more people watch the memorial service—over 1,700 now—and tell me of the impact it has had on them. I can see now that he was able to reach so many people because I stood with him, taking care of all the details of our life together, freeing him to serve in ways he wouldn't have been able to without me. I would have liked a better balance of family and ministry, but God used us even though we were imperfect.

I'm adjusting to this new life. I really miss having someone to pray with whenever something comes up. Chris and I spent many hours walking the trails near our home, always praying for family and friends as we went. Anytime I wanted to pray for someone, I only had to ask him, and he would put aside whatever he was doing and pray with me. I miss getting foot rubs while we watch old western movies. I miss being able to say, "Let's go to the coast," on the spur of the moment and just going. I miss adding to the years we've been married and planning our next big anniversary. I miss our Saturday morning trips to the Columbia River Gorge together.

On the other hand, widowhood has brought a deeper, sweeter dependence on God. I treasure His word in new ways, and I feel His love and closeness more tangibly. I'm learning that when I am weak, I am strong in Him. It's a new life, but it's still a good life.

Happily, God still has some surprises for me. On June 12, 2023, we are delighted to welcome Gabriel Christopher into Mikeah and Michael's family. He is named after his grandfather and is easygoing, happy, and energetic. *Lord, thank You for blessing us with our sweet Gabriel. May he come to know You at a young age and always follow You closely. May he find his strength in You and share Your love with everyone he meets.*

In August 2023, I travel to Kenya with a short-term team that is visiting the Agape Children's Ministries' new location in Nakuru. I have wanted to see this amazing work ever since Lynne told me about it years ago. It was during a visit to her daughter and son-in-law there that she was warned about the crocodiles in the river, and the title of this book was born. Agape[36] works in two other cities with street children who live in parks, sniffing glue and jet fuel to help them get through the hunger and loneliness of their dismal lives. Social workers visit them daily, sharing truth and offering a way off the streets. When they say they are ready, the team takes the child to their safe center, where they are cared for physically, emotionally, and spiritually while social workers look for any family members who can take care of them. Once an arrangement has been made, the children are taken to their new home, often with a grandparent or aunt. Agape workers visit every week to encourage the family and to help with any issues that arise. Agape provides money for school uniforms and fees. Caregivers are sometimes given goods they can use or sell to help with the cost of raising the children. The work in Nakuru is just beginning, and a center has not yet been set up to

---

36 Agape Children's Ministry, agapechildren.org.

house the children, but there is already an office building, and new staff are being trained.

Our second morning in Nakuru, we go with two social workers to visit some children who are still living on the streets, and we hear their heartbreaking stories. The next day, we go to see children who have been through the program in one of the other cities and are now living with relatives. The difference is astonishing. Children who once had no hope and were barely alive are now healthy and happy, talking about wanting to be a doctor or a farmer and proudly showing us their good school grades.

For the next two days, we help to train the incoming staff and visit the building Agape is hoping to buy to house the children. It is so impactful to meet the dedicated Kenyan workers and to see the huge difference they make in the lives of these vulnerable children. We connect quickly, and it is hard to say goodbye after our traditional Kenyan celebration meal of roasted goat, rice, beans, vegetables, and chapati on our last day. Before we leave Africa, we have one more stop—a short safari to see lions, hippos, rhinos, giraffes, hyenas, and water buffalo living their best lives in the wild. Spectacular!

Around the same time that I am walking around in Kenya, Joseph is in Uganda with a ministry that helps with job training in construction and farming. Because of the pandemic, he has had to wait a long time to fulfill his dream of being part of this exciting work. He helps on several building and farming projects and visits a center for needy children. He also gets to go on a safari before the long flight home. *Thank You, Lord, that we were both able to do these trips to Africa. What a joy to see the work being done in each country and to meet such loving and dedicated people who serve you there. Please bless the work of their hands.*

———————

In a full-circle moment, I find myself standing in front of Eilean Donan Castle in Scotland in April 2025! I've been dreaming of doing this since I was a little girl listening to Nan's stories of visiting this place when she lived in Scotland. Now that I'm here, I realize she must have seen the castle in ruins, as the twenty-year rebuilding by Major John Macrae-Gillstrap wasn't completed until 1932, when she had long since returned to New Zealand. The castle was originally constructed on this small island in the early thirteenth century to defend the lands of Kintail against Viking invaders. It was severely damaged in 1719 when it was attacked by heavily armed English ships during the Jacobite uprising. John Macrae-Gilstrap restored it to its original glory and added a walkway to the island to make access easier. I don't know why I feel such a connection to this place and the people who lived here so long ago. Many were described as "ecclesiastics" or ministers. Perhaps they prayed, as I do, for future generations to know and serve God, and by His grace, I joined the line of family members who know Him. *Thank You, Lord, for the opportunity to visit this land of unicorns, Highland coos, mysterious lochs, and famous missionaries like Eric Liddell and David Livingstone. I appreciate my Scottish heritage, but I hold more dearly to being part of Your family and the future we have together.*

As I prepare to finally finish this book, it's hard to imagine that three years have gone by since Chris went home to be with our Lord. The adjustment was certainly slow at first. Attending a GriefShare[37] group really helped, as I was able to work through so many of the feelings of loss, confusion, guilt, and loneliness with others who were experiencing similar situations. I did a workshop on emotionally healthy relationships[38] and learned about setting boundaries and expressing my opinion, and I am still part of a supportive and loving widows' group. My children and so many friends have supported me

37 www.griefshare.org.
38 www.emotionallyhealthy.org.

as we have walked through the ups and downs of grief together, and I'm finally finding my footing. The sweetness of our grandchildren brightens my days and pours love into my heart. Each one is truly such a gift, and it is my joy to pray for them often and to have regular opportunities to speak God's truth into their hearts.

Celeste (Nana) surrounded by love and giggles at Rockaway Beach, 2024.
Rhett (three), Nora (five), Gabriel (one), Naomi (nine), Saraia (four), and Joshua (six).

In conclusion, the three interconnected lives written about here are all part of God's story. My mother always had an awareness of the spiritual world, and she looked for truth in many places. She grew in self-confidence and worked hard to make a good life for her family, but she always carried a heavy weight of guilt and bitterness. I'm not sure if she ever truly found her way to a personal relationship with God, but I know she made sure her children were in Sunday school every week, and God used her searching for truth to lead me to Himself. I understand her reluctance to know Jesus after her last husband used Jesus's name to justify abusing her. I also know that God can reach people in comas, and I'm hopeful He did that during her last two days. So I trust Him with her soul and wait, grateful for all He taught me through her, hoping to see her again one day. **God sees and understands, and His is the final word.**

In my own life, I have endeavored to stay the course through some difficult times, even when the river's edge was tempting. Through the grace of God, He has kept me in the flow as evil watched from the banks. Looking back, I wish I had been less angry about some circumstances and more able to speak up, but He's gradually teaching me these skills as I keep trusting Him. In the past, I have struggled to feel loved and have often felt like it was "just You and me, Lord." God has been working on that in recent years too, and I now feel loved by Him and by family and friends. It was hard for me to understand why Chris and I struggled to figure out married life, but I've learned that the emotional trauma Chris experienced in childhood made it difficult for him to process negative feelings. He often shut down, and I was left feeling unseen and unloved. That combined with my always wanting to please others and my silence when I should have spoken up, made real communication difficult for us. Learning this has helped me to forgive him and myself. It's an ongoing healing process for sure. **God can heal fearful and weak people and give them strength, value, and usefulness in His kingdom.**

Chris dealt with low self-esteem and anxiety all his life, but he loved God, and his outgoing, smiling personality drew people to him. He always took every opportunity to point people to God and to share whatever he was learning in Scripture. Toward the end of his life, he had difficulty seeing the way for a while, but God pulled him back on course through his downtown service and the suffering of illness. He finished his journey well. Chris's legacy remains one of trusting God even when he couldn't see what was around the bend in the river. **God's grace can reach us in times of confusion and despair; He always goes after His children.**

Taking the time to write my story down has shown me how I have journeyed from being a nervous child, afraid to speak up but wanting desperately to be seen and heard, to an older adult who now firmly knows who she is and the calling God has placed on her. I have gone from knowing a lot *about* God to knowing Him personally as one of His adopted daughters. He has shown me His Father's heart, and I know I'm safe with Him. He is faithful . . . holy . . . loving . . . forgiving . . . just . . . powerful . . . and so much more! He has earned my trust and won my heart, even when there are circumstances that I don't understand or like. He is, after all, the Almighty Creator of everything—this is His world, His story, and His plan. He controls it all and has the right to do whatever He pleases. In His mercy, instead of designing a labyrinth of tasks we would need to complete in order to achieve forgiveness and a glorious life with Him, He stepped down into His creation, took on humanity, and graciously gave His life for us. *By grace we have been saved through faith, not of our own doing, for it is the gift of God (based on Ephesians 2:8).*

I am praying for you, dear reader, and entrusting you to God's care. **Stay in the river** of whatever He is doing in your life, knowing that He allows times of struggle and times of ease to show you your need of Him and that His power is made perfect in our weakness. Don't let the faithlessness of others or the enormity of your circumstances distract you—keep your eyes on Him, and He will lead you safely through.

[I] have not ceased to pray for you, asking that you may be filled with the knowledge of his will in all spiritual wisdom and understanding, to lead a life worthy of the Lord, fully pleasing to him, bearing fruit in every good work and increasing in the knowledge of God.

Colossians 1:9–10

The Kenyan school children were so excited to see us when we visited their schools.

Greg, Sandee, Shelby, Celeste, and Jim
heading to Kenya, August 2023.

Joseph makes new friends at a children's
center in Uganda, August 2023.

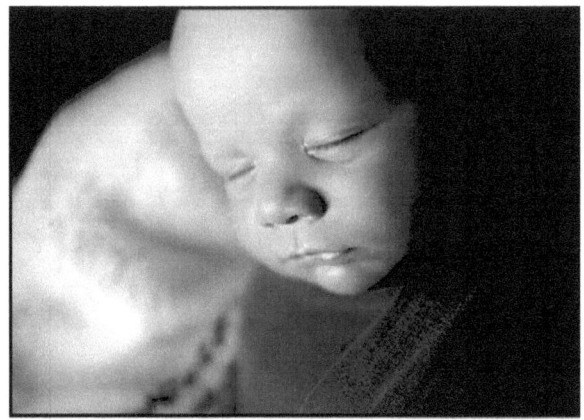

Gabriel Christopher Sleigh.
Born June 12, 2023.

Eilean Donan Castle near Dornie, Scotland. Home to the McKenzie and Macrae clans, it was originally constructed in the early 13th century to defend the lands of Kintail against Viking invaders. It was severely damaged in 1719 and reconstructed in 1932.

Family photo at Rockaway Beach, August 2025.
Back row: Erin, Trent, Mikeah, Michael, Gabriel (two), Celeste, and Joseph.
Front row: Rhett (four), Nora (six), Naomi (ten), Joshua (six), and Saraia (five).

Appendix

Appendix I: Clan Macrae

Clan Macrae (Macrath as it is written in Gaelic) was a small but important clan in the district of Kintail, in the northwest highlands of Scotland. The name means "son of grace" and first appears in 448 AD, where "Macraith the Wise" is mentioned as being a member of the household of St. Patrick in Ireland. The name appears in Scotland in the eleventh century with King Gregory the Macraith, who reigned during the last quarter of the ninth century and was one of the greatest of the early Scottish kings. The Macraes are related genealogically to the Mackenzies and the Macleans. They were known as strong warriors in the many battles they fought alongside the Mackenzies over the centuries, often protecting Eilean Donan castle from invaders. These "sons of grace" were also connected to many ecclesiastical endeavors and were known for being ministers in the church. They were men and women of God who went before us, serving Him and opening doors to His grace for generations to come. Memorial stones dot the landscape of Scotland, telling of their faithfulness and courage. These serve as a reminder for future generations to honor the God they served.

Clan Macrae family crest.
(Wikimedia Commons)

We have a godly inheritance. May all who come after us find us faithful.

Ewen Macrae (born in Scotland in 1852) moved to New Zealand and married Mary Eleanor Fantham in 1891. They had seven children, one of whom was my grandmother Annie Ethel Francis, or "Nan" as we called her. She often talked about living in Scotland and visiting the Eilean Donan castle, which is located near Ewen's family home.

Celeste visiting Eilean Donan castle near Dornie, Scotland, April 2025.

The Clan Macrae crest inside the banquet room.

Appendix II:
Macrae Family Tree (January 2025)

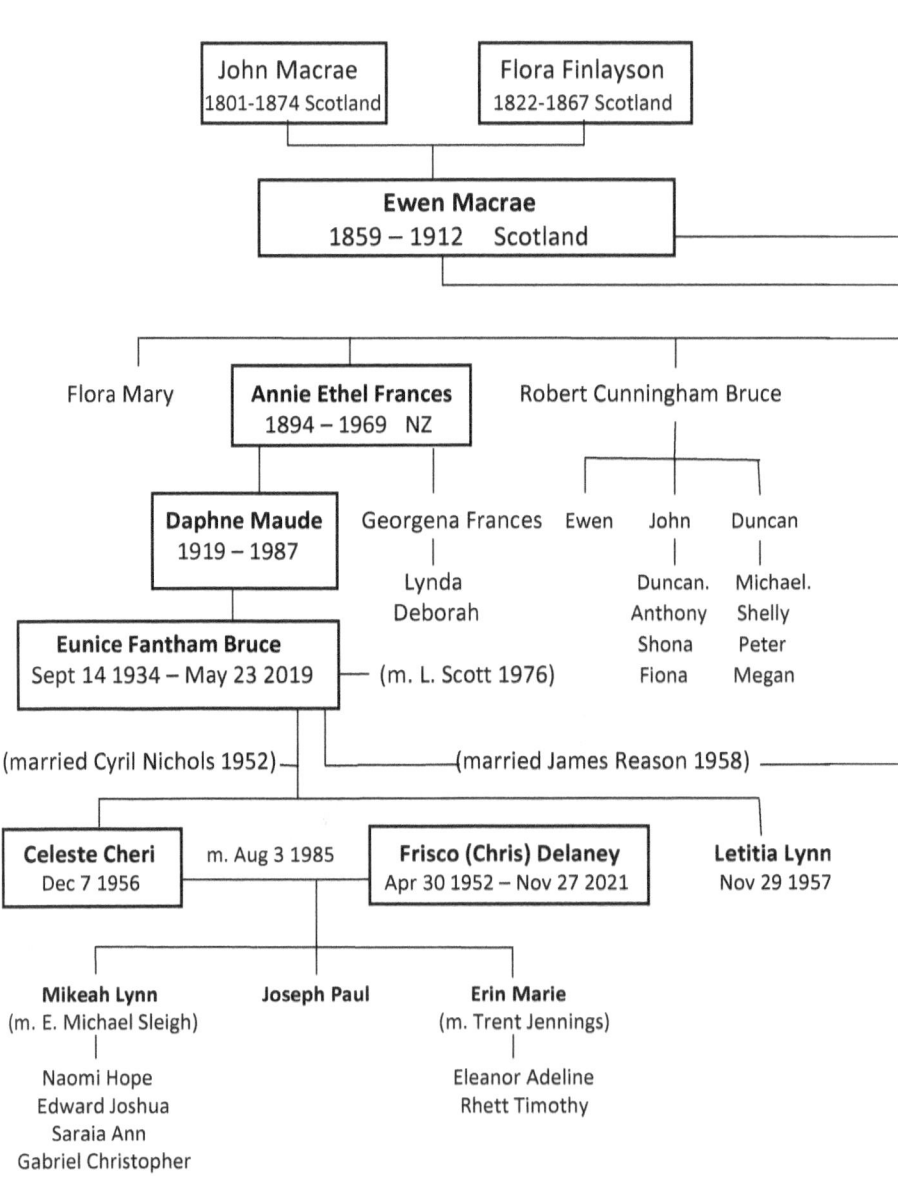

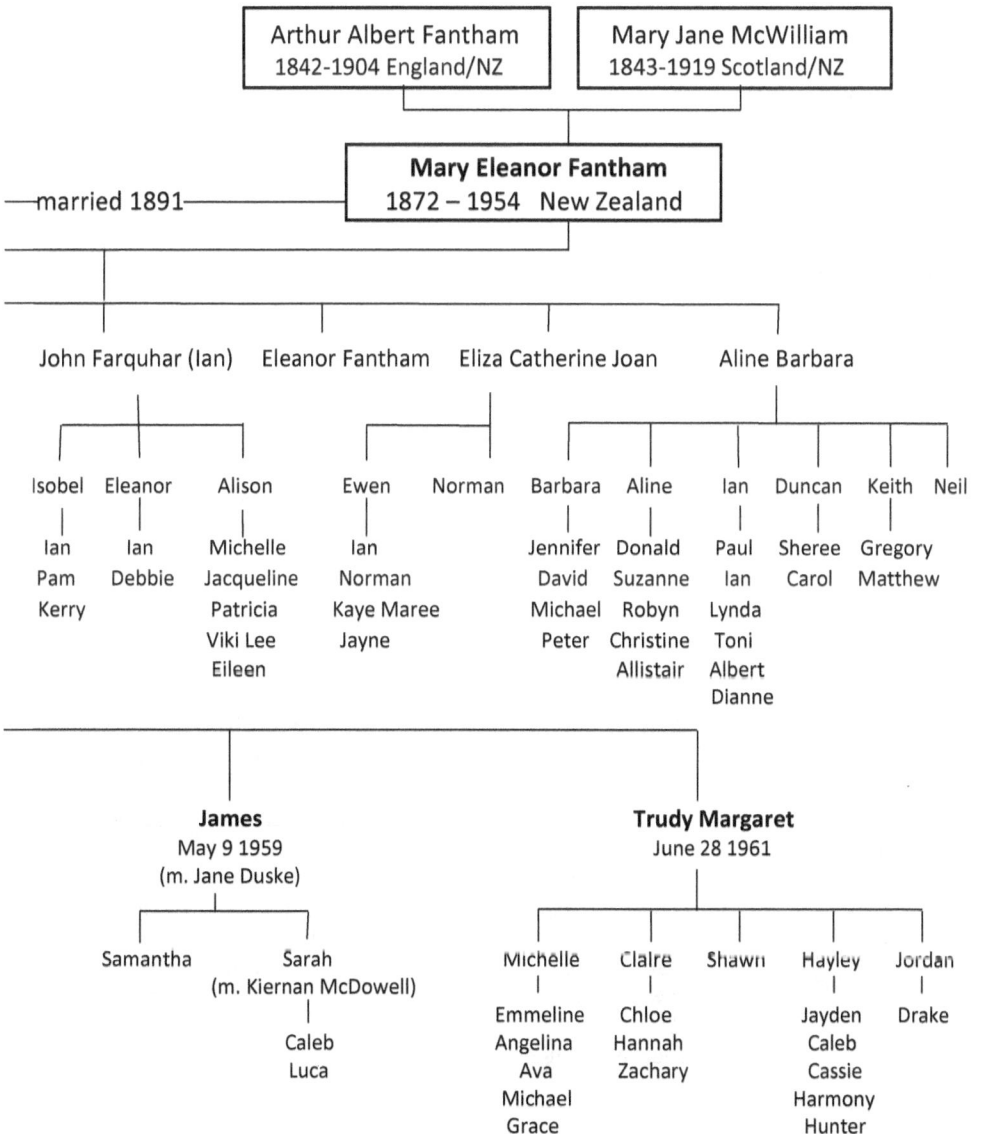

Arthur Albert Fantham
1842-1904 England/NZ

Mary Jane McWilliam
1843-1919 Scotland/NZ

Mary Eleanor Fantham
1872 – 1954   New Zealand

——married 1891——

John Farquhar (Ian)   Eleanor Fantham   Eliza Catherine Joan   Aline Barbara

Isobel	Eleanor	Alison	Ewen	Norman	Barbara	Aline	Ian	Duncan	Keith	Neil
Ian	Ian	Michelle	Ian		Jennifer	Donald	Paul	Sheree	Gregory	
Pam	Debbie	Jacqueline	Norman		David	Suzanne	Ian	Carol	Matthew	
Kerry		Patricia	Kaye Maree		Michael	Robyn	Lynda			
		Viki Lee	Jayne		Peter	Christine	Toni			
		Eileen				Allistair	Albert			
							Dianne			

James
May 9 1959
(m. Jane Duske)

Trudy Margaret
June 28 1961

Samantha	Sarah		Michelle	Claire	Shawn	Hayley	Jordan
	(m. Kiernan McDowell)						
	Caleb		Emmeline	Chloe		Jayden	Drake
	Luca		Angelina	Hannah		Caleb	
			Ava	Zachary		Cassie	
			Michael			Harmony	
			Grace			Hunter	

Appendix III:
Delaney Family Tree (January 2025)

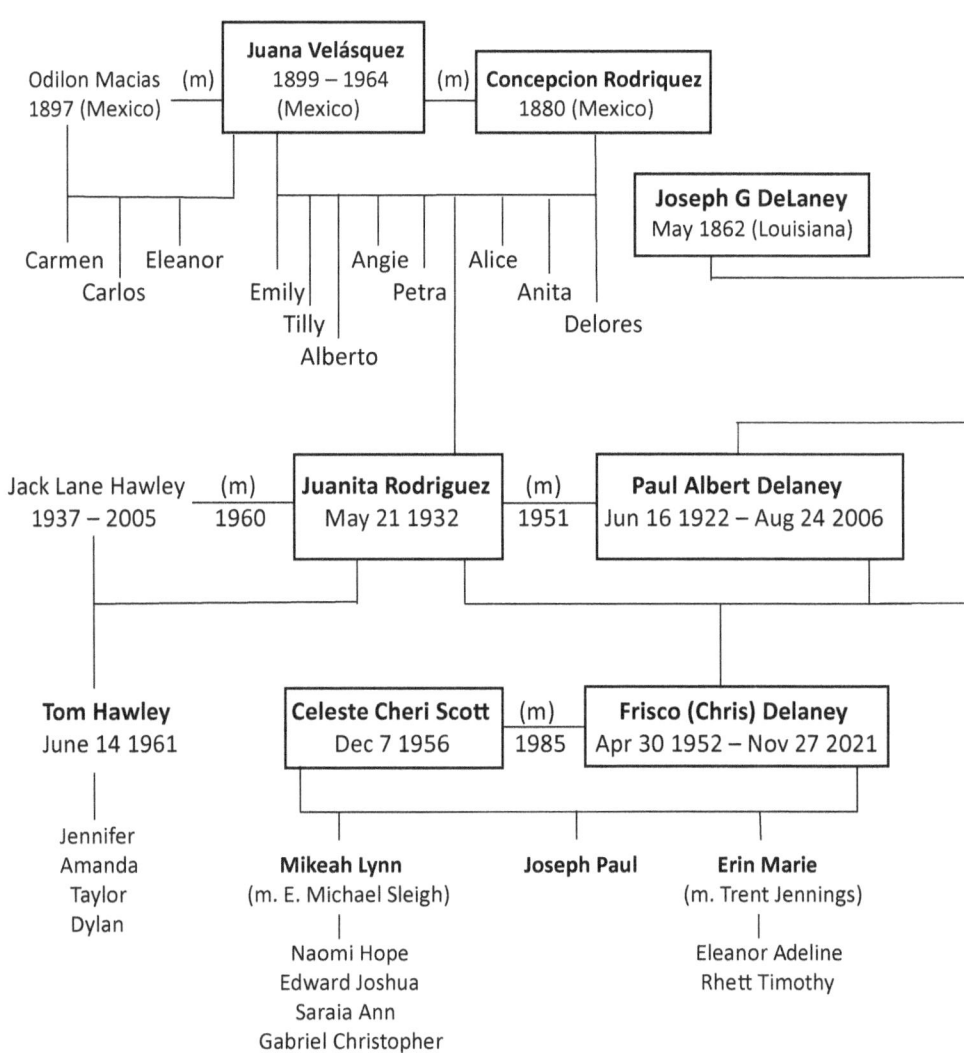

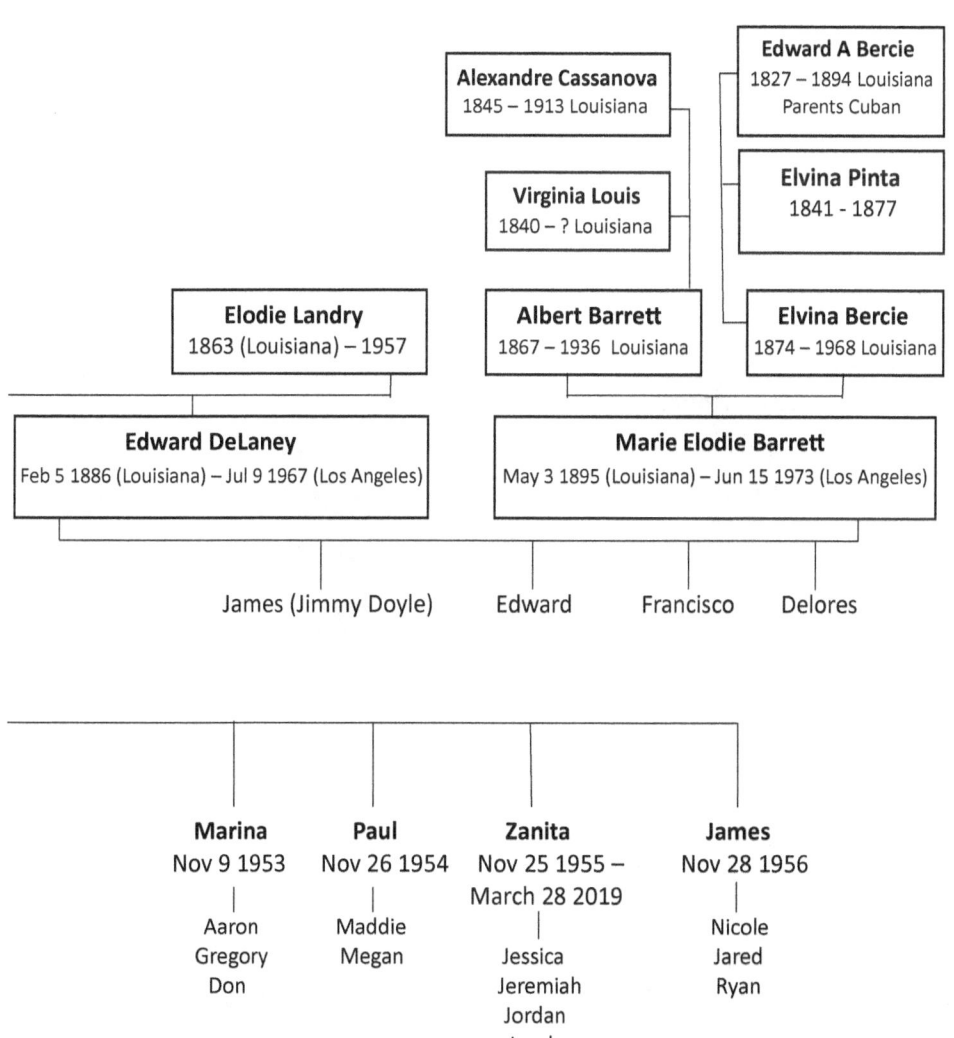

Appendix IV: Sibling Stories

Letitia's Story

Although my early years in New Zealand were filled with instability due to divorce, relocations, and difficult times for Mother, I felt, overall, that I had a happy childhood. I did well in school and had friends with whom I could enjoy weekends. I enjoyed learning; I enjoyed playing. I didn't read a lot, preferring more outdoor activities like making "huts" in the bush behind our house, collecting newspapers for the school recycling program, pressing flowers and leaves in old school notebooks, and  bringing stray kittens home. I went away for weekends with my girlfriends' families, often enjoying time at the beach with them. At fifteen, I took a part-time job in a local nursing home so that I had some money to spend.

Although people described me as "social," I never felt that way. I was not comfortable in groups and much preferred to have one or two close friends with whom I could build a deep connection. I have also always enjoyed being a friend, so I have managed to remain close to some of those early friends and now have many friendships with several decades duration. As a young girl, I was described as being "overly emotional" because I could go quickly from laughing (which I did a lot) to crying (which I also did a lot). Now in my later years, I see that sensitivity as one of my superpowers.

I didn't really have a plan for my life. My parents told me I was smart, so by the time I got to high school, I was enrolled in an academic path, excelling in foreign languages (French and German), math, and science. I was told not to be "ridiculous" when I suggested that I wanted to work training animals, so thoughts of a real career were little on my mind. My parents also said I wasn't creative, so those doors felt closed to me.

I left home at seventeen and ventured out into the world on my own, determined to find my own way. I started working, learning, and trying to discover what I should "do." I was taking classes at Auckland Technical Institute while working in a lab at Auckland Hospital when Mother hatched the plan for my sister and me to go to the U.S. This meant an opportunity to go to a university. After a long and involved process of Mum poring through books about schools (no internet then), Celeste and I headed out into the world together, traveling to the U.S. and starting a new life. I was enrolled in school at Oklahoma State University, with plans to study wildlife management. That turned into a focus on zoology, and in three years, I had a bachelor of science degree.

I relocated to Oregon after finding that Oklahoma was not really a lifestyle I could fully embrace. After working there for a while, I took a trip home to see my younger sister, Trudy, get married. On the return home, I met the man who would later become my husband, Jens. He was a Danish mink farmer. After he visited me in Portland and I spent the summer in Denmark, we decided to get married. I relocated to Denmark and became a mink farmer's wife. I worked in a few different jobs while there, always longing to continue my education and not feeling quite at home with my domestic role on the farm. We traveled some and enjoyed time with friends. I learned how to cook Danish meals and speak Danish, but I missed home terribly and did not feel fulfilled in that life.

I decided to return to the U.S. and attend graduate school. After discovering anthropology and doing a few classes at Portland State University, I ended up in a graduate program at the University of

Washington, studying anthropology and public health. No one could understand that combination of study at the time, but it turned into an incredibly interesting field of global health. Today, Seattle is considered a hub for this discipline, with large organizations like PATH (Program for Appropriate Technologies in Health) and the Bill and Melinda Gates Foundation, as well as the UW's own Department of Global Health. I paid my way through school with Research and Teaching Assistantships.

After spending a year in Ghana working at a research station in Navrongo and collecting data for my dissertation, I graduated with a Master of Public Health degree (MPH) and a PhD in Biocultural Anthropology. Mother organized an enormous surprise celebration to mark this achievement by bringing the family together for the ceremony. My brother, Jim, and his family came from New Zealand; my sister Celeste and her family came from Oregon; Trudy opted not to come, citing a fear of flying. It was an incredible time for me, as I felt I had found my footing and was finally being acknowledged for the path I had chosen in life.

During the writing of my dissertation, Mother helped me with the down payment for a small cabin on Vashon Island that has beautiful water views and easy beach access. I still live in my funky, beloved cabin at the time of this writing, enjoying spectacular sunrises, beach combing for rocks, shells, sea glass, and feathers, paddling in my kayak, and watching from my deck as orcas, seals, and sea otters frolic in Puget Sound.

During my global health career, I worked in a variety of different African countries, (Zimbabwe, Ethiopia, Botswana, and Rwanda), for about twelve years doing monitoring and evaluation of HIV programs. I conducted research and shared findings during the HIV/AIDS pandemic and taught our in-country colleagues data collection methods to ensure the success of their own efforts. Although I loved that work and the opportunities it gave me for travel, making a difference, cultural exploration, and developing a global network of friends, there was something in my soul that yearned to facilitate the awakening and spiritual development of others.

Jens and I divorced a few years after our marriage, and although I have dated other men since then, I have never remarried. I have lived with some of my partners for several years and shared many incredible adventures backpacking, going on safari in Africa, boating in Desolation Sound and the islands of the Pacific Northwest and Canada, campervanning in New Zealand, and discovering the joys of crabbing and digging for geoduck on Vashon Island. Having a man in my life has become of less importance in recent years as I developed a better sense of myself and a strong focus on spirituality and personal development. It is this commitment to being my authentic self and living a life of compassion and support for others on a personal-development journey that has led me to where I am today. I became a certified Life Coach and committed to my own journey of self-discovery and personal development. I did a course in training others in Mindfulness Meditation and hope to combine that with a strong interest in Nature and Forest Therapy. I believe strongly in treading lightly on Planet Earth and am committed to living sustainably and in harmony with nature.

After the coronavirus pandemic of 2020 hit, I was laid off from my local job on Vashon Island, and with the social distancing guidelines that were put in place, I spent a *lot* of time outdoors, walking Vashon's beaches, hiking forest trails, and enjoying Puget Sound from my kayak. A close friend and I went on several adventures off the island, taking our kayaks and camping and paddling in the great outdoors.

I am currently semi-retired, working part-time for the Vashon-Maury Senior Center with an amazing group of loving and heart-centered people. I also volunteer each week at the Vashon Food Bank and continue to learn and grow spiritually. I remain committed to being of service and living an adventurous and authentic life, always shining the light from within. A recent example of this comes from a trip I just took into the Ecuadorian jungle, where I spent seven weeks teaching the Achuar people English. It was an incredible experience, although not easy, and I was glad when my last teaching class was over. I gave myself an opportunity for some more lighthearted adventures with a few days in Quito and Mindo, as well as a boat excursion in the Galapagos Islands with my neighbor and friend, Steve. It was an extraordinary experience—the trip of a lifetime for sure! After being gone from home for almost two months, it was a real delight to return to my little cabin on the water and my dear, sweet Lagao kitty. I am extremely grateful for the wonderful life I have and am very happy with the simplicity and authenticity with which I choose to live.

Jamie's Story

Jamie is convinced that the separation was Mum's plan and that his father had no idea what was coming. He does not remember any plan for them to go to England and says Mum did not talk to him or Trudy before leaving that night. In fact, when he saw her at the court case a while later, she didn't talk to him, leaving him to feel totally abandoned by her.

Jamie was thirteen when the separation happened and went on to finish high school. His father sold the house, and they moved into a two-bedroom flat. Jamie then went to Trentham for police training in 1979 and worked in Wellington for two years before moving back up to Auckland and joining the CIB (Criminal Investigative Branch) as a detective. He met and married Jane, and they have two daughters, Samantha and Sarah. His last seven years with the police department were as a police prosecutor. Jamie left that job to become a legal assistant. He later worked as a supervisor at a steel mill, sold real estate, and worked with the EQC (Earthquake Commission) after the earthquakes in both Christchurch and Wellington.

He went back to a university to finish his law degree, but when he and Jane were divorced in 2005, he gave that up to return to work. He bought a place on the coast north of Auckland to get away to as often as possible. He is currently a Senior Body Corporate Manager and Team Leader for some of New Zealand's largest residential societies. He moved in with Robyn a few years ago, and they enjoy long rides on his Harley together. Fishing from his kayak is also a favorite pastime when he's not "writing to his sisters in America." Before his father died in 2009, Jamie took him back to England to visit family and enjoyed meeting cousins, uncles, and aunts that none of us had ever seen.

It is a joy to have seen him during trips I've made to New Zealand, and he has come to the U.S. to visit as well.

Trudy's Story

Trudy and I talked about what it was like after Mum took Teesha and me away that night so many years ago. She said their dad cried every night for a long time; he was absolutely devastated by the separation and never really got over it. In the account in this book, Mum makes it sound like it was all Jim's plan, and she was the victim. I'm not sure if that's the way it seemed to her or if she wrote it that way because admitting the truth was too painful, but I want to note that others saw it differently.

The choices Mum made deeply impacted the lives of all her children, but Trudy more than any of us. She was only eleven when that tearing apart happened. She was left with her father and brother but without a mother to guide her through her teenage years. She had Larry's baby, Michelle, alone at eighteen years old and went on to have four more children—Clare, Shawn, Hayley, and Jordon—by various men. Sadly, Shawn committed suicide in 2007 after a breakup with his girlfriend.

Trudy reports that she experienced repeated sexual abuse as a child, and although she never told anyone, she thought her mother knew. She always felt "unseen, unlovable, and unwanted." Trudy went on welfare when she had her first baby and continues to live on welfare in a state house, struggling to make ends meet. She cares for her children and grandchildren as best she can but doesn't take good care of her own health. She looks for the love she never knew as a child in her own children and grandchildren. She seeks truth and support by attending church and helps others along the way with yard work and grocery shopping. We keep in touch regularly, and I enjoy visits with her whenever I'm in New Zealand.

About the Author

Celeste Delaney is an author and speaker who grew up in New Zealand, where much of life was lived outdoors playing in the bush or at a nearby beach. Although she left the country after studying occupational therapy and lived and worked all over the world, she gets back to New Zealand whenever she can. In her twenties, she married the man of her  dreams, and they raised three wonderful children on the mission field. Now widowed, she lives in Oregon near her children and six grandchildren, who are her joy and motivation for writing this life story. She enjoys traveling, watercolor painting, reading, walking on the beach or along woodland trails, teaching, and writing.

Contact the Author

If you would like a copy of the booklet *Forty Days in Downtown Portland* or have comments or questions, please contact Celeste at stayintheriver25@gmail.com.

www.ingramcontent.com/pod-product-compliance
Lightning Source LLC
Chambersburg PA
CBHW021210130626
46554CB00004B/1157